D0886834

THE VIRGIN MARY
The Roman Catholic Marian Doctrine

THE VIRGIN MARY

THE ROMAN CATHOLIC MARIAN DOCTRINE

by

GIOVANNI MIEGGE

Professor of Church History
The Waldensian Faculty of Theology, Rome

Translated from the Italian by

WALDO SMITH

Professor of Church History
Queen's Theological College, Kingston, Ontario
Associate Professor of History
Queen's University

With a Foreword by

JOHN A. MACKAY

President, Princeton Theological Seminary
Princeton, New Jersey

THE WESTMINSTER PRESS
PHILADELPHIA

First published in English in Great Britain in 1955
by Lutterworth Press, London

This book originally appeared as *La Vergine Maria*, Editrice Claudiana, Torre Pellice, Italy, 1950; revised by the author for this English edition.

Library of Congress Catalog Card Number: 56-5884

PRINTED IN THE UNITED STATES OF AMERICA

CONTENTS

FOREWORD

FOREWORD

WHAT IS THE PLACE of Mary of Nazareth in the Christian religion? This question, because of recent developments, poses a crucial problem for contemporary Christianity.

Professor Miegge's book is a scholarly and discerning study of the Marian issue. With fine historical perspective and true theological balance, and without any taint of bigotry, the author recounts what has happened in the Roman Catholic Church with respect to the status and functions of the Virgin Mary. He focuses with great acumen the bearing of this development upon the unique and abiding significance of Jesus Christ in the faith which He founded and upon Christ's relevance to man and civilization in the world of our time.

Some years ago, a public address by a Roman Catholic Cardinal was printed in the press of a Latin American capital. The eminent prelate recorded this dream. He dreamed that he was standing in the Celestial City. A knock was heard at the gate. It was reported before the Divine Presence that a sinner of earth was begging admission. "Has he fulfilled the requirements?" the question was asked. The answer was, "No." "Then he cannot be admitted," was the verdict. Whereupon, the Virgin Mary, who was seated at the right hand of her Son, spoke up. "If this soul does not get in, I go out." The gate was opened and the sinner entered.

This night vision of the Roman hierarch is a perfect parable of the Virgin's new status and power in relation to human sin and redemption. Crowned Queen of Heaven by the Holy Trinity, as she is portrayed in the Shrine of the Virgin of Fatima, Mary is measureless in her compassion. In the exercise of that compassion, she asks no questions and lays down no conditions. She who in Michelangelo's famous painting of the Last Judgment stands with concerned countenance beside her Son, the Judge, seeking to restrain His hand, exercises in the present era an authority which the Trinity accepts. As pure Humanity beatified, miraculously raised into the realm of the supernatural, and endued with supernatural authority and power, the Virgin Mary becomes the fulfillment of the Trinity, the embodiment of a mercy that is unrelated to justice.

Today Mary, Immaculate and Ascended, has actually become the executive director of Deity, the ultimate mediator of God's grace to men. She is not only Queen of Heaven; she is also Queen of the Universe, Queen of Civilization. God has assigned her this mission: to maintain close and constant contact with the needs and desires of common folk, and with the course of human civilization as a whole. It is true that Mary is not worshiped as Divine; yet only through her can contact with the Divine be established. The Mass, with its Christocentric orientation, continues to be the official center of Roman Catholic worship; but, as the author of this book points out, "the heart of the people is rather with the Virgin Mary than with the tremendous and abstract mysteries of the altar" (p. 182). It is Mary rather than Christ who becomes increasingly relevant to the human situation today. The dream is growing of a new Marian civilization.

What is at stake is this. Is the Risen Christ a free and contemporaneous spiritual reality? Is He directly accessible to human longing? Is He close to the milling highways of life? Evangelical Christianity says yes. Can Christ's humanity be both inspiration and pattern for a vital Christian Humanism? The Protestant answer is: He can. Through the Holy Spirit, Jesus Christ is a living contemporary Presence, tender, strong, and righteous, Head of the Church and Ruler of the nations.

What then of the Virgin? Let Mary continue to be "blessed among women," the greatest and most honored woman who ever lived. But let us not do her wrong. That she was honored to bring Christ the Saviour into the world is no basis for believing that she should now be Christ's substitute in the world. Today, alas, the blessed Virgin, whom Protestants, too, love, devotedly, is being given a religious status for which there is no Biblical authority and a redemptive role for which there is no spiritual necessity.

JOHN A. MACKAY

TRANSLATOR'S PREFACE

To the Protestant Christian the cult of Mary is disquieting and perplexing. The devout and lowly maiden of Judah has become Queen of Heaven. She through whom the Son of God came to dwell among men in intimate fellowship has become the Mediatrix through whom they are now to approach Him and the Father. Mary in Roman Catholic devotion receives many times the prayers that are addressed to God or Christ. She is the preferred object of devotion. Mary has eclipsed her Son. There has been another eclipse too. The devotion to Mary, in its operation, hides and virtually negates the warmest and most profound truth in Jesus' teaching—the Fatherhood of God.

The movement goes on. The extravagances of the Marian Congress at Ottawa, in 1947, were a shock to Protestants who cared about their faith. For the secularists it is to be feared that they appeared as evidence that all religion is superstition. This is not an age in which Christianity is well served by such demonstrations. The Christian ethic is being undermined by amoral humanism and attacked by militant scepticism. The supreme need is to recall this generation to Jesus Christ in loyalty to His person and acceptance of His teaching. Instead of this the devotion of millions is being directed to one who has left us relatively little to direct our faith or conduct.

These are the more disquieting facts. Perplexing aspects of the Marian cult are the ascription to her of characteristics and virtues that represent her as something far different from the mother of Jesus whom the early Church knew and its Scriptures record. Apocryphal writings of the post-apostolic age are responsible for some of this. But devout imagination of modern times has been equally responsible. Orthodoxy and Anglo-Catholicism have taken part in this. The Marian writings of these communions as well as those of the Roman Catholic Church are compounds of Biblical references—frequently far-fetched—of devout and often very worthy meditations, and uncritical use of legendary material as historical fact for the establishment of doctrine.

All these things cause in Protestants an ingrained dissent that amounts almost to an aversion for special honouring of Mary. We feel no coldness toward the mother of our Lord as the other communions believe we do. But there is abhorrence of what too often accompanies the honouring of her: the sentimental invocations, the suspension of the rational faculty, most of all the making of Mary the object of prayers that ought to be addressed to God.

It will not do, however, for Protestants just to turn away in aversion and say that this special regard for Mary does not deserve consideration. The fact is that scholarly minds find values in it as well as the less tutored devout. Every branch of the Christian Church has the responsibility to try to understand the faith of other communions in the Christian fellowship. It can do us no harm to examine the cult of Mary to see what legitimately Christian ideas it may express. In the interests of Christian unity it may be possible for us to be more hospitable to some systematic honouring of her as mother of Christ. Our minds could well be open for new spiritual insights along the way.[a]

To the Orthodox Church the Virgin Mary belongs to the basic truth of the Incarnation; by her continued veneration and association with Jesus in the devotions of that Church it is felt that the approach of God to men is made more intimate. She deserves honour for the high function of being the mother of the Incarnate One, and it would be unworthy to lay her aside as an instrument that is forgotten when the need is past. In her person she "represents the whole of humanity, through the grace of God in her all the sanctity accessible to humanity is attained, even after the fall, in the Church of the Old Testament".[b] Her presence in the circle of devotion adds warmth and in her and by her the feminine receives a place in piety in

[a] Cf. Hans Asmussen, *Maria die Mutter Gottes*, Stuttgart, Evangelisches Verlagswerk, 1951, pp. 29, 30. In reference to the salutation of Elizabeth and Mary's "*Magnificat*":

"Wir lutherischen versetzen uns in Marias Lage und Maria in unsere Lage. Maria ist uns in erster Linie das Beispiel und das Vorbild. . . . Die Kirche, welche täglich das Magnificat singt, . . . meint sich selber, da sie bis zum Jüngsten Tage die arme Magd ihres Herren bleibt. Niemand kann das Magnificat verstehen, der es nicht als den *Lobgesang der Kirche* versteht."

[b] Cf. Sergius Bulgakov, *The Orthodox Church*, London, Centenary Press, 1935, pp. 137 ff.

connection with the Holy Spirit. The Orthodox Church does not accept the dogma of the Immaculate Conception of Mary in the sense that she was exempt at birth from original sin, for this would separate her from the human race and she could not then have transmitted to her Son this true humanity.

To represent the Anglo-Catholic position clearly is a matter of some difficulty. Here again there is the basic principle that Mary's continued honour is because she shared in the Incarnation. From this position on there seems to be considerable preoccupation with the "glories" of Mary through festivals in her honour. The sense of responsibility to basic Christian doctrine becomes less distinct. Some Anglo-Catholics accept the Immaculate Conception and laud virginity for its own sake. Assumptions are made without Scriptural warrant, as for example:

> "We must note that Mary's acceptance of the divine will implied on her part a real abandonment of a thought that God did not mean her to be the Mother of the Messiah, a thought which she must have had in her mind when she had determined to live in virginity and not to seek motherhood."[a]

The most familiar representation of Mary in the Roman Catholic churches is as the radiant young mother at the height of her beauty, as often as not wearing a crown as Queen of Heaven. In this representation Mary has become Our Lady, attracting to herself a chivalrous devotion. Most men have the capacity for chivalrous sentiment and it is understandable that for a celibate clergy Mary, as Our Lady, should be an outlet and focal point for this. A more sombre and realistic devotion, although less prominent, is towards the Mary of Seven Sorrows: not so much the transcendent Mary of Heaven but the human mother who mourns and needs human compassion. This has inspired some very fine devotional writing. Mention should be made of *The Seven Sorrows of Mary* by Father Gerard Corr of the Order of Servants of Mary. His treatment of the Presentation in the Temple, for example, is deeply moving and most of his little book could be used by an evangelical Protestant minister for Lenten sermons.[b]

[a] G. D. Carleton, *Mother of Jesus*, London, Pax House, 1942, p. 15.

[b] Gerard Corr, *The Seven Sorrows of Mary*, London, Sands & Co., 1945.

Again, if Mary is kept within the human circle, actually one of us in all essentials, then it is possible that to regard her as living on to-day can be a helpful reminder to us of the continuation of life after human death, eternity as one in time with our present.[a]

To a considerable degree there is an appeal in mariology to current interest in things mediaeval. The Virgin had an important place in the culture of mediaeval Europe, its art, its devotion, its folk ways. Its influence as a stimulus to art is too large a subject for these pages.[b] Mary's praise offered scope for whatever lyric impulses were permitted among the celibate clergy.[c] She had her place in numerous local customs and the popular demand for wonders was met by the reported miracles at her many shrines. One can believe that the programme in English Catholicism to-day of reviving pilgrimages to her rehabilitated shrines is planned to meet the well-known English interest in old folk ways.[d]

When the effort has been made to sympathize and appreciate, misgivings and reservations yet remain. This devotion to Mary appears to carry men away from strict responsibility to the basic truths of Christianity that God is a father of infinite love and compassion and understanding; that Jesus is still one with humanity; that each believer has direct access to both. The devotion to Mary carries men away from the Scriptural standards of the Christian Church; the rational faculty is suspended and the devout imagination is undisciplined. For example, Sergius Bulgakov writes:

[a] Charles de Koninck, in his thoughtful study, *La piété du Fils*, touches this point. One regrets that in general he does not take for his starting point ground on which Protestant Christians can stand together with Catholic Christians. Quebec, Les Presses Universitaires Laval, 1954.

Cf. also Asmussen, *op. cit.*, pp. 30, 31. "Das Einmalige an Maria ist das Bleibende. Um dieses Einmaligen willen ist das Magnificat das tägliche Lied der Kirche. . . . Maria muss auch *besungen* werden, man darf sich nicht darauf beschränken *mit* ihr zu singen. . . . Die Tatsache, dass sie schon so lange nicht mehr unter den Lebenden weilt, ändert daran nichts. Denn vor Gott leben die Toten alle."

[b] Cf. T. S. R. Boase, *English Art, 1100–1216*, Oxford, 1953, pp. 110 ff.

[c] Cf. *infra*, Chapter 8, Note (a) to page 158.

[d] Cf. The little book by the Reverend Giles Black, O.P., *Our Lady in England*, London, Bloomsbury Publishing Co., 1949. The twelve revived shrines are the twelve stars in her mystic crown. Each series of prayers includes one for the conversion of England to the Catholic faith.

"In her is realized the idea of Divine Wisdom in the creation of the world; she is Divine Wisdom in the created world. . . . Living in Heaven in a state of glory the Virgin remains the mother of the human race. . . . She covers the world with her veil." [a]

And George Carleton, concerning the Immaculate Conception:

"She was saved through the foreseen merit of Christ's death. She is the most wonderful of all the fruits of the redemptive grace of Christ."[b]

A regrettable side to the current mariology is its injury to Christian unity. It is widening the rift between the Roman and the Greek Catholic Churches. It makes an ever wider separation between Roman Catholics and Protestants. Among the latter there is more readiness than at any time since the Reformation to take up again particular occasions and ways of worship that were put aside then. A Protestant minister today can get a sympathetic hearing from his people when he commends a usage as catholic in the sense that it is common to all branches of the Christian Church and is grounded in a tradition that is in harmony with Scripture. On the Protestant side there is a relaxation of rigid and categorical protest against the old ways of the undivided Church and there is a movement to join again with non-Protestant Christians in ways of devotion that they have kept through the years. But Marian devotion has gone to lengths in belief and observance that the Protestant faith can never accept. Its promoters are carrying the Roman Catholic Church away from Christian unity faster than Protestants can approach it. Their policy is enlarging the doctrinal schism of Christendom.

Professor Giovanni Miegge, writing in the midst of the Italian scene, has surveyed the Marian movement and related it to current Christian problems. In undertaking a translation of his work I have been greatly helped by Professor H. W. Hilborn, of the Department of Spanish and Italian of Queen's University, who has brought his professional knowledge to the aid of my amateur effort. Professor Miegge has read the translation chapter by chapter. His footnotes have been kept with his

[a] *Op. cit.*, p. 139. Cf. *infra.*, p. 80.
[b] *Op. cit.*, p. 8.

numbering. A translator has opportunities to "slant" the translation so in various instances I have indicated the Italian wording where the reader may want to judge on this point. The translator's footnotes are indicated by letters of the alphabet. The critical scholarship of my brother-in-law, Mr John Ross, has been an invaluable help in the final correction of the proofs.

WALDO SMITH

Queen's Theological College,
Kingston, Ontario.

INTRODUCTION

The Problem

THE Virgin Mary occupies a place in Catholic piety and thought in our day the importance of which it is hard to exaggerate. This statement needs no demonstration. The spectacular manifestations of Marian piety, the Marian Congresses, the Marian Year of 1954, the consecration to Mary of entire nations, the pilgrimage of Mary, these are in the minds of everyone. Equally important is the doctrinal elaboration, the historical and theological study that flourishes on a scale seldom reached in the centuries preceding. There is the great work of propaganda and diffusion directed to popularizing among the laity the consciousness and love of Mary, served by publishing houses that specialize in this by all the arts of modern publicity. The importance of this endeavour is clear to its promoters. Catholicism in our time feels itself to be living in an age that in devotion to Mary is second to no other, probably not even those great centuries of mariology, the twelfth and thirteenth.[1] The twentieth century presents, moreover, a doctrinal superiority over that golden age of veneration of Mary. On the one hand, Marian theology through a century of work on it has reached a definiteness and an awareness of itself that the great Marian theologians of the Middle Ages, St Anselm, St Bonaventura and St Bernard did not attain. On the other hand, the desire to make the laity Mary-conscious has never been served by means so potent or a desire so strong.

What is the significance of this imposing Marian flowering? That it is not unrelated to the effort that the Church is making in our time to recover the masses, is at once evident. The Marian preaching particularly lends itself to this with its appeal to simple and elemental feelings. Mary, in her character of woman, virgin and mother, gathers to herself the most potent

[1] "Our century glories with good right, in being the century of Mary." E. Neubert, *Marie dans le Dogme*, Editions Spes, Paris, 1933: Italian translation, *Maria nel Dogma*, Pia Società di S. Paolo, Alba, 1944, p. 6.

and universal emotions. There is the subdued and nostalgic adoration of the drowsy child that is forever in us, desirous of caresses and protection. And there is the attraction, all the more heady the more it is sublimated and repressed, to which man is subject in the presence of the eternal feminine. In this fascinating symbol the most typical Christian qualities are brought together; goodness, pity, and the mercy that redeems and pardons. In the Marian preaching these qualities commend themselves, using as the vehicle of their appeal a symbol of tremendous psychological power. Will it perhaps come about that the cult of the Virgin Mother will be the means, the channel of grace, through which the eternal Christian values will come back and be accessible to the masses, barbarized and elemental, incapable of thinking yet capable of intense feeling? Will Mary be truly "mediatrix" in an historical and psychological sense of the Christianity of the century of the great apostasy?

Such is the thought that has been consciously expressed by the more thoughtful promoters of Marian piety. The new era will be the era of the triumph of Mary and the triumph of Mary will bring with it the triumph of Christ and the Church. So prophesied the French Father Chaminade in 1838 in a letter to Gregory XVI. In 1927 Father Doncœur gave an echo to this. "The present generation, grown and nourished by the dogmas and the eucharist, will achieve great things. But there yet remains the achievement of the discovery of the Madonna."[1]

All the same it would be an error to limit ourselves to this propaganda perspective, or, let us say more respectfully, missionary perspective. The present development of mariology is not to be interpreted solely as a resort to the most potent instrument of doctrinal diffusion. It has deeper roots that cannot be identified without penetrating into the most intimate recesses of the Catholic faith. In a book of deep piety, written for the younger generation and for seminarists in particular, Romualdo M. Giovanni Evangelista laments that the Catholic youth and even seminarists themselves remain impregnated with the "humanistic and naturalistic" spirit of the world of lay culture, from which not even the study of dogma or the practice of the eucharist succeed in freeing them. He maintains, and it is the thesis of the book, that a systematic study of

[1] Neubert, *op. cit.*, p. 6.

Mary, that begins with the secondary school and senior high school and extends through the seminaries, is the most exquisite means for the "supernatural forming" of the seminarist in preparation for theology and the theological life in pastoral or missionary work. Since "by Mary one goes to Jesus; yes, but only by the whole Mary does one come to the whole Jesus, by means of the theology of Mary to that of God in thought and in life." "Through Mary to Jesus and through Jesus to the Father!" Such is the way that Catholic piety follows, more and more consciously. The mediation of Mary, for it is not an abstract theological proposition. It is an experience lived, a method of education, a way that has been tried, the incomparable beauties of which are celebrated with enthusiasm afire.[1]

That a rebirth of Christian faith is not only to be invoked, but that it is the only remaining hope for our time if we do not want to go down into chaos, is a proposition that no person can doubt for a moment who thinks about the extreme gravity of the present hour and the eternal truth of the Gospel. But that this rebirth must necessarily follow the way of a Marian mediation that is psychological and pietistic, missionary and theological is not at all plain. The very insistence with which the promoters of the Marian cult stress this necessary mediation shows how this idea is felt by Catholicism itself to be a paradoxical novelty in little conformity with the constant universal and established traditions of Christianity.

Indeed there is no intrinsic evidence why the Gospel, the eternal Gospel of our Saviour Christ Jesus, the Jesus of Nazareth, prophet and master incomparable, of the Crucifixion of Golgotha and of the Resurrection, should not be able to address itself directly to a generation confused and lost as ours is, without going through the psychological and theological mediation of Marian piety. The fact that this mediation should be felt necessary, should be desired, invoked, preached with a conviction that no one can call in doubt, with a warmth that carries in itself the best graces of its sincerity, this very fact poses a problem for thoughtful minds of our time. However has the

[1] Sac. Romualdo M. Giovanni Evangelista, della Pia Società di S. Paolo: *Lo studio organico e metodico di Maria santissima in Ginnasio, Liceo e Teologia, per la formazione sopranaturale del seminarista.* Alba, 1944.

Catholic conscience come to this extreme? Has the Gospel lost for it its own intrinsic evidence to such a point; has it so lost its power of renewal and conviction that it has to be recovered and preached again through Marian piety and Marian thought? By what fatality, historical and spiritual, has Mary become the necessary mediatrix of Jesus?

The problem treats of the most important aspects of the piety of that Church, which through its organizations religious, scholastic and political, visibly aspires to the spiritual control of the world, or at least of Christendom. Further, the development of Marian piety, whether from the point of view of the history of religions or of religious psychology, or of dogmatic and liturgical development or of the Catholic ethic, presents such an abundance of interesting aspects that it constitutes by itself an attractive field for investigation.

In the pages that follow, the intention is to limit oneself to the problem's historical and dogmatic aspect. For obvious reasons of space we forgo liturgical research properly speaking. Besides, this would not belong within the limits of this book. Liturgy would concern us only as soon as the devout affirmations contained in it come to be received consciously as normative doctrinal principles according to the well-known principle, *lex orandi, lex credendi*, the law of prayer is the law of belief, which, however, is not absolute because there are expressions of piety that cannot be entirely translated into propositions of doctrine. Poetry is always a little beyond theology and its dogmatic responsibility is not to be over-estimated.

We shall refrain as a general rule from taking the problem to the attractive but uncertain and elusive ground of the comparative history of religions. This is not because we disregard the comparisons that can be established or the conclusions that can be deduced from them through critical study of the Marian dogma. It is because the historical-religious parallels do not give us information on the significance of Marian piety, and this is the only question that matters. It can be taken as certain, and indeed as obvious, that the cult of Mary has replaced that of the divine mothers of the Mediterranean world, but the recognition of this, apart from a generic reference to the symbol of divine maternity, does not tell us what Mary is for Catholic piety. To know this we have to seek at the sources of Christianity, that is, put ourselves inside its dogmatic development, and the coherent pattern that such development presents confirms our belief in the merit of the method. Whatever be the precedents and analogies offered by the history of religions, the cult of Mary is a phenomenon endowed with its own individuality; and this deserves observation in itself. The same observations present themselves in regard to Marian piety which are to be made concerning the origins of Christian asceticism, which is correlative to it and is intertwined with it by deep roots both psychological and moral. Christian asceticism has origins also outside Christianity, yet one does not truly understand it unless one brings it back to the impulses it received in the area of Christian piety of the fourth century, which made it an original phenomenon even though far removed from the ideas of New Testament Christianity.

It would be easy to write another kind of book by more general use of the parallels of the history of religions, drawing upon the turbid sources of popular superstition and applying to that material some elementary principles of psychoanalysis. But the end we set for ourselves is not to show a series of curiosities or scandals, or to carry water to the mill of the irreligious of our day. Rather it is to discuss among Christians a problem that however grave should not be insoluble, and, for a solution, must be treated with respect.

The limitation of our research in the history of the dogma has the advantage of fixing a ground of possible meeting with Catholic students who dedicate a whole life of research, and many large volumes, to this part of Catholic doctrine that is now promoted to the dignity of theology of university grade. We can approach these researches with confidence. Not only is the honesty of the Catholic students beyond question, but their conception of history is more ductile and trained than that of the theologians of the past. It is largely admitted that Marian piety has had a long development in the history of the Church and the historical interest of the phases of this development is accepted. The traditional position of finding in the sacred Scriptures the justification of all aspects of the Marian dogma, even at the cost of evident forcing of their meaning, has yielded to a more objective consideration. One may find in the popularized writing directed to the laity the admission that this or that aspect of Marian doctrine, such as her immaculate conception, her assumption, her participation in the redemption of men are not explicitly affirmed either in the New Testament writings or in the earliest fathers.[1] The Marian dogma is considered as a construction of the piety and the theological thought of the Church from certain premises contained explicitly or implicitly in the New Testament. The historical conception of Cardinal Newman appears to inspire the Catholic historians of dogma more and more widely. That great Catholic, who had preserved from his Anglican origin certain needs of liberty and modernity, taught, as is well known, that dogma is a living organism that develops on the lines of its premises and according to its intrinsic dynamic. This thesis was the great discovery of modernism and for having maintained it with the intention of dogmatic renovation many eminent Catholics in the first years of our century had to experience the rigours of excommunication. No one seems to remember that to-day when the dynamic conception of dogma has been put to the service of mariology. As it has been said, the Church chews slowly but always ends by assimilating useful discoveries, even if at first it has condemned them.

The adoption of this new position which is revealing itself in the Catholic camp cannot be displeasing to free students. It clears the air of many useless questions, leaving the field freer for open discussion of real problems. The critical study of the development of mariology is not made any easier by this. The time is past when one could have the illusion of confuting the Marian dogma by the simple demonstration that the word *Deipara* is not in the Gospel, or that Jesus had four brothers and some sisters. If the Catholic theologians continue to maintain the traditional interpretation of the data in the Gospels, they do it in deference to the exegetical tradition of their Church and

[1] Cf. Neubert, *op. cit.*, "The revelation in regard to Mary which was made to the first Christians does not contain the explicit assertion of the Immaculate Conception but allows it to be presumed and predisposes the mind to grasp it" (p. 82). "We do not possess reliable documents which inform us on the belief of the first Christians about the Assumption of Mary" (p. 174). "At that time there were no special reasons for drawing the attention of the faithful to the help given by Mary for such a work of redemption. It was the part taken by Christ that needed, rather, to be made understood. It could be divined from that time, however, the part the Virgin had in the mystery of our redemption" (p. 205).

within the limits in which such interpretations are at least tenable. But their main interest has long been turned elsewhere, and it is into this field that critical study must follow them. This is the field of the Church's dogmatic and liturgical creation, the field of that popular piety that chooses by its own laws its own objects of worship, and by the spontaneous expressions of its devotion creates the substance and designs the necessary lines of the doctrinal development. For such organic development it is enough to have its own point of departure in the New Testament, a geometric point, one would say, without dimensions.

Father Roschini, who is perhaps the greatest living specialist in mariology in Italy, in a short popular catechism, outlines clearly what might be called the intrinsic laws of the development of the Marian system and sums them up in one primary principle and four secondary. The primary principle is the divine maternity. "The most blessed Mary is the Mother of God and the Mediatrix of man." From this first principle, which he does not doubt he can establish explicitly or implicitly on the Gospel, "are deduced all the various conclusions of mariology and to it they all lead again." This is according to the secondary principles of singularity, propriety, eminence and analogy with Christ.

Here is the enunciation of this position in the actual words of Roschini.

1. "The most blessed Virgin being a creature altogether singular, constituting an order apart, rightly claims for herself privileges entirely singular which can fit no other creature." (*Principle of singularity*)
2. "All the perfections must be attributed to the most blessed Virgin which truly become the dignity of Mother of God and Mediatrix of man, provided they have some basis in revelation and are not contrary to faith and reason." (*Principle of propriety*)
3. "All the privileges of nature, grace and glory granted by God to the other saints must have been granted in some way also to the most blessed Virgin, Queen of the Saints." (*Principle of eminence*)
4. "Privileges analogous to the various privileges of the humanity of Christ are possessed correspondingly by the most blessed

Virgin and according to the condition of the one and the other." (*Principle of analogy* or *likeness to Christ*)[1]

It is easy to see how, with these principles, it is possible to justify all the historical developments of Marian piety and dogma. It is still more interesting to observe that they open the way to every possible development in the future. The Marian dogma, delimited by these four categories, is not a complete and closed theory in itself. It is a doctrine in evolution, an open dogma, one might say using a Bergsonian expression. One can accept *a priori* as Marian dogma all that it will be possible to assert as being the development of the divine Maternity and of the mediation of Mary according to the four principles put forward above. No celebration of Mary will ever be too hyperbolical according to the principle of singularity. No glorification of saints or martyrs but will add its potent contribution to the glory of Mary, according to the principle of eminence. Her greatness as mediatrix will find no other limits than those of a perfect likeness with Christ the Redeemer, according to the principle of analogy. And her apotheosis, according to the principle of propriety, will have no other limits than divinity itself. Indeed, these are the words of Roschini:

> "The divine Maternity raises her to a dizzy height [a] and places her immediately after God in the vast scale of beings, causing her to be a member of the hypostatic order (in the measure that through her and in her the Word is united hypostatically—that is personally—with human nature), an order superior to the order of nature and grace and glory. For this the Fathers and the Scriptures have almost exhausted their resources of language in exalting her without succeeding in giving her the glory that becomes her. Her greatness borders on the infinite."[2]

With this we are informed on the possibilities of the future. But let us see, meanwhile, what are the lines the Marian dogma has already taken in its historical development.

[1] Gabriele M. Roschini, *Chi è Maria? Catechismo Mariano*, Società Apostolato Stampo, Rome, 1944, pp. 12–14. See the full discussion of this question by the author in his large *Mariologia*, three volumes in Latin, A. Belardetti, ed., Rome, 1947–48, Vol. I, pp. 321–79.

[a] *ad un altezza vertiginosa.*

[2] Roschini, *Chi è Maria?* p. 39.

Chapter 1

MARY IN THE GOSPEL

An incident related by the three synoptic Gospels recalls that one day when Jesus was teaching, "his mother and his brothers came, and standing outside they sent to him", since the crowd made it impossible to get near Him. On that occasion Jesus said words that the first Christian community must have repeated often with deep appreciation in its troubles with hostile surroundings. " 'Who are my mother and my brothers?' And looking around on those who sat about him, he said, 'Here are my mother and my brothers! Whoever does the will of God is my brother, and sister, and mother' " (Mark 3: 31–35).

The challenging tone of this pronouncement surprises, and recalls another of the hardest sayings of Jesus, "If anyone comes to me and does not hate his own father and mother and wife and children and brothers and sisters, yes, and even his own life, he cannot be my disciple" (Luke 14: 25, 26). He who pronounced these bitter words was not merely a declarer of the unconditional requirements of discipleship in the unique hour of the coming of the Kingdom of God. He could only be a man for whom family life had reserved some of those bitter experiences of repulse and inner solitude that are often the lot of great geniuses and men of God. In fact, the explanation of the incident told by Mark is to be found in a brief and, as it were, modest admission made a few verses earlier. His relations, when they heard that, "went out to seize him, for they said, 'He is beside himself' " (Mark 3: 21). His relations, *hoi par' autou*, His people, must evidently refer to the same people named later, His mother and His brothers. They "went out", went home (*exelthon*) to go and get Him, according to verse 21. They arrived (*erchontai*), according to verse 31. Mark inserts between their departure and arrival the statement of the opinion which the scribes of Jerusalem held of Jesus, an opinion less charitable than that of his relations; "He has Beelzebub", that is to say,

He is possessed by the devil. And the severe answer of Jesus follows concerning the sin against the Holy Spirit which "has no remission in eternity". These exchanges fix a situation and create an atmosphere. We are at the beginning of Jesus' great conflict with the religious authorities of His people. The relatives of Jesus, who, perhaps, have never thought without a certain suspicion about His incomprehensible vocation which exalted Him above them and isolated Him, were now frightened and feared a scandal that would involve the whole family. Perhaps they feared more for His safety. Their words, "He is beside himself"—"out of his mind", are a commendable evidence of pity but they are certainly no credit to their spiritual insight.

One would like to know what part Mary had in this unhappy incident. That she was present along with her sons is explicitly stated by verse 31. Will her participation have been active or passive? We can safely suppose that it was only passive: the "brothers of the Lord" were now adults and the management of the family was definitely not in her hands. It could be that she came to temper the action of Jesus' brothers by her maternal love, to persuade her firstborn to think of Himself and not to compromise Himself but to moderate His zeal. It is easy to suppose the most affectionate motives on the part of the mother. Yet one would prefer to be able to think that Mary did not take part in this intervention of the "relations of Jesus".

One does not exaggerate the importance of this incident. If the earliest Christian tradition kept the memory of it, it was certainly not in order to displease the "brothers of the Lord" who held a place of honour in the Christian community in Jerusalem after the resurrection. The tradition kept it to honour Jesus. "He came unto his own and his own received him not", announces the prologue to the Gospel of John (John 1 : 11, A.V.). Jesus was to know to the depths the bitterness of this rejection. Not only the spiritual and temporal heads of the nation, not only the doctors and the pharisees—blind leaders of the blind,—not only the multitudes fickle and greedy for material benefactions, but His own family, His own dearest "did not receive him". "Even his brothers did not believe in him," observed the Gospel of John (7 : 5). The incident given by Mark is definitely authentic. The affectionate regard in which the family of Jesus was held in the primitive Christian community rules out the possibility that it could have been invented. The synoptic tradition on the contrary has carefully removed the traces of it, and while agreeing in keeping the episode of the intervention of Jesus' family for the sake of the beautiful and comforting word that it gave Him the occasion to say, it took care not to have us know the reason for their intervention. Only Mark has kept it.

This is the only information the synoptic tradition has given us about the relations of Jesus with His mother during the year or the three years of His public ministry. We have no grounds for presuming especially intimate relations between Mary and Jesus during His earthly career. The Gospels are quite silent in this regard. According to the synoptics Mary does not even appear among the group of women who, more faithful than the disciples, went with Jesus even to the foot of the cross. Only John has told us she was there. She appears again only at the beginning of the Acts of the Apostles, together with the brothers of Jesus, in the Jerusalem Christian community which invokes the Lord arisen and ascended to heaven and receives from Him the pentecostal Spirit. Then Mary disappears from sight again and for always.

The Gospel of John contains two episodes that refer to Mary. The first is that of the wedding at Cana in Galilee (John 2: 1–12), when it had come about that there was no more wine for the company and she said to her Son, "They have no wine." These words mean a certain [a] suggestion to intervene even though we do not know what form Mary thought the intervention might take. The answer of Jesus, which may be rendered "Woman, what has this to do with you and me? My hour has not yet come," has no irreverence. The expression "Woman" is the same that Jesus will address to His mother again from the cross, entrusting her to the care of the disciple John. It can have, therefore, only an affectionate meaning. The question "What has this to do with you and me?" means, practically, "What do you want from me?" But all the passages of the Old and New Testaments in which we find the same expression suggest an impression of a surprise that is not particularly welcome and a lack of inclination to give an affirma-

[a] *generico.*

tive response. The least that can be said is that it marks a limit between the one who asks and the one who should reply, and gives to understand that the request is too much or is untimely. And that Mary's request is considered by Jesus to be untimely is clearly expressed by the words that follow, "My hour has not yet come." The hour of Christ is that made plain by God for His manifestation. Christ waits upon God to get the sign of it from Him alone. He does not wait for this sign from His mother, whom he seems to reprove gently for a certain impatience to see the manifestation of his glory, as Chrysostom noted. If one would draw a general principle from this incident it would be that Jesus does not welcome His mother's interference in His messianic work, and it does not hold much to indicate an enhanced value in Mary's intercession even if Jesus, in the last analysis, does accede to her wish.[1]

The other incident is that of Mary at the foot of the cross (John 19: 25–27). "When Jesus saw his mother, and the disciple whom he loved standing near, he said to his mother, 'Woman, behold your son!' Then he said to the disciple, 'Behold your mother!' And from that hour the disciple took her to his own home." This delicate familiar incident does not seem to suggest theological deductions. It is natural that Jesus, dying, should think of the grieving woman who at the foot of the cross suffers everything that a mother can. And it is natural

[1] It is of interest to mention here the opinion of one of the more recent commentaries, that of Rudolph Bultmann (*Das Evangelium des Johannes*, Göttingen, 1941), according to which the incident of the wedding at Cana must come from a circle of disciples among whom a certain importance began to be given to the mother of Jesus, and perhaps holds a point of rebuttal against the incipient veneration of Mary. The refusal of Jesus has, above all, the object of underlining the tremendous and paradoxical character of the deed and of making it parallel with other similar rejections by Jesus (Mark 7: 27) or with declarations such as John 4: 48, Mark 9: 19, etc. The answer of Jesus to his mother is "rude" and the term "woman" is strange if not irreverent. Its significance is that "the ties of kinship and the motives that derive from them are not to be taken into consideration for the action of Jesus. The worker of miracles obeys his own laws and is to listen for another voice" (p. 81). But the rejection is not final, Mary understands and predisposes matters with a view to the miracle, the spiritual meaning of which is that "to the great difficulties of men there is offered the help of the miracle of the revelation. But the event of the revelation is independent of human desires and cannot be forced by human demand. It is fulfilled when and how God wills and above all human expectation" (p. 85). The account is not to be drawn out into allegory nor is Mary intended to be a symbol of the Judaizing church. The parallel is rather the request of the brothers of Jesus and his reply (John 7: 1–10).

also that he should entrust her to the favourite disciple who, according to a plausible interpretation of the familiar relations Jesus had with him, could be His cousin, particularly if it is remembered that, according to the statement of John, Jesus' brothers "did not believe in him". The words "Behold your son; behold your mother", simply refer to relations of affectionate regard which will be established between them. It is clear from the whole situation that if there is a protector it will be the youthful and vigorous disciple, and that the words, "Behold your mother", stress exactly the character of the sacred trust. There is no reason whatever to think that Jesus showed in Mary the spiritual mother of John and of all future believers with him. As far as we know, Mary never in her life exercised any influence that could in any way cause a belief in a spiritual motherhood in relation to the Church. Her position is modest and passive, a disciple among the disciples at the feet of the Lord.

If, however, one wants to give a symbolic meaning to the event—and in dealing with the Gospel of John one can always think of this—it might be said that Mary represents the Jerusalem Church and John the Church of the Gentiles, possibly in its mystic Ephesian character, of which the fourth Gospel is the sublime text, and that through the words on the lips of the dying Jesus the Evangelist counsels the Palestinian community to have maternal regard for the new Christianity that is about to grow out of the mission and this is to serve a grateful veneration for the mother Church.[1] But is it not preferable to think simply that this is an incident of biography, like others unedited,

[1] Such is substantially the interpretation of Bultmann, in his commentary cited. He does not consider the event historical, in view of the fact that the synoptic tradition says nothing of the presence of Mary at the foot of the cross. The symbolic meaning of the incident is this: "The mother of Jesus who stays faithfully at the foot of the cross is Jewish Christianity which rises above the scandal of the crucifixion of Jesus. The ethnic Christianity, represented in the person of the beloved disciple, is told to respect Jewish Christianity as the mother of which it is born, and to consider itself incorporated with it and feel itself truly at home in the large church community." And this instruction coming down from the cross is an order of Jesus that has been "elevated" and its meaning is the same as that of His prayer in John 17: 22 ff., that His disciples and all those who should come to the faith through them "shall be all one". Bultmann maintains that the interpretation of Hirsch is impossible by reason of the incongruence of the symbols when he says Mary represents the Church in general. The Church is the mother of the faithful and is not the mother of Christ but His bride (p. 521).

which is found embedded so singularly in the other meditations of the fourth Gospel?

The only important texts in regard to the Virgin Mary are the first chapters of Matthew and Luke which contain the account of the miraculous birth of Jesus. They are texts of a special nature that in their literary aspect are distinguished from the other parts of Matthew and Luke. They aim not so much to offer biographical particulars but to proclaim the Church's faith in the transcendent and divine nature of Christ. This character is common to all the Gospels, which are written not as biography and history but as testimonies to the manifestation of the Son of God. Yet there are certain moments in the life of Jesus which clothe this manifestation in a particular way. The virgin birth is not the only one nor is it the most important that is presented in the preaching of the Church. The most important is certainly the resurrection. It is enough to read the discourses of Peter, reported with liberty as to their form but in substance faithful to the book of Acts, to be certain that Peter preached "the man Jesus" whom God has accredited by "mighty works and wonders and signs", and that He was crucified by the hands of evil men. But God raised Him up, "and of that we all are witnesses. Being therefore exalted at the right hand of God, and having received from the Father the promise of the Holy Spirit, he has poured out this", on the same day of Pentecost when Peter speaks (Acts 2: 32–33). Christ crucified, Christ risen—this antithetic form is common to all the christological formulæ of Peter's discourses and its ancient character is clear. It corresponds with the "proclamation" of the Gospel of Mark which begins at the baptism of Jesus and goes on, as to its climax, to passion week. Paul makes this antithetic formula his own (1 Cor. 15: 3–5) and has perfected it, Christ was "put to death for our trespasses and raised for our justification" (Rom. 4: 25). Christ, according to him, has been "designated Son of God in power . . . by his resurrection from the dead" (Rom. 1: 4). But Paul adds to the antithesis, crucifixion—resurrection, a new double conception, pre-existence and incarnation. Christ "though rich became poor" (2 Cor. 8: 9). God has sent His Son in flesh, "in the likeness of sinful flesh" (Rom. 8: 3). The full expansion of this type of confession of faith is the notable passage, Philippians 2: 5–11:

"Christ . . . though he was in the form of God . . . emptied himself, taking the form of a servant, being born in the likeness of men. And being found in human form he humbled himself and became obedient unto death, even death on a cross. Therefore God has highly exalted him and bestowed on him the name which is above every name."

That is, the name Kyrios, Lord. The scheme of the Creed is already complete but the virgin birth is not a part of it. John perfects this scheme, identifying Christ with the pre-existent Word by which Creation was made, but he makes no allusion to Jesus' birth of a virgin.[1]

Yet it is the same truth announced by Paul and by John that the accounts of Jesus' birth proclaim in the episodes of the narrative. When Matthew (1: 18) declares that Mary, betrothed to Joseph, finds herself "with child of the Holy Spirit", he has no specific interest in the miracle of virgin birth as such, but wants to affirm solemnly that Jesus was born by the exclusive initiative and operation of that same Spirit that brooded over the waters of confusion on the first day of the world. The birth of Jesus is an event parallel to that of Creation; it is the new Creation in which will be restored the first that was spoiled by the fall of Adam (verse 21). According to the genealogy of Luke, Christ is the son of God and of Adam (Luke 3: 38). According to Paul (Romans 5: 12 ff.), he is the second Adam.[2] If this suggested exposition is true, the first chapter of Matthew is in spirit very close to the prologue of John.

Matthew stresses the annunciation of the virgin birth by citing an oracle of Isaiah (7: 14, A.V.): "Behold, a virgin shall conceive, and bear a son, and shall call his name Immanuel." This application of the prophecy has been able to establish itself only by a Christianity accustomed to read the Bible in the version of the Greek Septuagint. The Hebrew, actually, does not say "a virgin" (*bethulah*) but "a young woman" (*almah*). The Greek renders *almah* with *parthenos*, virgin. But Matthew appears to ascribe rightly a greater importance to the name of

[1] For this exposition see Ethelbert Stauffer, *Die Theologie des Neuen Testaments*, Oikumene, Geneva, 1945, pp. 221 ff.

[2] *Ibid.*, p. 98.

the child to be born, Immanuel, God with us. This admirably sums up the meaning of the incarnation of God in Christ.

The subject of the virgin birth gets no other reference in Matthew, whose content is that of Mark, combined with the *Logia*, discourses of our Lord. The real thesis of Matthew's Gospel is that Jesus is the Messiah, the son of David. But Jesus' descent from David is made to go through the paternity of Joseph. This makes a difficulty, but its importance is not to be overrated. For the gospel writer the important matter was not so much to establish the bodily descent of Jesus as His being in the legitimate line of David. Now, this could not be valid except by the paternal line and according to the rules of the Talmud it was enough for this purpose that Joseph was the legal spouse of Mary.[1]

The first two chapters of Luke form a cycle narrative which in various respects is distinguished from the synoptic tradition that the third Gospel elsewhere follows faithfully. These chapters are full of Biblical recollections, contain lyric passages in the style of the Psalms, and introduce grave personages who seem to be transferred from the Old Testament. The whole atmosphere is Judaic-Messianic while the general tendency of Luke is towards the heathen.

To this fine cycle narrative we are indebted, for the most part, for the poetry of the Nativity and to it Mary owes the beginning of the veneration that accompanies her in the following ages. The idea that these accounts want to inculcate is the same that we have seen in Matthew. And if the beautiful interpretation of Stauffer, already referred to, is right, we have here an allusion, if possible even more explicit, to the creator Spirit of the beginning, an allusion to the "power of the All Highest"

[1] An ancient Syriac version contains the verse Matthew 1 : 16 in this form: "Jacob begat Joseph, Joseph with whom the Virgin Mary was affianced, begat Jesus who is called Christ." The majority of the critics believe that we have here the original form of the genealogy of Jesus, that this ignores the virgin birth and considers Joseph as the father of Jesus and makes Him go back by this way to the house of David. The form that we know would be a later adjustment to harmonize accounts. But it must be observed, with K. L. Schmidt, that this version also designates Mary by the term, the Virgin, and makes her equally in the same line in which Joseph is said to have begotten Jesus. The ancient translator saw no contradiction in this approach and must have meant the paternity of Joseph in a juridical sense as our synoptic version does (K. L. Schmidt, *Kanonische und Apokryphe Evangelien und Apostelgeschichten*, Majer, Basel, 1944).

that initiates our creation. The annunciation, that is to say, is in the setting of the Biblical conception of Creation and not in the Greek-Oriental myth of the virgin birth of heroes and demigods.[1]

All the personalities in the account and all the thoughts of it gravitate about the wonderful declaration of this new manifestation of God's creative power. This does not bring, at least not directly, glory to Mary. The young woman affianced to Joseph, in the account of the annunciation and the birth of Jesus, has the subordinate rôle of the chosen instrument and faithful witness of the great event.

The angel's greeting in the Latin version, "*Ave Maria gratia plena*" (1 : 28) arbitrarily gives an excessive meaning[a] to the Greek verb which is passive: "*chaire, kecharitomene*", "hail thou who hast received grace". And if one takes account of the current meaning of the Hebrew expression "to find grace in the eyes of someone", it means simply, "Hail thou who hast had the fortune to be the object of the kindness [b] of God, who has chosen thee as the instrument of His ways". This is assuredly an expression of the highest distinction, but it does not in any way authorize the idea that Mary can dispense graces with which she is superabundantly endowed. And Mary's reply stresses with great simplicity that rôle of pure instrumentality. She is, in all aspects of the term, the "handmaid of God", completely at His disposition, as is right and logical. Her consent, "Let it be unto me according to thy word", her "fiat"—"let it be", as the Catholic mariologists express it for us, is not charged with all the theological responsibility that they wish to attribute

[1] There are not sufficient reasons for considering Luke 1 : 34–36 as an addition to bring into harmony with the idea of virgin birth an older account which knew nothing of it. It certainly conceived of the birth of Jesus according to the Biblical scheme of the predestination of the man of God to be born of a mother, whereas the idea of virgin birth (parthenogenesis) would be exclusively hellenistic. (Thus Bultmann, *Geschichte der Synoptischen Tradition*, Göttingen, 1921, pp. 175 ff.) On the contrary, the general tendency of the account is to oppose the absolute uniqueness of the birth of Jesus to the birth of John the Baptist that was conceived of in the style of the Old Testament. Thus the demur of Mary: "How shall this be since I do not know a man?" (verse 34), is of course hardly natural in one betrothed on the verge of marriage, but in the pattern of the account this saying has evidently the purpose of emphasizing the wonder of the event, as in the case of the dialogue of Jesus and Mary at the wedding in Cana.

[a] *sovraccarica.*

[b] *attenzione benevola.*

to it. They draw from it proof of the contribution of human freedom to the solicitations of grace with a meritorious worth *de congruo* [a] and therefore having a "co-redemptive" significance.

In the sequel Mary goes to visit her relative Elizabeth, who has received a similar annunciation, yet how different. The two women together, related according to the flesh, but related in a quite different way by the hope and the faith that now unites them, i.e., the trusting expectation of the redemption that has been declared,—these women, if we wish, can be considered in a certain sense the representatives of the Church in the presence of God's declared plans that are fulfilling themselves, representatives of the great divine hour that is about to strike. This is the Church, let it be noted, as it receives a tremendous message from God, accepts it with faith and waits and hopes for its realization, the Church that already feels present in itself the event of the future. It is not the Church that collaborates and distributes grace and is actively associated with the redemption. It is, so to speak, the Church of the Old Covenant on the threshold of the New that is about to be achieved. Otherwise the Church in reality were not one, identical itself through the age of waiting and of prophecy no less than in the age of fulfilment.[1]

Elizabeth salutes Mary, "Blessed are you among women, and blessed is the fruit of your womb! And why is this granted me, that the mother of my Lord should come to me?" What do this meeting and greeting mean? Christ and John, the Lord and Precursor are present, meeting in the persons of their mothers and in the words of Elizabeth. The Precursor bows to his Lord. Such is the meaning of Elizabeth's greeting. It is directed not to Mary personally but to Him whom Mary carries with her. He is "my Lord", *Mar-an*, the divine Messiah promised and awaited: only in this carefully circumscribed sense can it be said that the salutation of Elizabeth anticipates the title *Theotokos*, given to the Virgin Mary.

[a] The ideas of merit *de congruo* and of merit *de condigno* are not too easily grasped, partly because the theologians who use these terms do not always mean exactly the same thing by them. In general one can say that merit *de congruo* means merit of the same character as that of Christ, while merit *de condigno* means merit that is superlatively worthy.

[1] It is of interest to note here the fine interpretation of Karl Barth, *Advent*, French translation, Roulet, Geneva, 1948.

Mary's answer is the Magnificat:[1]

"My soul magnifies the Lord,
And my spirit rejoices in God my Saviour,
For he has regarded the low estate of his handmaiden.
For behold, henceforth
All generations will call me blessed;
For he who is mighty has done great things for me . . ."
(verses 46–49).

Mary, replying to the deferential greeting of her relative, so much more advanced in age and dignity than herself, puts away from herself all reason for praise in order to praise (magnify, make great) "the Lord" only, that is God, who is the only author of the salvation declared. Her sole glory is that God "has regarded the low estate of his handmaiden", has let His regard fall upon her, Mary. "It is enough that God so condescends to look upon us. . . . In this there is already contained the mystery of the virgin birth in which God is present already. . . . That brief moment is filled with eternity, an eternity always new. There is nothing greater in Heaven or on earth. We speak of Mary but it is really to speak of the Church as well."[2]

The song of Mary is entirely of Biblical substance: a mosaic of citations from the Psalms with particular reminiscences of the song of Hannah, mother of Samuel (1 Samuel 2: 2–10) and of the triumphal song of Miriam, Aaron's sister, after the passage of the Red Sea (Exodus 15). Mary is clearly not expressing herself only. In her is the purest tradition of Israel. In her are the highest aspirations, the most unconquerable hopes, the expectation deferred but never abandoned which are lifted in the song. The maid of Israel personifies her people, the people of the promise that sees the hour of fulfilment come.

"He has shown strength with his arm. . . .
He has helped his servant Israel
In remembrance of his mercy,
As he spoke to our fathers,
To Abraham and to his posterity forever." (verses 51, 54–55).

[1] Even though certain manuscripts, supported by the authority of Irenaeus and Nicetas of Remesiana, attribute the *Magnificat* to Elizabeth, we see no sufficient reasons for giving up the general opinion that puts it on the lips of Mary.

[2] Karl Barth, *op. cit.*, pp. 71–72.

The praise of the Almighty's regard that has come down to rest upon the humility of His handmaid suggests the proclamation of the overturning of all customary values:

> "He has scattered the proud in the imagination of their hearts,
> He has put down the mighty from their thrones, and exalted those of low degree;
> He has filled the hungry with good things,
> And the rich he has sent empty away." (verses 51–53).

Does one not seem to hear an echo of the *Beatitudes* in the drastic version that the same Gospel of Luke has given?

> "Blessed are you poor, for yours is the kingdom of God.
> Blessed are you that hunger now, for you shall be satisfied. . . .
> But woe to you that are rich . . .
> Woe to you that are full now . . ." (Luke 6: 20 ff.).

Thus the past joins itself to the future. The Church of the promise, of the expectation, is conscious that it has no power but must wait upon all the infinite and unpredictable grace of its Lord. It desires no other greatness than its need, its hunger and thirst, upon which the creative care of the Lord rests to-day at this time of the changing of the ages. Such is the true Church in every age. So Mary presents herself to her immoderate devotees [a] of future centuries.

The gospel declaration of the virgin birth of Jesus, therefore, has not as its purpose the glorification of Mary. It is rather to proclaim that Christ is Lord, that His birth is the work of the Almighty, that His coming breaks the chain of human generations and events that are exclusively rational and historical. This declaration of the virgin birth of Jesus is to proclaim that in Him is manifested the absolute Principle as at the day of Creation. In the setting of this solemn declaration the miraculous physiology of the virgin birth has a very modest place. This does not mean that we can do without it. The idea of the incarnation must be bound to the presentation of the virgin birth by deep roots indeed if, whenever a doubt has appeared in the Church about the symbol "born of the Virgin Mary", the very idea of the incarnation has then declined to-

[a] *eccessivi ammiratori.*

wards the extremes of Ebionism and docetism,—that is, a Jesus entirely human, Son of God in a solely messianic sense, or a mythical Christ stripped of all historical reality. This is assuredly the reason for the presence of the Virgin Mary in the Creed. She stands there as the faithful witness to the actual historicity of Christ and, at the same time, of His real divinity. She is not only a witness but the chosen instrument of the incarnation. In this is the true, the great glory of Mary. This is enough, according to her words, to "make her blessed" for all time. And in truth she has need of no other glory.

Chapter 2

THE ETERNAL VIRGIN

In the sub-apostolic literature of the first half of the second century almost complete silence reigns concerning the Virgin Mary. The Didache, Clement of Rome, Pseudo-Barnabas, Hermas, Polycarp, the Epistle to Diognetus (in its authentic part), the earliest apologists, Athenagoras, Tatian, Theophilus, the surviving fragments of the Apologia of Hermias, Quadratus, Aristo, Miltiades, none of these mention her at all. Ignatius of Antioch, in his authentic letters, refers to her a few times, and Aristides once, in the Armenian fragments of his Apology to Hadrian; these are the first rudiments of the symbol "apostolic" that begin to outline themselves in opposition to the docetic theories of gnosticism.

The gnostic teachers in the imposing cycle of their cosmogony brought in the Saviour Jesus at a certain point, one who came down into the material world to free the souls that had fallen. But, spiritualists to excess, they maintained that the purest "*eon*" could not really have incarnated himself in a man. They thought that the Christ had temporarily united himself to the man Jesus from his baptism to the crucifixion only, or that he manifested himself with a seeming body without true material substance (docetism, from *dokei*, seems). This second conception had the advantage also of not requiring a real maternity in the physical sense on the part of Mary, whom the *eon* Christ simply passed through as water passes through a conduit. The virginity of Mary in the bringing forth was the legitimate consequence of these speculations, although it was not one in the strict sense.

The Church reacted decisively to the gnostic docetism that denied the real humanity of the Lord and transferred salvation to a mythical plane away from the historical and human. The traces of this reaction are plain to be seen, first in the later writings of the New Testament, then through the references and confutations of the anti-heretical writers, and also in the elaboration of the oldest symbols of the faith. The so-called Apostles' Creed has an anti-docetic tone that is quite recognizable in the emphasis of its affirmation of the real humanity of the Lord and His historical life, "Begotten (*gennethenta*) by the Holy Spirit and by Mary", "*qui natus est de Spiritu Sancto et Maria Virgine*", as the Roman Apostles' Creed affirms. Or "conceived by the Holy Spirit, born of the Virgin Mary", "*conceptum de Spiritu Sancto, natum ex Maria Virgine*", according to the more accurate rendering of the definitive Gallican wording. The Creed expresses the same insistence on the humanity and historicity of Christ in its particularizing of the Passion: "suffered under Pontius Pilate, was crucified dead and buried".[1] The Church did it directly again with the stress these expressions receive from Ignatius of Antioch: "Jesus Christ of the progeny of David by Mary, who was truly begotten, ate and drank, was truly persecuted under Pontius Pilate, was truly crucified and died, in the presence of beings celestial, terrestrial and subterrestrial, who was truly brought to life from the dead, His Father raising Him up."[2] Mary and Pilate! The two pillars on which stands the affirmation of the real historicity of Christ, truly born in a human body at a definite point in history, and truly crucified in that body at an equally definite point in time. Mary and Pilate, the two witnesses of the humanity of the Saviour, that is of the reality of the incarnation. Mary owes her inclusion in the Creed—as does Pilate—to this her function of witnessing, but she assumes, besides, the other function of testifying to His divinity by the adjective that describes her, the Virgin Mary. This function she shares with the affirmation of the resurrection and ascension of Christ which ends the central article of the Creed, *Vere homo et vere Deus*, according to the concise formula of Irenaeus.

To the same exigency of opposing the docetism of the gnostics we owe the first extensive treatment in orthodox Christian literature; that is, the parallel between Eve and Mary, found in Justin Martyr's *Dialogue with Trypho*, which, taken up shortly

[1] Gallican text. The old Roman Creed says more simply: "qui sub Pontio Pilato crucifixus et sepultus, tertia die resurrexit a mortuis". Cf. Lietzmann, *Kleine Texte. Symbole der Alten Kirche*, Berlin, 1931.

[2] Ignatius, *Ad Trallianos* 9, 1. Cf. the other allusions to Mary in his *Ephesians* 7: 2; 18: 2; 19: 1.

afterwards by Irenaeus, has had a large result [a] in centuries following.

> "We have understood," [writes Justin] "that He (Christ) became man by the Virgin so that by the way in which disobedience had its beginning through giving heed to the serpent, by the same way it should meet its end. Being virgin and incorrupt, Eve, having received in herself the word pronounced by the serpent, brought forth disobedience. Mary, having received faith and joy when the angel Gabriel gave her the glad word that the spirit of the Lord would come upon her and the power of the Most High would overshadow her, and that therefore the one who should be born of her would be the Son of God, made answer, 'Let it be unto me according to thy word.' Therefore there was born of her He by whom God destroys both the serpent and the angels and men that resemble it and frees from death those who repent of their bad deeds and believe."[1]

This parallel is evidently inspired by that of Christ and Adam that is found with the apostle Paul (Romans 5: 12 ff.). The parallel of Eve and Mary stresses the historicity of salvation as of sin as well, and expresses the thought that salvation must in some way follow in an inverted sense the way of the fall. It must therefore be on the same level as the other limited enunciations of the second century with which it shares the concern for controverting docetism.

But if the affirmation of the real humanity of Christ seemed to have as consequence the reality of His birth, with all the usual physical effects of maternity, the gnostic idea of a perpetual virginal integrity [b] for Mary was too attractive, too much in accord with the idealizing requirements of piety not to be received by the orthodox, even at the cost of making the miracle greater and more incredible. We see it appearing, with some uncertainty, in the opinion discussed by Clement of Alexandria, that great conciliator, who strove for a gnostic orthodoxy in the extremely spiritualistic circle of the intellectual metropolis of Egypt.[2] His disciple Origen tries to avoid the difficulty presented by the "brothers of the Lord", by attribut-

[a] *fortuna.*

[1] Justin Martyr, *Dialogue with Trypho*, cap. 100, 3.

[b] *incolumnità.*

[2] *Stromata*, VII.

ing an earlier marriage to Joseph alone.[1] Tertullian also, in the same period, ignores the matter or takes no part in the discussion, restricting himself to a consideration of Mary as the ideal example of the "monogamy", i.e., one marriage without a second one, which he strove to inculcate. "Christ was born of a virgin who was to marry once only after the birth in order that in Christ should be manifested both titles of sanctity, through the mother both virgin and married to one man."[2]

The perpetual virginity of Mary, to the great and realistic African doctor, meant less than the reality of the incarnation. He therefore felt no need to yield to the pressure of the gnostics and so put it in doubt that Jesus had brothers and sisters. "*Non recipio quod extra Scripturam de tuo infers*", he wrote to one who contradicted him—not accepting what you infer by your reasoning outside the Scripture.[3] But on the other hand he was glad to show the reality of the forming of the body of Christ in the womb of His mother, with expressions the crudeness of which must appear excessive to-day. "Thou hast drawn me from my mother's womb, *avulsisti me ex utero matris meae*," he writes, applying to Jesus Psalm 22 (Vulgate 21), verse 9. "What is drawn away if it is not that which is adhering, fixed and immersed in that from which it is drawn from outside? If there was no adhering to the womb how was there a drawing away from it? And if that which was drawn away adhered, how did it adhere if not by means of the umbilical cord? . . . And when a distinct thing has been amalgamated to another distinct thing it becomes at that point one flesh only, *ita concarnatur et conviseratur*, with that to which it is so amalgamated, so that when it is drawn away from it, it takes with itself something of the body from which it is drawn."[4]

After these precise details, no one will wish again to doubt the reliability of the Christ of the flesh. But what remains of the perpetual physical integrity of Mary? Tertullian indeed denies it without ambiguity. "Mary is virgin as regards man; she is not virgin as regards birth. . . . Therefore one must call

[1] *Commentary on Matt.* 10: 7, and *Homilies VII on Luke.*

[2] *De Monogamia*, cap. 8: "Christum quidem Virgo enixa est, semel nuptura post partum, ut uterque titulus sanctitatis in Christi sensu dispungeretur, per matrem et virginem et univiram."

[3] Tertullian, *De carne Christi*, cap. 7.

[4] *Ibid.*, cap. 20.

her rather non-virgin than virgin, having been, by a sort of inversion of the natural order, a mother before she was a wife."[1]

Such are the opinions held by the doctors of the third century, at least insofar as they refer to the virginity *in partu* and *post partum*, since about her virginity *ante partum*, that is, the miraculous conception of Jesus through the Holy Spirit, there is general agreement so far. The few Jewish Christians in Palestine who still think of Jesus as the Messiah descended from David by the paternal line, and therefore the son of Joseph and Mary, are now reduced to a negligible sect, the Ebionites.

The agreement in the other two aspects of Mary's virginity, in birth and after birth, was the work of the doctors of the fourth century, but the decisive impulse did not come from theology, nor even chiefly from the requirements of piety or cult. It came from the amazing favour which ascetic ideals acquired after the political victory of Christianity, particularly the ideals about virginity. This is not the place to give the history of Christian asceticism, even briefly. What is important to note here is that with the sudden spread of the ascetic ideal and of the attempts to attain it either in solitude or in the monastic community, there is associated a novel and fervid praise of the perpetual virginity of Mary. To the ascetics of both sexes the Virgin Mother of Jesus offered the ideal model, the inspiring image, and at the same time stimulus and comfort in the hallucinated vigils and in the self-tormenting efforts of the self-discipline of continence. Thus it is no wonder that the greatest promoters of ascetic piety are also the most fervid advocates of the perpetual virginity of Mary; to mention one only, Jerome, *Adversus Helvidium, De perpetua virginitate Beatae Mariae.*

Helvidius, a Roman churchman, was a disciple of the Arian bishop of Milan, Aussensius. It is therefore possible that the controversy which the great exegete carried on with him had a christological background. In this period the glorification of Mary is still closely connected with the work of elaborating the Trinitarian dogma. Mary is the witness of the divinity of

[1] *Ibid.*, cap. 23: "Virgo quantum a viro, non virgo quantum a partu. . . . Utique magis non virgo dicenda est quam virgo, saltu quodam mater ante quam nupta."

Christ and is the "sacred asylum" in which Jesus "lived for ten months" and must be kept free "of the suspicion of all physical intercourse".[1] Yet it would be hard to maintain that this christological preoccupation is the dominant note in the writing of Jerome. He writes in the first place about "the honour of the Virgin" against which Helvidius "turns his rage", comparing him to Erostratus who, to get fame, burned the temple of Diana of Ephesus.[2]

The theological question is already seen to be in process of becoming a theme of chivalry. It is possible to discern in the tone of Jerome's works the vibrant ardour, the sublimated passion that the chaste ascetics of succeeding ages consecrated to the Virgin Mary. The christological theme begins to pass into the second pattern. The virginity of Mary is in process of acquiring a value in itself; better, let us say, it is the value of virginity in itself that comes to be celebrated in the virginity of Mary, that same virginity to which Jerome consecrated shortly afterwards the hyperbolical apologia of his book *Adversus Jovinianum*.

Helvidius maintained that Mary had certainly conceived Jesus by the Holy Spirit and had been virgin up to His birth, but after the birth of Jesus she had become the wife of Joseph in the normal sense and by him had other sons, called by the Gospel "brothers of the Lord". Jerome replied that if the Gospel of Matthew states that Joseph did not know Mary "until she had borne a son" that does not necessarily mean that he did so later, and that according to a Hebrew custom easily demonstrable, the "brothers of the Lord" can be relatives, and in the particular instance, cousins, sons of Cleopas and of Mary, a sister of Mary the mother of Jesus.

With this writing Jerome posed the problem in the terms in which it continues still to be discussed among Catholics and Protestants, without either side succeeding in convincing the other. One must admit that the relations of kinship existing in the group of Jesus' first disciples is complicated by the paucity and lack of clarity in the information we have, by the frequent identity of names, and by the imperfect agreement of the traditions brought together in the Gospel writings. There are three

[1] Jerome, *Adversus Helvidium*, cap. 1.
[2] *Ibid.*, cap. 16.

Marys: the mother of Jesus, Mary mother of James (and wife of Cleopas or Alphaeus) and Mary Magdalene. There are three James: the brother of the apostle John, a son of Zebedee and Salome, James called the less who was son of Cleopas and Mary, and James "the brother of the Lord". Are we to take the last two as the same person and believe that James the brother of the Lord is no other than James the less, as Jerome would have it? But James the less is one of the "twelve", that is the group of disciples who follow Jesus constantly and are therefore the apostles, while the "brothers of Jesus" did not follow him but rather "did not believe in him" (John 7: 5).

There is possibly another case of identity of names. The brothers of Jesus, according to the list in Matthew 13: 55, are called James, Joseph, Simon and Judas. But according to Mark 6: 3, in place of Joseph there appears Joses, which can be an abbreviated form of the same name, and Mary of Cleopas has another son with the name Joses, although this does not prove that she had four sons. But such repetition of names must have been frequent.[1] Jerome's explanation could have only a certain plausibility—it is not impossible that such was the situation. Actually, one who reads the Gospel accounts without dogmatic preoccupation finds no reason for trying to avoid the natural sense of the texts, according to which Jesus had by Mary four brothers and some sisters. Indeed he will find it

[1] On this question see the concise exposition of Neri Giampiccoli: *La famiglia di Gesu*, Claudiana, Torre Pellice, n.d. Also Paolo Bosio, *La figura storica di Maria madre di Gesu*, Conference paper, Claudiana, Torre Pellice, 1935. The idea that Mary of Cleopas is the sister of Mary mother of Jesus rests upon a contestable interpretation of John 19: 25; "Now there stood by the cross of Jesus his mother and his mother's sister, Mary of Cleopas and Mary Magdalene." The question is whether the women are four, three or two. That is: (1) the mother of Jesus; (2) her sister (perhaps to be identified with Salome, Mark 15: 40); (3) Mary of Cleopas; (4) Mary Magdalene; or whether they are three: (1) the mother of Jesus; (2) his mother's sister, that is Mary (wife?) of Cleopas; (3) Mary Magdalene; or whether they are two: the mother of Jesus and her sister, that is Mary (daughter?) of Cleopas and Mary Magdalene. The second interpretation, which is Jerome's, comes to grief on the reef of homonymy: two sisters both called Mary? The third, in addition to the same difficulty, is contrary to the common opinion that Mary is not the daughter of Cleopas but of James the less. It cannot be meant that Mary mother of Jesus is the wife of Cleopas, being the wife of Joseph. The only possible interpretation then is the first. The identification of the sister of Jesus' mother with Salome has nothing impossible in itself. In that case Jesus would be first cousin to John the Evangelist and his brother James (sons of Zebedee). We do not know definitely, however, how far it is legitimate to harmonize two different traditions such as the synoptics and John.

almost psychologically impossible to interpret them differently. Jesus' fine word of consolation in which He contrasts His disciples to His near kin,[a] "These are my brothers," loses its wonderful meaning if the contrast is not with true brothers of his own but with cousins. Again, the argument of those who said of Jesus, Is not this fellow[b] "the carpenter, the son of Mary and brother of James and Joses and Judas and Simon? And are not his sisters here with us?" and, as Mark adds, "they took offence at him"—all this loses the force of identification, loses its savour of scandal if these brothers are in reality cousins, from another father, from another mother; in short, a quite different family.

In his book against Helvidius, Jerome does not touch the problem of virginity "*in partu*" of Mary. In his book against Jovinianus there is an allusion to it but only in passing. Jovinianus had offended the Christian circles at Rome. Having made profession of ascetism he had given up the struggle—vows then not being perpetual—and had become in speech and writing a severe critic of the disproportionate honour in which virginity was held by its new devotees.[c] He gave further offence by seeking to prove his thesis by maintaining that although Mary was virgin in her conception she had lost her virginity in giving birth to the Lord. A Roman synod, called by Bishop Siricius, had excommunicated Jovinianus, describing him as *luxuriae magister, pudicitiae adversarius*. He was summoned before the emperor Theodosius who was at Milan. Ambrose had the Roman excommunication ratified by a synod of Milan, with the emperor's tacit consent.

The letter by which Ambrose told his Roman colleague Siricius about the decision of the synod of Milan can be considered as the basis of the doctrine of Mary's virginity during the birth.[1]

In the first part Ambrose affirms against Jovinianus the eminent worth of virginity:

"Those persons make pretence of bringing honour to marriage. But what is the honour of marriage if virginity has no glory? We

[a] *sui familiari.*
[b] *costui.*
[c] *preconi.*
[1] Ambrose, *Epistola 48, ad Syricium.*

do not deny that marriage has been sanctified by Christ. . . . It is right to praise a good wife but it is still more right to set a godly virgin before her. . . . The former is held in the bonds of marriage; the latter is free of bonds. The former is under the law; the latter under grace. The union is good by which human posterity is obtained; but virginity is better by which is gained a celestial heredity and a succession of heavenly merits. Through a woman care came into the world; through a virgin it left it (*per mulierem cura successit, per virginem cura evenit*). Finally Christ has chosen for himself the gift of virginity and in himself has represented and illuminated the honour that he chose in his mother."

"What is incredible in that, if contrary to the use of nature the sea saw and fled and the waters of Jordan were driven back to their source (Psalm 114 [Vulg. 113])? It is not at all incredible that a man should issue from a virgin if an abundant spring issued from the rock (Numbers 20: 11), if the iron swam upon the water (2 Kings 6: 6), if a man walked upon the waters (Matthew 14: 26). If the waves carried a man could not the virgin bear a man? And what man? He of whom we read, 'And the Lord will show them a man who will save them and the Egyptians will know the Lord' (Isaiah 19: 20, 21). Then in the Old Testament a virgin led the army of the Hebrews across the sea; in the New Testament a royal virgin, chosen by heaven, is the way of salvation."

All this is nobly said but cannot be called very perspicacious. The recourse to the argument of the possibility of the miraculous is too general. It is not a matter of knowing whether such a prodigious event is abstractly possible—this is always admitted *a priori*, *credo quia absurdum*—it is right to say so here. But one wonders what purpose this marvel serves, what verity of faith it expresses. It cannot be said that Mary's virginity *in partu* has a real christological interest. The conception by the action of the Holy Spirit suffices for the idea of the incarnation. The problem of the physical integrity of Mary has no interest except in the ideas about Mary herself, or better, in an ideal of virginity that wants to see itself incarnated in Mary. The mariological interest begins to take precedence over interest in the person of Christ, and one could almost say, over the ascetic interest also, its two forerunners.

Not only this. The declarations of faith, even when they go

beyond the limits of reason, are subordinated to a sort of law of disposition or of interior suitability,[a] to adopt a word dear to the mariologists. Now, one understands perfectly the affirmation of the virginity "*in partu*" in a conception like the docetic that does not consider the body of Christ as real. The reduction of the offence of the incarnation and the idealization of Mary's motherhood go along together mutually supporting each other. But the affirmation of the reality of the incarnation, with all the consequences it implies, seems to have as corollary an emphasizing of its consequences for Mary. To try then to transform a theory of the birth of Jesus of docetic tendencies to an anti-docetic doctrine of His person gives the impression of incomprehensible incongruity, and the appeal to the prodigious event presents itself as the mantle designed to hide the difficulty of a conception logically contradictory.

In his discussion with Helvidius, who objected ironically that the subsequent married life of Mary was not a more difficult idea than the painful physiological reality of her childbirth, Jerome has a spasm of his irate temper and, referring to an analogous expression of Tertullian, exclaims:

> "Put together if you like all the other unpleasant things that belong to nature: the internal disturbance for nine months, the birth, the blood, the cloths [b]—we shall not blush or be silent. The humbler are those things that Christ suffered, the more I am debtor to Him. And when I have named them all I shall not have spoken of anything more shameful than the cross, which I profess and believe, in which I triumph over all enemies."[1]

This, one must agree, is the right tone. This is the ardour of faith that is not offended at the ordeal of the incarnation because it knows that in the Gospel there comes a great revolution of values, that the birth of Christ is the sign of this revolution at the beginning of His life as is His death on the cross at its end. But perhaps the time was not ripe for this recognition, which will be the conquest of mediaeval piety. Jerome took up again against Jovinianus the argument of the bishop of Milan. He did this in a letter to Pammachius that he wrote to defend his

[a] *convenienza.*
[b] *pannilini.*
[1] Jerome, *Adversus Helvidium*, cap. 18. Cf. Tertullian, *De carne Christi*, cap. 4, 5.

book against the charge that he had disparaged marriage too much and had exalted virginity. He added another argument in favour of Mary's virginity "*in partu*":

> "Christ is virgin; the Mother of our Virgin is the perpetual Virgin, mother and virgin. Jesus entered by the closed doors and in His sepulchre which was new and hewn in hardest rock, no one was laid, either before or after. . . . Let them tell me in what way Jesus entered by the closed doors when He gave His hands to be touched and His rib to be seen and His flesh and His bones because His real body was not replaced by a phantasm, and I will answer and tell in what way the holy Mary is mother and virgin at the same time. Virgin after the birth, mother before she was married!"[1]

But is not this recourse to the comparison of Christ's post-resurrection body a little misleading? The Gospel accounts seem to suggest that the body with which Christ came out of the sepulchre is a glorified body made capable of ascending to the highest spheres. Is it possible simply to transfer to the body of Jesus' humiliation what is said about His glorified body? And in this transfer does there not perhaps again appear, involuntarily, a docetic sensibility?

Indeed, as soon as one goes beyond a simple postulating of the wonder, as soon as one tries to make it in some measure intuitive, one seems inevitably to enter a realm of docetic character. Father Roschini, trying in his *Catechismo Mariano* to make Mary's virginity in giving birth understood, writes, "As a pure ray of light passes through a crystal without injuring it but rather giving its own splendour to it, so the incarnate Word, true light of the world, passed through His most blessed Mother, not merely without causing her any harm, but making her radiant with His light."[2] One can suppose that the gnostics would not have disdained this comparison.

[1] Jerome, *Epistola 48 seu Liber apologeticus, ad Pammachium, pro libro contra Jovinianum*, cap. 21. The last words: "mother before she was married" are an allusion and an answer to the verdict of Tertullian, *De Carne Christi* 23, cited above.

[2] Roschini. *Chi è Maria? Catechismo mariano*, p. 61; cf. *Mariologia*, II, 2, p. 260. The imagery goes back to Bernard of Clairvaux. The objection we have made is already noted by Jovinianus and is included by Thomas Aquinas, *Summa Theologica*, III, quaestio 28, art. 2. He objects that humility and glory are united in Christ's body: "To show the reality of His body He was born of a woman, to show His

The elements of the doctrine of Mary's perpetual virginity are all present at the end of the fourth century. The miraculous conception of Jesus receives the belief of the Church from the end of the New Testament period. Her virginity in giving birth and after are subjects of discussion and definition. They will be declared a dogma of the Church by the Lateran Council of A.D. 649, Martin I being Bishop of Rome.

The dogmatic decision was preceded by popular imagination. Toward the end of the fifth century there began to circulate in western Christendom a tract entitled *Book of the birth of the Blessed Mary and the infancy of the Saviour.* It purported to be the translation of the Hebrew of a certain Gospel of St Matthew, made by Jerome at the request of two bishops. Its attribution to Jerome is of course a literary fiction that shows the fame this great writer enjoyed not only as an hebraist but also as a supporter of Mary. The book is a compilation of not very ancient materials that show numerous affinities with the legends that were going to appear about the same time, the *Protevangelium of James.*

When Augustus' decree for the census was issued, relates *Pseudo-Matthew*, Joseph and Mary set out for Bethlehem. On the way, Mary says to Joseph: "I see two people before me, one weeping and the other joyful." Joseph urges her not to be upset and not to speak or tire herself, but an angel in the form of a shining youth explains that the two people are the Jews, who have gone away from God, and the Gentiles who "will be blessed in the seed of Abraham".

> "At this point the angel causes the animal that Mary rides to stop, for the time of birth has come. He told Mary to dismount and enter a subterranean cavern where there was never any light but always darkness because the light of day did not penetrate it. But at Mary's entry the whole cavern began to shine with light as if the sun were there and the divine light illuminated the cave as though it were full noon. Night and day that light remained while Mary was there. And there she bore a male child whom the angels adored as they surrounded him in his birth, saying

divinity He was born of a virgin." He does not concede that Christ's body assumed at birth a special gift of "*subtilitas*", or that it possessed already the qualities of the glorified body, and he confines himself, in the last analysis, to the affirmation of the miracle.

'Glory to God in the highest and on earth peace to men of good will.'

"Meanwhile Joseph had gone to look for midwives. When he came back to the cavern Mary had already borne the child. Joseph said to her, 'I have brought you the midwives Zelomi and Salome who are outside the cave but do not dare come in because there is so much brightness.' Mary smiled as she heard this. Joseph went on, 'Do not smile, be careful, lest you need medicine.' Then he had one of the women come in and Zelomi, having entered, said to Mary, 'Will you let me touch you?' And Mary having permitted her, the midwife cried out with a loud voice, 'Lord, great Lord have mercy! Never has this been heard or imagined! The breasts are filled with milk and the baby born shows that his mother is virgin. There is no blood on the child and no pain of childbirth. As a virgin she has conceived, as virgin she has given birth, a virgin she has remained!' (*Virgo concepit, virgo peperit, virgo permansit.*)

"Salome, the other midwife, hearing these words, said, 'I will not believe what I hear unless I have the proof myself,' and having gone in she said to Mary, 'Allow me to touch you to make sure whether Zelomi has told the truth.' And Mary having allowed her to do so Salome put out her hand. And when she put out her hand and touched her it dried up and began to pain violently so that in her desperation she wept and cried out, 'Lord, thou knowest that I have always feared thee and have always cared for the poor without pay and have taken nothing from the widow and orphan and have never sent the poor away empty handed. And here I am afflicted for my unbelief because I have ventured to doubt thy virgin.' And as she spoke there appeared close to her a youth all shining who said, 'Come near to the child, adore him and touch him with thy hand and he will heal thee, for he is the Saviour of the world and of all those who hope in him.' And she went to the child forthwith, and adoring him touched the hem of the swaddling clothes about him and at once her hand was healed. And going out she proceeded to declare the marvellous things she had seen and suffered and how she had recovered, so that many believed in her word."[1]

We have quoted this version of the account, characteristic of the main narratives among the apocryphal gospels known to us. It may have gained currency because its Latin rendering was

[1] *Liber de ortu B. Virginis Mariae*, cap. 13, in the volume: *Les Evangiles Apocryphes*, Textes et documents, ed. Hemer et Lejay, Paris, 1911, pp. 96 ff.

what gave credit to these legends in the Roman church circles, while the rigour of the juridical and theological proof that it purports to give brings us a clear indication of the interest which it answers. The problem of virginity *in partu* is resolved with the expert technique of two skilled witnesses. Its meaning is supported by the punishment Salome brings on herself by her incredulity, while without that incredulity the proof witnessed to would be less valid. And the result of the legal verification is formulated with all the theological rigour that was necessary and possible in the fifth century, "*Virgo concepit, virgo peperit, virgo permansit!*"

Through these characteristics our account presents a progression over that earlier and also more poetical *Protevangelium of James* which proceeds thus.

When, after the vision of the two people (which is not explained by any angel nor needs to be) Mary was placed in the grotto, Joseph goes in search of a midwife. Then a wonder takes place. For a moment everything in nature and the world of men comes to a stop. The air of the sky is "filled with fear" and the birds stop in their flight. On the earth some men who are kneading bread stop motionless, bent over the kneading trough. Sheep that move about stop, and their shepherds remain with staff upraised, the kids at the watering place stand without drinking; then all starts to move again. Joseph, having by chance found a midwife, comes back to the grotto with her. This is covered with a bright cloud, clearly a sign of the divine presence. The cloud melts away and in the grotto appears a dazzling light that grows dim little by little until the newborn one appears and attaches himself to Mary's bosom. Are we to see in these imaginings the poetic description of the descent of the Word that unites itself with the baby Jesus at His birth, or is it just a case of poetry without theological responsibility?

However that may be, the wonder suffices for the midwife who praises God and goes out, meets Salome, announces the wonder to her which the other does not believe and the story becomes like that of *Pseudo-Matthew*, without the intervention of the angel which is superfluous in any case. In all these details, and in the fact that the first of the two women is not designated by name, we have the indication of the greater antiquity of the legend. In the Arabic-Armenian narrative of the infancy the legend is still more developed. There is one person more, Joses, the youngest of Joseph's sons, who stays by the entrance of the grotto while his father goes in search of the midwife. In this way the unfortunate necessity is avoided of leaving Mary alone in that anxious time, and the midwife, by chance met by Joseph, is represented as Eve, the mother of the living, who comes "to take part in her redemption". It is she who goes to meet Salome and announces the wonder to her. Salome not only disbelieves but passes condemnation upon Mary for her illegal pregnancy. The rest of the account seems to be a compilation of the *Protevangelium of James* and of *Pseudo-Matthew*.

What value have these legends? The central core of the *Protevangelium of James* is certainly very old, for it was known by Justin Martyr and by Origen, but one cannot with certainty trace it back beyond the mid-century. The period was marked by the beginning of a whole outgrowth of Gospels and Acts of Apostles around the nucleus of our canonical gospels, the purpose of which was to set forth definite theological interpretations of the coming of Christ, or, more simply, to supply an answer for the desire of the faithful for particulars and, above all, for wonders. The extent of this production is shown by the fact that about fifty apocryphal gospels are known by title and from twenty to thirty Acts of Apostles.[1]

[1] K. L. Schmidt, *Kanonische und Apokryphe Evangelien*, p. 37. Roschini, *Mariologia*, I, p. 63, cites the lament of Thomas of Villanova (1488–1556) for the silence of the Gospels about the Virgin Mary: "I am thinking and wondering why the Evangelists deal so fully with John the Baptist and the other apostles and so meagrely with the Virgin Mary who is above them all through the dignity of her life. Why, I say, has it not been handed down to us how she was conceived, how she was born, how she was brought up, with what virtue she was adorned or what she did with her Son in the human relationships, how she was accustomed to conduct herself with him or how she lived with the apostles after the Ascension? These were great matters and worthy of being remembered, of being read devoutly by the faithful, of being meditated on by the people. Oh Evangelists, I say, why do you deprive us of such joy by your silence? Why are you silent about things so happy, desirable and joyful?" Roschini adduces certain reasons. God has wished it so as to glorify her the more. The author applies to Mary the words of Philippians 2: 9, "He has given her a name which is above every name." God has wanted to warn us against earthly glory. It was not necessary to add to her glory other than this:—she was the mother of Jesus. Her glory was so great that silence is the greater praise. And added to this is the fact that the Gospels were occasional writings, having a scope limited and precise, and that Mary's life does not present itself favourably to being described, being entirely an inner life, and the Gospels having been written (at least the synoptics) while she was still living, their authors

At the beginning the Church adopted a severely critical and healthy attitude towards this literature, whether because of its gnostic tendencies or for its absolute lack of sobriety. The accounts of our canonical Gospels generally exclude from all their treatment the purely narrative and romantic interest in order to focus their readers' attention solely upon the central figure of Christ as the Messiah who suffered and was glorified. But the natural desire to know more of Him, to give a name to the secondary personages, to explain certain circumstances on which the Gospel is silent, the desire to glorify the Redeemer by an abundance of striking wonders flows on in the apocryphal literature.

The Church did not always persevere in the sane and critical spirit of the first centuries. When the discussions provoked by the gnostics calmed down and the dogma of the great councils of the fourth and fifth centuries was firmly fixed, the legendary material of the apocryphal gospels began to circulate more freely in versions expurgated to make them orthodox, as the preface of *Pseudo-Matthew* states, and their theme entered the common patrimony of the Church. From the apocryphal literature comes almost everything that is believed and thought about the Virgin Mary: the names of her parents Joachim and Anna, her late birth, announced by an angel, her education in the Temple, her vow of perpetual virginity on account of which she was betrothed to Joseph, who was old and a widower, marked by the wonder of the dove issuing from the rod. From this apocryphal literature come the circumstances we have cited of the birth of the Saviour, which are preceded by a long and tragic story of the difficult situation in which Joseph and Mary came to find themselves as a result of her virginal conception, of the "judgment of water" to which both are subjected by the action of the priests and from which they emerge victorious; and after the birth of Jesus the wonders of His capricious infancy as a little divine despot. The interest of the legend soon changes from the figure of Jesus to that of the secondary personages, especially the Virgin Mary, with a particular predilection for the theory of her perpetual virginity. From the *Protevangelium*

did not want to trouble her modesty. Some of these reasons are indeed plausible; would it not be appropriate to remind Mary's faithful followers of them sometimes?

of James in particular Origen had learned that the "brothers of the Lord" were sons of Joseph by an earlier marriage. In the last analysis that explanation, even if it has no support in the canonical Gospels, could be more plausible than the theory that we have seen elaborated on the Gospel texts by Jerome but at the cost of forcing them; a theory that became official in catholic theology.

One can suppose that it was the desire to give precision to the form and circumstances of the Virgin Mary's life, on account of the importance she assumes as supreme symbol of the ascetic ideal of the fourth century and as a result of the eminent position given her by the Council of Ephesus in 431 as Mother of God, that induced the Church to relax its earlier mistrust of the apocryphal traditions and to accept their content. But notwithstanding the wealth of their contribution to piety and Christian art, a sober historical judgment must recognize their complete inconsistency. The intensive work of the scholars on the extra-canonical sources of the life of Jesus, with the help of valuable papyri that have been recovered, has done nothing but confirm what has always been the conviction of the Church. All that we can know about Jesus, apart from some sayings of quite secondary value, is contained in the canonical books of the New Testament.[1] And that is also true of the Virgin Mary.

[1] Joachim Jeremias, *Unbekannte Jesusworte*, Zwingli-Verlag, Zürich, 1948, p. 33.

Chapter 3

THE MOTHER OF GOD

IN 325, barely twelve years after the political victory of Christianity, the Council of Nicaea, condemning Arius' theory, defined the "consubstantiality" of God the Son with the Father; that is, the perfect divinity of Christ. As a result of this definition Mary could be said to be, in a certain sense, the Mother of God (*Theotokos*). It is not possible to show with certainty the origin of this description which, according to a statement of the historian Socrates that cannot be verified, goes back to Origen and was certainly used many times by Athanasius, the great promoter of the Nicene orthodoxy. The first purpose of the title *Theotokos* (*Deipara*, *Dei genetrix*) is not to glorify the Virgin Mary but to express in a term clear, impressive and popular the real divine humanity of Christ. God in Christ is made man in such a precise and realistic sense that Mary can be called His mother. This expression is a paradox which pleased faith, in that it could adore the humiliation of God come down into the world in "the form of a servant" (Phil. 2:7) to save men. It does not seem, moreover, that through the fourth century the title "Mother of God" had any wide diffusion except in Egypt. Alexandria had already been the spiritual forge of a mystic christology radical in character in the preceding centuries, while in the discussions of the fourth and fifth centuries the school of Antioch and the Anatolian Church represented in opposition to it the standards of sober criticism and of rational theological temper.

It was around the title *Theotokos* that the most animated and occasionally violent christological disputes turned in the first half of the fifth century, disputes confused and envenomed by the rivalry of patriarchal sees and settled temporarily by interventions of political authority. In a limited way the doctrine that is our concern here had a place in the Councils of Ephesus (431) and Chalcedon (451).

In these discussions it was essentially a question of christology

—the person of Christ. Mary is not the object. Her person, the preoccupation about her "honour" has no part there, at least officially. The true problem is to define accurately the Nicene conception of the substantial identity of Christ with God (*homoousia*), avoiding at once interpretations that are insufficient or excessive by which the faith might be troubled. Among these the expression *Mother of God* was not the most problematical. From the earliest time Christians had repeated with a shudder of devout horror and unbounded love, "God has suffered for us: God was crucified for us." These expressions, in their latitude, could mean that divinity itself in its greatness and serenity had known suffering and death and was that not, perhaps, stating too much? Already, towards the middle of the third century, Tertullian was offended by the modalistic christology of Praxeas, which did not draw the distinction between Father and Son with sufficient clarity. "Praxeas has committed two offences at Rome," the great African roared; "he has crucified the Father and driven out the Holy Spirit!" He was referring, it is well known, to his beloved and inspired Montanists whom Praxeas opposed.

In what sense can it be said that God was crucified or that God was born of the Virgin Mary? Here is the problem that wearied the minds of the fifth century, and the heat of the passion that accompanies the fluctuations of the doctrine makes it clear that the problem was not just an arbitrary theological abstraction but was vital to faith. The first phase of the dispute begins with Nestorius, archbishop of Constantinople, and Cyril, archbishop of Alexandria, and ends with the Council of Ephesus and its condemnation of Nestorius. In the second phase the quarrel is between the Nestorian party represented by the school of Antioch and the archimandrite of Constantinople, Eutyches, and ends with a conciliatory formula suggested by the bishop of Rome, Leo I, a man of theological and diplomatic genius and the first bishop of Rome who had truly papal stature. His formula was substantially adopted by the Council of Chalcedon.

The first reserve in considering the term *Theotokos* is not associated with Nestorius but with his teacher Theodore of Mopsuestia, a colleague in the priesthood of John Chrysostom, then for thirty-three years bishop of the city of Cilicia from which he gets his name and where he died in 428, celebrated for his orthodoxy and greatly venerated. He combated the idea expressed by Apollinarius in the preceding century, who, in teaching the union of the Word with a human body without a rational soul, had come to deny the true humanity of Christ. Theodore vindicated the completeness of Jesus' humanity possessed of a body and a rational soul, declaring that Mary had borne Jesus but not the Logos, which has always been and has no beginning, even though it had dwelt in a particular way in Jesus. Mary is therefore in a proper sense the mother of Christ and not the mother of God. She cannot be called mother of God unless in a figurative sense and because God is in Christ in a narrowly particular way.[a] She has actually given birth to a man,[b] to whom the Word is united, initially, from His birth, but still imperfectly inasmuch as Christ is not declared Son of God until after His baptism. According to Theodore, it was therefore not true sense to say of God that He was born of a virgin, that is, what is born of Mary is not God but the temple in which God has made His abode.[1]

Nestorius, raised to the episcopal seat of Constantinople in 428, found opinion divided: some called Mary "Mother of God" and others wanted to give her only the name "Mother of the man" Jesus (*Anthropotokos*). Nestorius tried to reconcile the two to what he wrote himself, proposing to them the obvious name of Mother of Christ. According to another version it was rather Nestorius who divided people's opinion by suggesting his own doubts about the expression "*Theotokos*" that was generally allowed. However this may be, there was much agitation and Nestorius had to define his doctrine in sermons. He declared that Christ is two-fold in His natures but one in the honour given Him:

> "When the Holy Scripture speaks of the birth of Christ or of His death, it does not call Him God but Christ, or Jesus, or Lord, terms which are appropriate for the two natures. Mary ought to be called *Christotokos*, because giving birth to the son of God she gave birth to a man who, by his union with the Son of God, can be called Son of God. In such a sense one can say that the Son

[a] *in modo particolarissimo.*

[b] *propriamente dato i natali ad un uomo.*

[1] Hefele-Leclercq, *Histoire des Conciles* (Paris, 1908), Vol. II, part I, p. 233.

of God died but one cannot say that God is dead. . . . We desire to keep intact but without confusion the union of the two natures. We want to recognize God in the man and venerate this man united with God in a divine manner and that makes him worthy of our prayers."[1]

Nestorius went on to say in another sermon that whoever taught in any absolute fashion that God was born of the Virgin Mary made the Christian dogma ridiculous in the eyes of the heathen, who could reply, "I cannot pray to a God who was born and died and was buried." But seeking to calm his adversaries and to find a way of conciliation he declared also that "that which is born of woman is not solely God or solely man, but humanity united to divinity", and declared himself ready to accept the title of Mother of God provided it was clearly intended in the sense he indicated.[2] Writing to Pope Celestine he proposed the formula, "The two natures which perfectly united with each other and without confusion are adored in the one person of the Only Begotten" (*utraque natura quae per conjunctionem summam et inconfusam in una persona unigeniti adorantur*). It is hard to say in what way this formula is distinguished from that which will be the orthodox formula of Chalcedon and was the formula of the Roman faith.[3]

These quotations indicate clearly what gave Nestorius concern. He did not deny the reality of the two natures or their union in the person of Christ, but he wanted them to be distinguished. He denied that divinity "in itself" could be born and suffer; he accepted the expression "*Theotokos*" in certain cases but rejected it in the heretical sense that "divinity in itself" could have a mother.[4] But Nestorius conceived the union of the divine and human in Christ as the moral and spiritual union of a holy man with the Son of God, come down to live in him as in a temple. Jesus and Christ, in the final analysis, were two distinct persons, intimately united by a sacred will and to be held in honour as one. The paradox of the incarnation

[1] Hefele, II, 1, p. 242.

[2] Hefele, *loc. cit.*

[3] Epistula II, *Nestorii ad Coelestium*; cf. Harnack, *Dogmengeschichte*, Italian translation, *Storia del Dogma*, Mendrisio, Vol. IV, p. 221. Referred to hereinafter as *History of Dogma*.

[4] Thus Hefele, II, 1, pp. 246, 7.

was becoming dangerously thin and the Church, all things considered, could do no other than reject the christology of Nestorius as too close to the spirit of Arianism.

But if it was easy to reject an inadequate solution it was no easier to formulate one satisfactory at every point. As soon as the union of the Word and the Man in Jesus Christ is considered seriously and the attempt is made to conceive this union clearly, the idea inevitably presents itself that the humanity of Jesus has been absorbed, transfigured, annulled and transcended by His divinity. The "monophysite" conception which recognizes only one nature in Christ, and that divine, thus comes forward and it can be avoided only by the most careful and subtle theological distinction.

In the precision of doctrinal conception that was the result of the Nestorian dispute, the difference between the monophysite and the orthodox interpretations of the union of the natures in Christ found expression in two closely related formulæ: physical union, *henosis physike*, and hypostatic union, *henosis hypostatike*. By physical or natural union was meant the union of divinity itself and humanity itself, and this conception was set aside as responsible for the confusion that had stirred up the Nestorian trouble. The hypostatic union meant instead the union of a divine being (*hypostasis*, rendered imperfectly by the Latin *persona*), and the actual divine Word with the man Jesus. This was a union of "God" in a positive and limited sense and not of divinity in its full sense. It was a union with a man in the fullness of his personal attributes, body and rational soul, and not with an abstract idea of humanity, much less with a human body without rational soul as Apollinarius had argued in the preceding century, entirely resolving the human individuality of Christ in the divine Word. It is a matter of subtle distinction but of fundamental importance, for the title *Theotokos* can be accepted in the second sense but must be rejected in the other.

If the ideas of the Alexandrian party and of their leader Cyril in their controversy with Nestorius are examined in the light of this essential distinction, it cannot be denied that Nestorius was seriously exposed to the charge of monophysitism. Cyril believed he was simply opposing Nestorius with the Nicene orthodoxy. Actually he was making large use of the formula "physical union" and considered it as synonymous with the "hypostatic union". It was not that he failed to distinguish their difference, it seems, but because he resolved the hypostatic union in the physical, at least on the side of the man, for through him the Word united itself truly to a "human nature". (Unlike Apollinarius, Cyril said that it was a complete and natural man with body and rational soul.) The two natures before their union were distinct but after it they became one nature only. This is the nature of the incarnate Word, of the Word become flesh, and in consequence of the union of the two natures in one, the properties (*phonai*, *idiomata*) of one can be attributed to the other. This means that what can be said of Christ according to His divine nature can likewise be said of Him according to His human nature and vice versa (*communicatio idiomatum*) and it is therefore accurate to say that God has suffered and that Mary is the Mother of God.[1]

If, then, one looks beyond the formulæ and regards the sentiment, the devotion, the state of mind of the masses of the simple believers, and especially if one takes note of the Egyptian monks who formed Cyril's great supporting army, one cannot doubt for a moment that the contest with Nestorius was carried on by monophysitism in the name of Nicene orthodoxy. One sees too that the Council of Ephesus in its very failure to give any new formulation is a monophysite victory, and it is in the name of monophysite devotion and feeling that the title *Theotokos* was triumphally launched in 431.

There is nothing for wonder in this. As we have been compelled to recognize an affinity not fortuitous between docetic sensibility and the theory of Mary's perpetual virginity, so here in the sphere of personal piety we see beyond the subtle theological distinctions a natural affinity between the idea of the complete fusion of the two natures in Christ and the title *Theotokos*. It will be said: that piety was just the orthodox Nicene piety. No. The orthodox piety, on the contrary, was as concerned not to confuse God and man in Jesus Christ as to conserve their union. The scruples of Nestorius (not his theology) are part of orthodox Christian piety, as much as the mystic exaltation of the Egyptians. In fact, the orthodox christological formula will be that defined by the synod of

[1] See Harnack, *History of Dogma*, Vol. IV, p. 214.

Chalcedon and will be such with the help of Rome, always interested in affirming the two natures. But an undiscriminating unitive title like *Theotokos* would not have come out of orthodox piety with its requirements of unity and distinction. This title conveys the same enraptured enthusiasm with which the crowds greeted Jesus in His every aspect, and indirectly in His worship, in His sacraments, in His mystical body, in the martyrs and their relics in which they adored the transfigured presence of the divine. That piety reflected, substantially, belief in the incarnation, but it needed to be tempered and guided in order that its demand for the divine in tangible form should not turn into a deification of all that is of Christ. Precisely such a restraining rôle in the dispute was filled by the critical school of Antioch.

The Council of Ephesus was called by Emperor Theodosius II as a result of the appeal by the parties of Cyril and Nestorius after each had been excommunicated by the other. Cyril had issued twelve anathemas and had been the target of an equal number in return.[1] The place of the council could not have been more unfavourable to Nestorius.

The province of Ephesus brought a particular interest to the question. The generally received tradition put the death of the Virgin Mary at Ephesus. A building was still there that was said to be her tomb and not far from it was the tomb of John the apostle. The council itself consecrated that tradition. The people of Ephesus showed for their protectress an enthusiastic devotion that had completely cancelled out their earlier ardour for the great Diana of the Ephesians. There was the same susceptibility that had almost cost Saint Paul dearly four centuries earlier. The man who would have dared in Ephesus to contest with Mary the title of Mother of God would have been considered not only a blasphemer but an enemy of the city. It would have been hard to prevent such a setting from influencing the assembly which it surrounded—and to some degree oppressed—on every side. The bishop of Ephesus shared the devotion of his fellow citizens.[2] Here is a new factor, not to

[1] The texts in Hefele, II, 1, pp. 270 ff.

[2] Thus Leclercq, in a note on the cited work of Hefele, II, 1, p. 292. This opinion, general among historians in the past, is contested among others by Jugie, *La Mort et l'Assomption de la S. Vierge*, Vatican City, 1944, pp. 96 ff. It is based on the statement contained in the official letter, in which the Council of Ephesus

be disregarded. In the victory of the title *Theotokos* how much weight must be given to the popular devotion to the Virgin Mary? Again a strict question of theology became a matter of chivalry: the honour of Mary was at stake and had to be defended.

The council was called for Pentecost, 431. Count Candidianus was to preside at the assembly in judicial capacity, for both parties had asked for an award by imperial authority. His instructions stipulated that the assembly should not be constituted until the parties to the contest were all there. That, obviously, was dealing with a council that was to work a pacification. But at the date given there were present only the Egyptian delegates and those from Asia Minor who were for Cyril (about two hundred) while those of the Antioch school—who were not so much favourable to Nestorius as opposed to the Egyptian monophysite position—were delayed on their journey by a series of misadventures. The papal delegates were also late. After waiting two weeks, although it was known that the men from the east were only a few days distant from Ephesus, Cyril decided to begin the council, against the opinion of the representative of the Emperor and sixty-eight bishops. Candidianus who tried to oppose this was put out of the council forcibly. The council constituted itself, cited Nestorius who refused to appear, excommunicated him and deposed him from his patriarchal rank. All was settled in one session lasting from morning till evening, June 22nd. When it was spread abroad through the city that the Holy Virgin's honour had been saved by the council, a crowd came rejoicing to acclaim the bishops at the door of the cathedral, escorting them with torches to their lodgings while the city proceeded with a festive illumination.

The council, held by Cyril with such precipitateness against the express arrangements of the Emperor, was not only illegal

conveyed to the people of Constantinople the notice of Nestorius' excommunication: "Nestorius, the renewer of the impious heresy, having been the first to arrive in the city of Ephesus, where (are) John the Theologian and the Virgin Theotokos, the holy Mary, having withdrawn from the assembly of holy fathers and bishops. . . ." The verb is missing but can easily be supplied. But in what sense "are" John and the Virgin Mary in Ephesus? It seems natural to think of their relics. Jugie interprets it that there were two churches dedicated to their names and that the council was held actually in the one dedicated to Mary Theotokos. But this interpretation seems less natural.

but contrary to the very purpose of making peace that had presided at its convocation. One of the two parties had been entirely absent. Of the bishops present, many in their uncertainty had submitted to Cyril's energetic and intransigent will and the pressure of the city that surrounded them. Nestorius' sentence of excommunication had 198 signatures: a forced unanimity, how sincere there is no knowing.

A few days later the eastern delegates arrived, led by John, Patriarch of Antioch. On being informed of what had happened he held a counter-council with the imperial representative in which Cyril and Memnon were excommunicated and deposed. Later the Roman delegates had the first council reconvened and sanctioned its decisions.

Once again the two parties appealed to the Emperor. He ratified the deposition of the leaders of the two factions, then initiated conciliation using persons who were in his confidence. The negotiations were long and laborious and after dramatic vicissitudes reached a formula of agreement, proposed by John of Antioch and accepted by Cyril. It declared, after a preamble that confirmed the Nicene faith:

> "We confess that our Lord Jesus Christ, Son of God, Only Begotten, is perfect God (*teleion*) and perfect man (*teleion*), of a rational soul and a body; before the ages he was begotten by the Father in his divinity and in these last times for us and for our salvation, by Mary, according to humanity. He is consubstantial with the Father (*homoousion to patri*) according to divinity and consubstantial with us (*homoousion hemin*) according to humanity, since the union of the two natures took place. Therefore we confess only one Christ, only one Son, only one Lord. And through this union, free of all confusion, we confess that the holy Virgin is Mother of God (*Theotokos*), by the fact that God the Word is incarnated and made man, and from her conception has united to his very self the temple taken from her. As for the gospel and apostolic statements (*phonai*) about the Lord, we know that those which apply to the two natures refer to only one person, and those that distinguish the two natures refer to only one nature, and the expressions which refer to God are transmitted to us by the divinity of Christ and those that are more humble, by his humanity."[1]

[1] Text in Hefele, II, 1, p. 396.

This formula of agreement was perfectly orthodox. If the debatable aspects of Cyril's theology were the result of the relative imprecision of his terminology more than of anything else, it is understandable that he was able to subscribe to the formula and then defend it. Yet it cost him notable renunciations. The distinction of the two natures was expressed in a form much more rigorous than that which Cyril had been accustomed to use. The theory of the *communicatio idiomatum*, so dear to him, was practically denied or at least severely circumscribed. The perfection of Jesus' humanity was defined so as to exclude all trace of Apollinarianism and was fixed by the two complementary expressions: consubstantial with the Father, consubstantial with us. It is possible that his decision to accept was dictated more by considerations of church diplomacy than by conviction.

However this may be, it appeared to his party as a victory and recovery [a] of Nestorianism and the dispute broke out again, especially after Cyril's death in 444. The most influential leader of the monophysites then was Archimandrite Eutyches, of Constantinople. He was an old man, an ascetic, the head of a respected convent. He could not accept it that two natures of Christ should still be spoken of after they were united in one person, and he denounced as heretics those who professed such an opinion. Tempers grew bitter. The patriarch of Constantinople, Flavian, cited the old man before an assembly of thirty bishops where the attempt was made in vain to get his adherence to the formula of concord. "Up until this day I have never taken the liberty of discussing the nature of my God. . . . Until this day I have never said that his body is *consubstantial* with ours. . . ." So he spoke with warmth, letting it be understood that he considered that expression a dangerous innovation. He was ready to submit but maintained his point of view. The council excommunicated him. His party, however, had a revenge in a new council at Ephesus in 449, which, for the violence that characterized it, was called the "Robber Synod". The bishops present were forced to disavow the decisions of Constantinople and to depose Flavian and his adherents. Flavian, beaten and wounded, died from the ill treatment he received.

[a] *rivincita*.

At this point began the action of Leo the Great for peace, action decisive, shrewd and energetic. In the first phase of the controversy Rome had acted against Nestorius, but now it lined up definitely on the side of the doctrine of the two natures, defined in the formula of John of Antioch, accepted by Cyril. The doctrine of the Roman see was expressed by Leo in a letter of dogma addressed to the patriarch Flavian, that stands as a monument to those qualities characteristic of the Church of Rome—its genius for balance, for what is practical, its preference for devotion and action rather than subtle theological distinctions. After confuting the utterances of Eutyches, *homo imprudens et nimis imperitus*, the pope sets forth, with arguments that are simple and concrete, the real humanity and real divinity of Christ.

"The Son of God came into this world below, coming down from His heavenly seat and without losing His paternal glory, by a new order and a new nativity. By a new order, in which being invisible by its own order it made itself visible in ours, and, incomprehensible, He willed to be comprehended. And He who was before time began to be in time. And the Lord of the universe, the greatness of His majesty being hidden, took the form of a servant. God who is not subject to suffering (*impassibilis*) did not disdain to become a man subject to all suffering, and the immortal to submit Himself to the laws of death. He was born by a new birth, because the virginity that was inviolate did not know concupiscence but offered the material of the flesh. From the mother the Lord received the nature of flesh but not the guilt. Although the Lord Jesus Christ was born of the womb of the Virgin, because His birth is wonderful, it does not follow that His nature is different from ours. He who is true God is also true man. And there is no falsehood in this unity in which are joined (*invicem sunt*) the humility of the man and the loftiness of God. As God does not change His nature by His humbling Himself in mercy (*non mutatur miseratione*), so man is not absorbed into the divine by his elevation (*non consumitur dignitate*). Each of the two forms completes, in communion with the other, what is proper to it. The Word works what is proper to the Word, the flesh fulfils what is proper to the flesh. The one is resplendent by its miracles, the other succumbs under its injuries. And as the Word does not recede from its equality with the paternal glory, so the flesh does not give up the nature of our race. . . . The birth in the flesh is a manifestation of its human nature; the virgin birth is evidence of a divine virtue. The weakness of the baby is shown by the lowliness of the cradle, and the greatness of the Most High is declared by the voice of the angels. . . . To suffer hunger and thirst, to be weary, to sleep, is clearly human. But to feed five thousand men with five loaves, to give to the Samaritan woman the living water [after] which he who drinks will never thirst again, to walk upon the sea, to command the tempest, is incontestably divine. . . .

"To pass over many things, does it not belong to the same nature to pity a friend who has died and bring him to life again from the sepulchre where he has been for three days; or else to be hung upon the cross and change day to night and make all the elements tremble; to be pierced by nails and open the doors of paradise to the faith of the thief? Thus is it not of the same nature to say, 'I and the Father are one' (John 10: 30) and 'The Father is greater than I' (John 14: 28)? Indeed even if in the Lord Jesus the person of man and God is only one, the humiliation and the glory, common to both, have a different origin. From us He has His humanity which is less than the Father; from the Father, His divinity, which is equal to the Father. For this unity of the person in two natures one reads that the Son of man is come down from heaven, though it is the Son of God who has put on the flesh of the Virgin of whom He is born. Thus, moreover, it is read that the son of God was crucified and buried, though He did not suffer this in His divinity itself by which He is the only begotten coeternal and consubstantial with the Father, but in the infirmity of human nature. Therefore we all confess in the Creed that the only begotten Son of God was crucified and buried, according to the apostolic words, 'If they had known it they would never have crucified the Lord of glory, (1 Cor. 2: 8). . . ."[1]

We have quoted at length, because this letter, that stays so close to the requirements of piety, shows what is the interest for the faith in the doctrine of the two natures in Christ, their personal union and their necessary distinction. It shows also in what sense and within what limits the title, Mother of God, is intended.

The Council of Chalcedon produced its creed. This ecumenical council was called by Emperor Marcian at the request

[1] Text in Hefele, II, 2, pp. 722 ff. Cf. L. H. Heurtley, *De Fide et Symbolo*, London, 1887, pp. 209 ff. (*Trans.*)

of the pope and was held in that city on the Bosphorus. In its fifth session this creed was drafted to put an end to the disputes aroused by that title of the Virgin. It brought together in its sober formulary both the point of view expressed in the dogmatic letter of Leo the Great and the old formula of conciliation of the parties of Cyril and Antioch. It defined the faith in the following words:

> "Following the holy fathers we confess all together one and the same Son, our Lord Jesus Christ. And He is complete in divinity and complete in humanity, truly God and truly man, being a rational soul and a body, consubstantial with the Father according to divinity and consubstantial with us according to humanity, in all things like us except without sin. He was begotten before time by the Father by divinity and in the last days for us and for our salvation by Mary, the Virgin, the Mother of God according to humanity one and the same Christ, Son, Lord, Only Begotten, whom we acknowledge to be in two natures without confusion or transformation, division or separation. The difference of the two natures is not suppressed by the union, but rather the properties of each nature are kept and united in one person only and in one hypostasis only, not divided or disjoined in two persons but one and the same Son and Only Begotten, God, Word, Lord Jesus Christ, as the prophets have taught us of Him from the beginning, and as He Himself the Lord Jesus Christ taught us, and as has been transmitted to us in the Creed of the fathers."[1]

And now, after all this weary detail, we can ask what then is the orthodox and legitimate meaning of the title Mother of God? The theological errors that offended Nestorius having been laid aside, the hypostatic union of the two distinct natures in Christ having been accurately defined and each having been kept in possession of what is its inalienable due, the expression Mother of God means exactly that the Virgin Mary is mother, according to the flesh, of the incarnate Word in its aspect of humanity. None of the foregoing words can be left out without the sense of *Theotokos* being falsified. Mary is mother of Christ "according to the flesh", because Christ "according to the spirit" is son of God and conceived by the Holy Spirit. She is

[1] Text in Hefele, *loc. cit.*, and in Lietzmann, *Symbole der Alten Kirche*, p. 35. Cf. Heurtley, *op. cit.*, pp. 26, 27. (*Trans.*)

mother not by divinity in herself—a blasphemous idea—but by the hypostasis of the Logos; but not by the Logos in itself, which has no mother, but the Logos incarnated. And she is the mother of the incarnate Logos by its aspect of humanity because the properties of the two natures must be respected and what is said of Christ as God is not to be said of Christ as man. This notwithstanding, in virtue of the hypostatic union, since there is only one Christ, one can say, with all the reservations and explanations above, that the Mother of Christ is the Mother of God and that such is the paradox of the faith.[1]

This paradox could and ought to have remained such. Its christological function freed, rigorously defined by its help, the hypostatic union of the two natures in Christ ought to have been able to re-enter the armament of theological formularies, useful for them yet dangerous for the undesirable implications that can be suggested. It cannot be said that the title "Mother of God", in its grandiose and emphatic expression, corresponds exactly with the orthodox definition that has been given of it which suggests simply the idea that Mary is the mother of the incarnate Word in its human aspect. The formula, so much more sober and evangelical, suggested by Nestorius, if only with a bad theological motive, was yet the right formula, devout, respectful, capable of bringing together the reverent support of all Christendom; Mary is the mother of Christ. And also the expression that the Evangelist puts on the lips of Elizabeth (Luke 1: 43), "The mother of my Lord", clearly refers to the messianic dignity of Jesus. But the name of God, notwithstanding all the theological definitions, remains by universal consent the term that designates divinity in its infinite fullness. There is no reason why any person, unless he has been duly warned and has thought about the results of the christological dispute of the fifth century, should make a distinction between God and divinity and should consider the title Mother

[1] The explanation of Roschini is, if possible, still more cautious. "If we look carefully, the formulae Mother of Christ and Mother of God are synonymous and mean one and the same thing only. The Blessed Virgin, indeed, is not called Mother of God in that she gave birth to Divinity or the divine nature of the Word (that would be heretical), but because she gave birth to the human nature assumed by the Word in the unity of the person (*humanam naturam in unitatem personae a Verbo assumptam*), or rather because she bore, by humanity, a person having humanity and divinity (*genuit secundum humanitatem personam habentem humanitatem et divinitatem*)." *Mariologia*, II, 1, p. 143.

of God as inferior to that of Mother of divinity, or should translate the legitimate paradox into something much vaster and more disputable than what it is intended to mean. Perhaps for this particular reason, Calvin, who in theology recognizes the legitimacy of the title "Mother of God", never adopts it in practice, unlike Luther and Zwingli and the theologians of Protestant orthodoxy who make frequent use of it for its christological significance.[1]

But the success of the term *Theotokos* is not due to its christological meaning. The delirious crowd that at Ephesus in 431 acclaimed the removal of Nestorius, or demonstrated twenty years later for the insertion of that title in the Creed of Chalcedon, was probably not in a position to appreciate the subtleties of the hypostatic union and the *communicatio idiomatum.* It saw just one thing clearly: Christ is God and Mary is His Mother. But the full divinity of Christ had been for more than a century the indisputable heritage of the Church universal. The innovation was the solemn emphasis that the new discussions indirectly put upon Mary's name. The formula Mary *Theotokos* had been the banner of one party in the christological dispute, the impressive formula of the two natures in one person: but the standard now acquired an importance in itself and for itself. It was the official and ecumenical proclamation of the incomparable glory of Mary. All that which, for whatever reason, merged and flowed towards a more and more deliberate veneration of Mary gained an enhanced status from the solemn formula. The destiny of the Virgin Mary as an object of worship began from this date.

[1] Cf. Karl Barth, *Kirchliche Dogmatik I,* 2 (1939), p. 152. He quotes, among others, Luther's interpretation: "Mary did not give birth to a separate man as if on her part she had a son, and God on his part had his Son. But he himself whom God begot from eternity, him she bore in time." (*Enarratio 53 cap. Esaiae*, Erl. op. lat. 23, 476.)

Chapter 4

QUEEN OF HEAVEN

Apuleius, the platonist of Madaura, in his autobiographical novel *The Metamorphoses*, relates how after various misfortunes due to his ardent temperament he won release and inward peace through initiation into the mysteries of Isis. His invocation of the goddess and her answer make an interesting page in the history of the religions of imperial Rome in the second century.

> "Queen of heaven," [the philosopher invoked] "whether thou art Ceres mother of the grain . . . whether thou art heavenly Venus who first united the sexes in love—whether thou art Phoebus' sister who dost help women in confinement and art worshipped in Ephesus, whether thou art Proserpina with her nightly howlings—or thou who with feminine lustre lightest all cities and with thy humid light dost nourish the tender buds and diffuse a radiance that changes with the travelling of the sun, whatever thy name, whatever the rite, in whatever form it is permitted to invoke thee, come to help me in my utter misery."

The goddess appears in answer to his invocation, arising out of the sea, clothed in the attributes of the several divinities by whose name she has been called, and answers the afflicted one.

> "Behold me, Lucius, moved by thy prayers. I am the Mother of Nature, Mistress of all the elements, first Progenetrix of the ages, Supreme among the divinities, Queen of the dead, First of celestial beings, Figure alike of Gods and Goddesses. With my nod I govern the heights of heaven in their brightness, the health-bringing winds of the sea, the mournful silences of the underworld. My divinity in its uniqueness is worshipped by all the world in many forms, by various rites, under diverse names. The Phrygians, first born among the peoples, call me Mother of the Gods of Pessinus, the autochthonous Athenians, Minerva Cecrops; the islanders of Cyprus, Venus Paphia, the Cretans who draw the bow Diana Dictynna; the Sicilians who speak three tongues,

Stygian Proserpina, the Eleusinians, the ancient Goddess Ceres; some call me Juno, others Bellona, Hecate, Ramnusia. The Ethiopians, lighted by the first rays of the rising sun, and the Arii, and the Egyptians wise through ancient lore, honour me with rites that are proper to me, and call me by my true name, Isis Regina!"

Having received the gracious answer and become a faithful devotee, the initiate turns to her again.

"O thou holy one, perpetual saviour of mankind, always bountiful in nourishing mortals, thou dost give a mother's sweet affection to the wretched and unfortunate. No day goes by, no night, no slightest moment that is empty of thy benefits or that thy protection is not over men by sea and land. Thou dost assuage the tempests of our life; thou dost hold out thy helping hand and drawest out the tangled threads of the Fates; thou calmest the storms of Fortune and restrainest the stars in their hurtful course. The supernal beings honour thee, the infernal deities do thee reverence; thou dost make the world revolve and to the Sun thou givest its light; thou dost rule the world and hast the powers of hell under thy feet. The stars obey thee, by thee the seasons come again, in thee the gods are joyful and the elements are thy servants. At thy nod the winds blow gently and clouds gather, seed comes to life and crops grow up. The birds of heaven fear before thy majesty and the wild beasts of the hills, the serpents hiding in the earth and the monsters swimming in the deep. To celebrate thy praises my talent cannot suffice. . . ."[1]

This very beautiful invocation lets us understand what could be the religious vision and the piety of a pagan philosopher of the second century. The philosophical criticism and the syncretistic combination of traditional cults are complete. Gods and goddesses are now only intuitive forms behind which divinity hides itself, one, spiritual, invisible. We must not let ourselves be misled by the fantastic description or by the feminine appellation. Isis the queen is above the sexes; she is the essence of all the gods and goddesses but the female form in which she presents herself is the symbol of a majesty that has pity. Such is the most apparent attribute in Apuleius' invoca-

[1] Apuleius, *Metamorphoses*, lib. IX.

tions. And it is in the quality of mercy that she dispenses the blessings of nature that are the prerogative of the various goddesses of agriculture whose mystic images are merged and resolved in her name. This devotion is not nature worship, at least not confessedly. Plutarch in his *De Iside et Osiride* already has rejected as puerile the naturalistic interpretation that seems still to-day to be the high point of scientific objectivity to so many historians of religion. But it has a pantheistic tone. "I am all that has been and is and is to be, and no mortal has taken away my virtue"—so reads the inscription to her on the temple of Sais. But above all she is the Goddess "knowing and philosophic to the extreme degree", whose name, by Plutarch's etymology, expresses wisdom.[1]

Isis the merciful, the wise, the universal mother, dispenser of the blessings of life, thought of as Pallas Athena, the Virgin Cecrops, but also thought of as *Khochma*, Sophia, who in the Hebrew wisdom literature is the joyful collaborator of Jehovah in the morning of the world and is identified with the Word in the syncretistic judaeo-platonism of Philo. Is it possible that this divine female figure, in which is centred so much spirituality and so much light of merciful goodness, has been without relation to or influence upon that evolution which has brought the Virgin Mary to the place we know in Christian piety, an evolution that is marked by growing intensity after the Council of Ephesus?

Clearly the problem cannot be evaded. But the answer is neither as easy nor as obvious as might appear on superficial comparison.

Until the mid-fifth century there is nothing in orthodox Christianity that with certainty can be defined as a cult of Mary. One might suppose that the fear of assimilating the mother of Christ to some female figure of pagan syncretism had a delaying effect on the emergence of her cult. But there is certainly a more basic reason: in the Christian consciousness of the first centuries Mary had nothing in common with a personality that was divine or quasi-divine and merciful. She stayed characteristically on the human plane as "witness" of the incarnation, and, we can say further, a secondary witness. In

[1] Plutarch, *De Iside et Osiride*, cap. 9. The inscription of Sais, *ibid.*, cap. 2. He makes the name Isis derive from the same root as *eimi*, I am.

Christian piety of the first three centuries the position of Mary is less important than that which the martyrs were assuming, whose veneration is already attested by the *Martyrdom of Polycarp* about the mid-second century. The first great impulse towards the veneration of Mary is the rise of asceticism in the fourth century; the second, the christological definition of the fifth, the *Theotokos*. Before these there is no determining motive for raising Mary to the dignity of the altars.

The position is otherwise in the marginal currents such as gnosis. Here it is evident that the syncretistic motive is at work. The spiritual atmosphere of the gnostic communion is the same breathed by Apuleius and Plutarch, or more exactly, the same as that which must have prevailed in the cults of initiation which were not comprised exclusively of cultivated people of the intellectual understanding of our two philosophers. We find in gnosticism the same tendency to merge myths and interpret allegorically, and moreover, a phantasy at times exuberant, which is not always kept within the bounds of informed and critical thought, as it is in the case of greater gnostic teachers such as Valentinus. Hippolytus of Rome, in the first decades of the third century, could base all the confutation of heresy, contained in his *Philosophumena*, on the thesis that gnosis was none other than the Christian transposition of Greek philosophy and mystery religions. We are therefore to expect to find in gnosis a Christian equivalent of the cult of the Mother, celestial and polymorphous, that was celebrated by Apuleius. And in fact such is the case, but once again the results are less decisive than what one could suppose from the analogies suggested by the history of religions.

We find in the gnosticism of certain more noted teachers such as Valentinus the continued concern to represent intelligible essences as emanating from the one unfathomable and primordial Abyss—and it was also furnished with a female equivalent, *Sige*, Silence—essences in bisexual pairs, thus assuring to the idea of femininity its presence in the transcendent world of divine archetypes. But there is no hint at an identification of one of these feminine entities with the Virgin Mary. The gnosis that offers the most favourable prospect in this regard, if we go by the information of Irenaeus and Hippolytus, is that of the Ophites or Naasseni, who adored the serpent in Eden.

Irenaeus tells us that there are those who have it that in the primordial Abyss there is an original light, holy and inscrutable, called Father Universal, and it is represented as the First Man.[1] Projecting from himself his idea of himself he begot a son, the Son of Man, the second man. Below these is the Holy Spirit which brooded over chaos and is the First Woman (*Ruach*, the Spirit, in Hebrew is feminine). Impregnated with light by the Father and the Son, the First Woman becomes the mother of the son Christ. Then, unable to bear the excess of light by which she is overwhelmed, she emits from her left side a potency that is besprinkled with light, Prunicus-Sophia, which goes down into the primordial waters, troubles them, and gives origin to the sensible cosmos. This comes under the dominion of seven powers born of Sophia in whom can be recognized equally the hypostasis of the evil Demiurge, the Creator of the Old Testament. The greatest of these powers, Ialdabaoth, created Adam in his own likeness and gave him Eve for companion. But the *eon* Sophia has now repented of having given life to this wicked world of sensibility, and is offended by Ialdabaoth's pride, who has had the audacity to proclaim himself the only God, ignoring the existence of the First Man. He seduces Eve by means of the serpent, or, according to others, seduces her personally by taking the form of a serpent, to induce her to rebel against the evil Demiurge, giving her the "gnosis", that is the knowledge of her true nature, luminous and immortal. Adam and Eve are condemned by Ialdabaoth and there begins a long battle between him and Sophia, who seeks to free the souls, luminous sparks, that are submerged in matter. The Mother, the First Woman, seeing her weariness and having compassion, prays to the First Man to send Christ to help her. The *eon* Christ comes down, recognizes his sister Sophia, and the two make their dwelling in the most wise, pure and just man who has ever been, Jesus, born of the Virgin Mary. They remain in him until the moment of his crucifixion. Actually only the man Jesus is crucified and is then raised up again by Christ as a sign of gratitude for his service.

[1] Irenaeus, *Adversus Haereses*, lib. I, cap. 30. For brevity we omit the other forms of gnosis that gave an important place to a female figure. Among Montanists also there was a sect, "the philomarianita". Cf. Cecchelli, *Mater Christi*, I, pp. 137, 149.

Such in brief is the Ophite gnosis[a], in which the constant themes of gnostic speculation are easily recognized: the antithesis of the world of ideas and the world of sense, the hostility towards the "inferior" system of the Old Testament which in this case is pushed to a rehabilitation of the fall of Eve considered as a glorious rebellion and a conquest of truth jealously opposed by the Demiurge. By this topsy-turvy relationship of values comes the name of the sect that glorifies the serpent, wise and clever, as a symbol of wisdom.

But Sophia also, the Wisdom of Hebrew gnostic writing, is after all an *eon* of lower nature. The rejection of the Old Testament involves, as well, the idea of wisdom personified in it. In Valentinus' system Sophia is the last of the *eons*, the farthest from the infinite[b] Father, from whom comes, instead, the Mind (*Nous*), the Word, the Man, with whom are the feminine correlatives, Truth, Life, and the Church. It is not possible in this general review to identify Sophia with the Word as in Philo. Anti-semitism projects itself into the world of divine perfection: the Word and the Holy Spirit are at one extreme, the highest; Sophia is at the other, the lowest. Her figure in the gnosis of Valentinus is that of a weak and transcendent Eve who with her restless curiosity disturbs the perfection of the Pleroma, the divine fullness.

In the same way in the gnosis of the Ophites, we have the figure of a heavenly Mother of Christ, not of the incarnate Christ, however, but of the *eon* Christ. As a result we have the representation of Sophia as associated with Christ in His redemptive work, an evident concession to the Christian identification of the Hebrew Wisdom with the hellenistic Word. And on the same human and historic plane we have the Virgin Mary, mother of Jesus but not of Christ. We must resist, however, the temptation to a hasty identification of these figures because there metaphysical dualism and the religious-historic dualism of the system are opposed. The mother of Jesus in the gnosis is a small weak human creature who belongs to the tiny sphere of influence of the guilty Sophia. There certainly appears to be no promise of the honours of an apotheosis.

That the identification should come—as come it did—one

[a] The Greek *ophis* means serpent.
[b] *insondabile.*

must suppose that the double dualism of gnosticism was overcome, that the idea of the reality of the incarnation triumphed over the docetic conceptions and that the hostility towards the theories of the Old Testament was forgotten. Then the celestial Mother of Christ will be able to come down to meet the Virgin mother of Jesus, the Virgin Mary; on the wings of the hypostatic union she will have power to rise to the heavenly Mother of Christ and they will be able to form one person. This is not to affirm that such was actually the way followed by the cult of Mary, but one wants to indicate the psychological possibility and the historical possibility of this identification.

In reality everything that came out of gnosis was the object of energetic repudiation by the Church and one can take it that the gnostic speculations, with their transcendent sexual dialectic and with their evident and avowed affinities with the pagan mysteries, may well have put the Church on guard against a deification of Mary of which it felt no need and which did not conform with the virile style of hebraic-Christian symbolism.

But the identification of the Virgin Mary with the heavenly mother of Christ was effectually accomplished in the realm of heresies. Epiphanius, at the end of the fourth century, in his catalogue of heresies described a sect of women in Arabia, of Thracian origin, and in upper Scythia, who offered to the Virgin little cakes of barley flour on a small squared altar, adorning themselves with the title "priestesses of Mary".

This suggests a Biblical parallel. In the sixth century B.C., Jeremiah, among his reproaches to the people of Judah, denounced a cult of the "queen of heaven":

> "The children gather wood,
> The fathers kindle fire,
> And the women knead dough,
> To make cakes for the Queen of heaven;
> And they pour out drink offerings to other gods,
> To provoke me to anger.
> Is it I whom they provoke? says the Lord.
> Is it not themselves, to their own confusion?"
>
> (Jer. 7: 18, 19)

The queen of heaven to whom the women of Palestine were giving their homage and devotion was at the time of Jeremiah the Canaanitish goddess Astarte, the semitic Venus, goddess of the earth's fecundity, sometimes worshipped in her astral Babylonish form of Ishtar, star of the morning and evening. Epiphanius vehemently rejects the strange cult of this confraternity of women, declaring that Mary is not a goddess and sacrifices are not to be made to her. His indignation shows clearly that in orthodox Christianity at the end of the fourth century the very idea of worship of Mary could still cause scandal.[1]

After the Council of Ephesus the situation changes; and to find the reason we must think not so much about the theological content of the title *Theotokos*, which means strictly "the mother of Christ" and was not an innovation, but we must think rather of the vague and high sounding tone of the title itself, suggesting more than the actual dogmatic meaning. The "divine maternity" was the expression used—inappropriately—by the Catholic theologians, translating the concrete *Theotokos* into an abstract, which the Council of Chalcedon would probably have refused because it seems to suggest that Mary was mother divinely or that she was a divine mother. This title exalted Mary effectually to the extreme limit of humanity and brought her close to the realm of the divine. There she was to meet with the other Virgins and the other Mothers, the spiritualized conception of which Apuleius saw mystically prefigured in Isis of many forms.

This assimilation is to be seen in Christian art. The representation of the enthroned Virgin with the infant reproduces the typical Isis with her son Horus on her knees, in the same hierarchical positions and with faces the same.[2] She wears the mural crown like the *Magna Mater*, Cybele, protectress of the Roman Empire.[3] She shows affinity with the figure of Athena with the Gorgon at her breast. Some Byzantine likenesses have the baby enclosed in an oval medallion on Mary's breast.[4]

[1] Epiphanius, *Panarion*, n. 78, 79. Cf. the discussion and bibliography in Carlo Cecchelli, *Mater Christi*, Francesco Ferrari ed., Rome, 1946, Vol. I, p. 136. He arbitrarily limits Epiphanius' criticism, it seems to me, to the form of the worship rendered by those simple and ignorant women.

[2] Carlo Cecchelli, *Mater Christi*, cit. I., p. 83. Cf. the Byzantine likeness of the Madonna della Clemenza in S. Maria in Trastavere, pp. 80, 81.

[3] *Ibid.*, I, p. 235. Cf. Table V, pp. 98, 99 (S. Maria Antiqua, in Rome).

[4] *Ibid.*, I, p. 88; cf. p. 217 ff. The fact that the infant is enclosed in the sacred oval (the mandala) could mean that Mary is the "temple" of God more than

Equally characteristic is the erection of churches dedicated to the Virgin Mary on the foundations of temples to various pagan deities or in their proximity. Santa Maria Antiqua, in Rome, stands in an area consecrated to Pallas and before that again to the Etruscan Minerva.[1] Santa Maria in Aracoeli is built on the Capitoline hill where the celestial Virgin—the Carthaginian Tanit—used to be worshipped.[2] Santa Maria above Minerva, near the Pantheon, whose very name means that it was a reconsecrated pagan sanctuary, arose in the vicinity of a sanctuary of Isis.[3] Santa Maria Maggiore, on the Esquiline, according to a mediaeval record, was built on the site of a temple of Cybele, Mother of the Gods, and if the belief is not confirmed by excavations it is true that less than three hundred yards away stood a temple dedicated to Juno Lucina, protectress of women with child.[4] The most suggestive of these superimpositions were perhaps those which occurred on former dedications to Minerva. Besides the Roman temple, the *Athenaion* in Syracuse was reconstructed to the Madonna, seemingly before the seventh century.[5] A still more striking instance was that on the hill in Athens sacred to Pallas, where the Erechtheum was reconsecrated to the Virgin Mary. It is not possible to verify the statement that the greatest sanctuary in Constantinople, Saint Sophia, was built where the pagan temple had stood.[6]

In this instance the supersession means an assimilation that has an explicit theological meaning. In the Byzantine theology of the eleventh century the Virgin Mary will be identified with Wisdom and with the Church.[7] There is going to be a transposition of the terms of the early Christian theology by which Wisdom is Biblically identified with the Word, that is Christ, a transposition that is in harmony with certain gnostic views.

"Mother of God", *Theodokos* and not *Theotokos*, according to the distinction of the Nestorians. The resemblance to *Athena Clipeata* is therefore only external. It is interesting, however.

[1] Cecchelli, I, p. 53.

[2] *Ibid.*, p. 43.

[3] *Ibid.*, p. 89.

[4] *Ibid.*, pp. 198, 199.

[5] *Ibid.*, p. 89.

[6] *Ibid.*, p. 64.

[7] *Ibid.*, pp. 238 ff. Bibliography and discussions in the notes. See also the Appendix, "Ancora della Sophia e del Logos," pp. 279 ff.

It can be supposed that the mere grammatical fact that Sophia is feminine has helped toward its identification with Mary rather than with Jesus, but it can be doubted that such identification would have been possible if Mary had not already succeeded Minerva, the wisest of the goddesses.

The superimposing of Mary upon the Virgins and Mothers of the ancient pagan pantheon has had the result of continuing their functions. Mary takes the place of Juno as protectress of women with child. She replaces Athena Polias as protectress of cities, or, according to the localities, Tyche or Fortuna.[1] She becomes protectress of sailors in succession to Isis, star of the sea, and replaces Cybele as protectress of Rome, and similarly with all the propitiatory goddesses of the pagan nature cults.[2]

This substitution of Mary for the pagan divinities took place partly through a spontaneous transfer of the popular piety of the converted masses, and, after Constantine, imperfectly converted. In part it corresponded with a programme of exorcising of the pagan cults by the Church which destroyed paganism when it could, and when it could not, or found it preferable, took its place by transforming it. The reconsecrations of temples, the location of new sanctuaries in the vicinity of pagan shrines are evidently intentional. It can be presumed that they were done with careful thought in the knowledge of the dangers they presented, and to this knowledge can be attributed the fact that on the whole the reconsecrations were rare and in general it was preferred simply to build in the neighbourhood of the most celebrated pagan sanctuaries, as though to oppose the true worship to the "diabolic". In this setting up of Mary above the pagan goddesses the polemic motive was certainly more important than assimilation. One can therefore agree with Cecchelli when in the course of his investigations of the origins of the worship of Mary, rich in artistic, archæological and theological lore, he writes:

> "The contribution of the pagan devotion to the female divinities was a factor that was subsequently to make itself felt more strongly

[1] *Ibid.*, pp. 198, 90.

[2] In the Coptic liturgy, as we shall see when we deal with the Assumption, the feasts of Mary, December 26, May 15 and August 13, are set to secure Mary's blessing on the sowing, the harvests and the vintage.

in manifestations of popular piety. . . . On the other hand it cannot be denied that in the impulse it took at a particular moment, the cult of the Madonna may have been part of that general turning of Mediterranean deference towards the heavenly woman, Virgin or Mother or else an associate in a love mystery."[1]

These prudent expressions, confirmed by ecclesiastical approbation, can be considered to represent the more serious Catholic study on our subject. They are, to be sure, rather below truth than above it. The field in which the creative and assimilative phantasy of popular piety displayed itself was truly vast. Official pronouncements in part guided the popular sentiment but in part they were subject to it. The uncritical transfer of the attributes and functions of the mother goddesses to the Virgin Mary was like a rising tide to which the guiding organs of the Church could offer no effective resistance because in its own mind it had connived in their expression.

The admission is important, however, that a generic impulse was there through the working of the Mediterranean cult of the goddess mother and we must take account of it. It is not without interest to bring to it the statement of a Protestant theologian who is not suspected of any nostalgia for Catholicism, Karl Barth.

"Our objection to the cult of Mary does not rest essentially on the affirmation that it is the result of the transfer of paganism, of the representation of a feminine or maternal divinity more or less central and original contained in many religions outside Christianity. . . . The Biblical writings themselves that contain the testimony of the revelation work all along the line with elements that are 'pagan' or are so represented and they do so of necessity: just as it is true that the world to which they shut their ears is that pagan world. . . . That affirmation is in no case an article of evangelical faith. And it certainly cannot constitute a serious problem set against Catholicism."[2]

These statements of Barth are to be taken in the climate of a reaction against the "religious-historical" school with its

[1] Cecchelli, *Mater Christi*, I, p. 150. Of course we do not care to subscribe to the rest of his sentence: "An impulse that was very general, as is seen, which does not at all lessen the Christian importance of the worship of the Madonna, because there we must perceive a predestination and an expectation."

[2] Karl Barth, *Kirchliche Dogmatik*, I, 2, p. 157.

specious and hazardous parallels in comparative history of religions, a reaction quite extensive among Protestant theologians particularly of Barth's generation. In substantial accord with what we have cited of Cecchelli they circumscribe a problem and define a method. They tell us that the worship of Mary is a subject of the history of dogma and in only a secondary way of the history of religions. But perhaps the very character of the reaction that they show in some measure limits its importance for our problem. We are entitled to ask whether the cult of Mary, in borrowing from the female pagan cults, took only their language and their symbols or did it not assume from them some element of substance, whether, in short, the impulse was truly "generic" only or did it have some specific content.[a]

If we pay attention only to the most apparent aspects of the official cult of Mary on the one side, and the cults of the mother goddesses on the other, their difference appears great. On the one hand we have an organic construction—we do not say normal, that is another matter—which develops thoughts and feelings that come out of the margin of the faith in the incarnation of God in Christ. On the other hand we have a cult of naturalistic origin and in essence pantheistic which seems to have nothing in common with the preceding. If a parallel had to be established on the plane of the history of religions, one would have to say that Mary is a very modest competitor of the syncretistic goddess of many forms worshipped in the Mediterranean world, since after all Mary is not a goddess but the figure of an historic woman who slowly mounts the steps of apotheosis—the most modest form of cult in the ancient world and the expression of divinity that is most problematical. On the other hand Isis, Cybele, Minerva are authentic goddesses and different expressions of a really divine idea. But these antitheses lose something of their apparent evidence and this is due to another factor which, for all its obscurity, was the real meeting place of Marian piety and the cults of the Mediterranean world, gnosis.

The gnostic motif of the celestial Mother of Christ, identified more or less clearly with the Holy Spirit, a female, and with the Wisdom of the Bible, a belief which although not included in the official theology of the West had a large place in that of

[a] *aspetto.*

the Christian East, contained the germ of an assimilation of the Virgin Mary to the cosmic functions proper to female divinities.

"In her," writes Bulgakov, "is realized the idea of Divine Wisdom in the creation of the world; she is Divine Wisdom in the created world. It is in her that Divine Wisdom is justified, and thus the veneration of the Virgin blends with that of the Holy Wisdom. In the Virgin there are united Holy Wisdom and the Wisdom of the created world, the Holy Spirit and the human hypostasis. Her body is completely spiritual and transfigured. She is the justification, the end, the meaning of creation; she is, in this sense, the glory of the world. In her God is already all in all."[1] Mary, in fact, is "the creature glorified, and completely deified."

Now it is interesting to observe that Bulgakov explains these ideas in antithesis to the pagan cults: Mary is not a goddess precisely because she is the creature deified. In reality, in the pantheistic atmosphere of Mediterranean syncretism, it is hard to mark out rigorously the boundaries between divinity in its proper sense and the creature deified. In all the religions of the Eastern Mediterranean in certain archaic phases is to be found the idea of a female divinity which, in antithesis to male divinity, personifies the cosmic principle, the earth, the passive matter that waits to be fertilized—Rhea, Demeter, Cybele, Isis herself—and upon which is wrought the activity and initiative of the divine masculine principle. The assimilation of the Virgin Mary to the symbol of the creature glorified and fully deified is not in contrast but is in continuation and analogy with that archaic and essential aspect of the Mediterranean female cults. And in this it seems clear that the relation of the pagan cults is not general only but offers a specific and important contribution to Marian doctrine.

These speculations were not accepted by the official theology in the West. They were accepted in part in the East by reason

[1] Sergius Bulgakov, *op. cit.*, pp. 139 ff. See pp. 10–13 *supra*. Vladimir Soloviev, in his interpretation of orthodoxy that is personal but by no means unfaithful, contemplates a triple incarnation of the divine Wisdom in the masculine humanity of Christ, in the feminine humanity of the Virgin Mary, and in the collective humanity of the Church, thus debasing the absoluteness of the incomparable moment of the Christian revelation. Cf. *La Russia e la Chiesa universale*, Edizione de Communità, Milan, 1947, pp., 245 ff.

Bulgakov, *loc cit.*, refers to the differences between the West's "chivalrous" cult of Our Lady and the sober spirit of the Orthodox Church. (*Trans.*)

of the speculative genius of that Church never wholly free from the gnostic influences. But in the West too we observe its presence, submerged, in the heretical and esoteric currents where the identification of the Virgin Mary with the cosmic principle is most clear and most conscious of its pantheistic content. In Mary the principle of cosmic life is intimately associated with divinity. In a mediaeval engraving she sits upon a throne, apart, close to the three figures of the enthroned Trinity and at a level slightly lower, and the four figures are enclosed in the sacred oval of the mandala, symbol of the unity of God and the cosmos.[1] In the Holy Quaternity, symbol of the divine-cosmic totality, there manifestly lives again—personified by the Virgin Mary—the pantheistic motif of the Mediterranean cult of the fecund earth.

These ideas, when they were not directly rejected and prohibited, continued to be marginal in the orthodox Christianity of the West, but they continued. It is not easy to establish what part they actually had in the development of the Marian cult, just as the possibility is not to be excluded that in our time they may be knowing a wide revival. They are the deep and seductive mystery in the orthodox developments of mariology.

These are limited, consciously, to the border themes of the Christian tradition which we have mentioned, and to which we must now turn, for it is these that give Mary her traditional mien and make mariology an original creation.

The Byzantine representations of the *Basilissa Panhagia*, the All-Holy Queen, which compare with those of the *Kyrios Pantokrator*, Lord Christ Omnipotent, with equal ecstatic power and numinous expression, do not represent the starry perfections of a new Isis shining with light or a new Cybele filled with inexpressible mysteries of fecundity. They represent her whom the litanies of Loretto celebrate much later as Queen of the angels, of patriarchs, prophets, apostles, martyrs, confessors, virgins, and all the saints.

But the Virgin Mary could not have become the Queen of the Church militant and triumphant if she had not been seated on the throne of Isis, and if she had not put on the turreted crown of Cybele. To understand psychologically the exaltation

[1] Cf. C. G. Jung, *Psychology and Religion.* Ed. Communità, Milan, 1948, table between pages 80–81, and p. 91.

of Mary in the realm of Christian dogma and piety, to understand how it was that out of the doctrinal dispute about the two natures of Christ and the paradox of the *Theotokos*, there issued the hyperbolical veneration of the Virgin Mary, it is necessary to consider the devotional climate of the Mediterranean cult of the Virgin and the Mother. We must consider whether the historical reason lies in the fact that the great centres of impulse to the veneration of Mary are Egypt, sacred to Isis, Ephesus, the seat of Artemis, and Phrygia, home of the Great Mother Cybele; while the northern countries, to which the Mediterranean cult of Mary remained foreign, only followed slowly and without enthusiasm and were decisively freed from it with the Reformation.

Chapter 5

THE ASSUMPTION

THE growth of the cult of Mary was not rapid, not as rapid, at least, as appeared possible, in view of the very great possibilities of development in the title *Theotokos* and the analogies of the various Mediterranean cults of the celestial Mother. But possibly it is as well to believe that there was a certain discounting of the titles honouring the Virgin Mary as Mother of God, and a disinclination to draw out from this one the very extensive theological consequences that eventually came. As for the general influence of the pagan female cults, notwithstanding the highest praises that came to be given to the Virgin Mary, she remains in the Christian thought simply a human creature however lofty and venerated. Account must be taken of the wise and prudent traditionalism that slowed the liturgical and theological evolution, tying it to the criterion of the Holy Scriptures and the most ancient and constant tradition of the Church.

On the eve of the Council of Ephesus, Cyril and Nestorius were substantially in accord over this point. If Nestorius said, "Do not make a goddess of the Virgin!", Cyril answered, "We have not made a divinity of her who must be numbered among the creatures. . . . We know she belongs to humanity as we do!"[1] This position conforms with the oldest tradition. At the end of the fourth century, Epiphanius, denouncing the sect of the Collyridians, declared, "The saints are not to be honoured beyond what is right but we must honour their Lord. . . . Mary, indeed, is not God, nor has she received her body from heaven but by a conception by a man and a woman." "The body of Mary is holy but she is not God; she is Virgin and worthy of great honour but she is not given to us in adoration, rather she adores Him who is born of her flesh." "Let Mary be honoured but let the Father, Son and Holy Spirit be adored. Let no one

[1] Cyril, *Adversus Nestorium*, I, 9.

adore Mary."[1] And these words Ambrose of Milan echoed in the same century, "Mary was the temple of God, not the God of the temple. Therefore only he is to be adored who worked within the Temple."[2]

It is not possible to fix the date of the origin of the Marian cult with certainty. We can refer with confidence to the judgment of a most learned mariologist such as Jugie: "Perhaps at the end of the fourth century and certainly at the beginning of the fifth, in certain churches of the East and West they began to honour her in a public cult and with a special festival."[3] This festival appears to have been closely connected with the celebration of the birth of Jesus and constituted a sort of ancient Advent celebrating the Sunday before Christmas. It was consecrated to the "memory" of Mary and was meant to commemorate the Annunciation and the other episodes contained in the synoptic Gospels. In this Mary is before all else the testimony of the incarnation. After the Council of Ephesus such a practice became widespread. But we have to come down to Justinian to find a series of festive days—few in number—dedicated always to the commemoration of the same Gospel events, the Annunciation, Nativity, Presentation in the temple.

Now, between the Council of Ephesus and the beginning of Justinian's reign an entire century intervenes. Only after Justinian in the second half of the sixth century is the organization of the Marian festivals completed by the celebration of her birth, September 8th, and her conception, December 9th, and finally, her death—let us say, rather, her "passing over" or her "falling asleep" (*koimesis*). These festivals are distinguished from the preceding in that they are concerned with Mary as herself, her own person. In particular one is to perceive at an early date the desire to celebrate the day of her death. Death

[1] Epiphanius, *Panarion*, 78: 11, 24; 79: 4, 7.

[2] Ambrose, *De Spiritu Sancto*, lib. III, cap. 11, n. 80. In the preceding paragraph he asks himself what he is to adore: not the earth that corresponds to the body of Christ, but one must adore Christ in that He is the Son of God. "Also the Holy Spirit is adored because He is adored who was born of the Holy Spirit according to the flesh." And in para. 80, very briefly, he adds, "and in order that a deduction in favour of the Virgin Mary be not made from that (*ne quis—ad Mariam deducat*), Mary was the Temple—*Maria erat templum Dei, non Deus templi. Et ideo ille solus adorandus qui operabatur in templo*."

[3] Martin Jugie, A.A., *La mort et l'Assomption de la Sainte Vierge. Etude historico doctrinale*. Vatican City, 1944, p. 58.

was looked on as the day of birth to the true life, the day of ascent to heaven. The festivals of the martyrs are all observed on the anniversary day, actual or supposed, of their martyrdom. An assimilation of Mary to the holy martyrs could seem natural. The words of the aged Simeon, "And a sword will pierce through your own soul also",[a] could cause them to think of a violent death. In reality this was a matter of arbitrary interpretation. "Neither Scripture nor history inform us that Mary left this life by a violent death," wrote Ambrose of Milan, commenting on this passage in Luke.[1] Rather, the uncertainty itself surrounding the blessed transition of Mary suggested diverse suppositions: who knows whether Mary truly died or was taken alive into heaven as the Bible tells of Enoch and Elijah? Epiphanius echoes these suppositions in the mariological passage we cited *à propos* of the Collyridians, "Search the Scriptures, you will not find either the death of Mary or whether she died or that she did not die, or that she was buried or was not buried."[2] And in his uncertainty he concludes, "If the Holy Virgin died and was buried, her falling asleep (*koimesis*) was surrounded with honour. Death found her pure and her crown is in her virginity. If she was killed—according to Luke 2 : 35—she is glorified among the martyrs and her holy body is blessed by which the light shone forth upon the world. Or whether she continued in life here, because nothing is impossible to God. . . . No one knows her end."[3]

Actually the good Epiphanius made a superfluous display of hypotheses. If in his time no tradition existed about the end of Mary's life, that is simply due to the fact that her death happened in a time when the practice of venerating the memory of martyrs or of persons eminent in the Church had not yet arisen, and it passed unobserved. She departed life humbly and modestly as she had lived it and none remembered the place of her burial, even if a tradition toward the mid-fifth century gave her a sepulchre near Jerusalem in the garden of Gethsemane.

But piety, now turned towards an ever increasing and ardent

[a] Luke 2 : 35.

[1] "Nec littera nec historia docet ex hac vita Mariam corporalis necis passione migrasse." *Expositio Evangelii Lucae*, II, 61.

[2] Epiphanius, *Panarion*, 78, 11.

[3] *Ibid.*, 78, 24.

celebration of Mary, could not content itself with the silence of tradition, and made up with imagination for the death of Mary as it had done for her life. In the second half of the fifth century apocryphal accounts of the *Transitus* of Mary the Virgin began to circulate. Pope Gelasius (492–96) condemned them together with the apocryphal Gospels, as we have already noted, yet in spite of official condemnation they continued and fed popular piety.

The apocryphal legends of the Transition of Mary can be traced to two main origins. These are the "*Transitus Mariae*", said to be from the *Pseudo-Melito* because it purported to be the work of the bishop of Sardis and apologist of Christianity who lived in the second century, and the *Book of the falling asleep* (*Koimesis*) *of the Holy Mother of God*, from the *Pseudo-John the Evangelist.*[1]

Here, briefly, is the account of *Pseudo-Melito.*

After the death of Jesus, Mary stayed for twenty-two years in the home of John's relatives, which was close to the Mount of Olives. One day as she was praying to be reunited with her Son, an angel appeared to her who gave her a palm from God's paradise, telling her to carry it to her bier because in three days she would be dead. Mary asked to be attended by the twelve apostles in that supreme moment. The angel vanished, Mary dressed herself in her festal clothes, took the palm and went to the Mount of Olives. There she addressed a prayer to Jesus asking to be saved from the assaults of the infernal powers during her passage. Then she returned home.

In that same instant the apostle John, who had been caught up by a cloud at Ephesus as he was praying, appears on the threshold. Then all the other apostles similarly caught up and carried find themselves at Mary's door to the amazement of all. Paul also is there and Peter invites him to offer a prayer to God

[1] These apocryphal writings were edited by Tischendorf in his collection: *Apocalypses apocryphae Mosis, Esdrae, Pauli, Johannis, item Mariae dormitio, additis Evangeliorum et Actuum apocryphorum supplementis*, Leipzig, 1866. There are less developed traces of our apocryphal writings that are somewhat more ancient. The condemnation by the decree of Gelasius at the end of the fifth century refers to one of these writings. The decree, on the other hand, is a compilation that came to its present form only later on. This is why the mention of the *Transitus*, even if attributed to *Pseudo-Melito* as some think it should be, would not necessarily imply a greater age for this apocryphal work. Cf. Jugie, *La Mort et l'Assomption de la S. Vierge*, p. 110.

in the name of all that He will make His will known. But Paul demurs, declaring the primacy of Peter. (The writing of *Pseudo-Melito* is Latin.) The apostles are pleased with the humility of Paul. Peter prays and as he says "Amen" the apostle John comes out of the house where Mary has told her vision. All go in. Mary tells the apostles that the Lord has sent them to comfort her in the anguish of the last passage and asks them to watch.

The three days pass in devout converse and prayers. At the third hour of the day all those present in the house fall into a deep sleep except the apostles and the three virgins who are attending Mary. Jesus appears with a multitude of angels and asks Mary to come with Him into the rest of eternal life. Mary repeats her desire not to see the infernal spirits and Jesus tells her that He has had to bear their assault on the cross and that she too will see them, for such is the condition of humanity, but the demons can do nothing to her and she will be defended by the hosts of heaven. Then the Holy Virgin lies down upon her bed and renders up her spirit while the apostles see a dazzling light. Jesus entrusts her soul to the archangel Michael, prefect of paradise and head of the Hebrew nation, and orders the apostles to bury her body. While the heavenly train mounts to the supernal regions the virgins prepare Mary for the funeral. She has turned white as a lily and from her comes a perfume of incomparable sweetness. Then the funeral cortège starts on its way, preceded by John who carries the heavenly palm in his hand. The coffin is carried by Peter and Paul, the former at the head, the latter at the foot. All sing, *In exitu Israel de Egypto, alleluia!* A crown of light appears on the coffin and the angels sing with surpassing sweetness.

At the sound of the heavenly music a multitude of fifteen thousand people comes together, for the Jews have sworn to burn Mary's body. One of them, the chief priest, filled with fury, flings himself upon the coffin to overturn it. But the hands and forearm of the evil man become shrivelled and he remains fastened to the bier. The cortège goes on while the Jew leaps up and down howling with pain. The other Jews cannot come to his help because they are blinded by the angels. Finally Peter tells the Jew that if he will confess Jesus Christ he will be healed. He not only confesses but eloquently praises Jesus

Christ, with quotations from the books of Moses. Then, recovered, he receives from Peter the heavenly palm carried by John and is told to go back into the city and preach to those who have been made blind. Those who will confess Christ will be healed and the others will stay blind. And so it comes to pass.

Meanwhile the apostles, having come into the valley of Jehoshaphat to the place the Lord showed them, place Mary in a new tomb and seat themselves at its entrance. And then, unexpectedly, the Lord Jesus comes down from heaven with an innumerable company of shining angels. He greets the apostles, "Peace be with you." They answer, "Let thy mercy be upon us, O Lord, as our hope is in thee." Then Jesus, reminding them that according to His promise they will sit on twelve thrones and judge the twelve tribes of Israel, asks them to decide what Mary's future is to be. Peter answers for all, "Lord, thou hast chosen her, thy servant, that thy dwelling should be immaculate. As for us, thy poor servants, thou hast taken us into thy service. From all eternity Thou knowest all things, with the Father and the Holy Spirit, with whom Thou art one divinity only, a power equal and infinite. Here, then, is what has seemed right to us Thy servants: as Thou dost reign in glory after having conquered death, so let the body of Thy Mother be given life again and be brought with Thee into celestial joy." Jesus said, "Let it be according to thy word." He orders Michael to take the soul of Mary. The archangel Gabriel opens the sepulchre, Mary emerges from the tomb and embraces Jesus, who gives her into the care of the angels who carry her into paradise. Then Jesus embraces the apostles and disappears caught up by a cloud. Other clouds carry the apostles away to their fields of work.

The *Pseudo-John* offers a somewhat different version.

Mary receives the annunciation of her death on a Friday as she prays by Jesus' sepulchre. She then returns to her house in Bethlehem and asks the help of the apostles, including those who have already died. John arrives from Ephesus on a cloud. Mary tells him that the Jews will want to burn her body and John reassures her that her body will not see corruption. The apostles come, including Andrew, Philip, Luke and Simon momentarily arisen from their tombs, but the Holy Spirit warns them that it is not yet the final resurrection and they will have to go back into their tombs after the passage of Mary. A peal of thunder announces the arrival of angelic legions. In the meantime the inhabitants of Bethlehem give the alarm at Jerusalem from whence come a troop through Bethlehem to take possession of the Virgin, but an invisible force stops them a mile from Bethlehem. They then return to Jerusalem to get reinforcements, and the Roman governor, after vacillations like Pilate's, gives them a chiliarch with a battalion. But they find the house empty. Mary, laid upon her bed, and the apostles are transported through the air to Mary's house in Jerusalem. The Roman officer takes revenge upon the people of Bethlehem, arresting some of them.

The Jews look for Mary for five days and finally find her, as she sings the praises of the Lord with the apostles. They try to burn the house but the flames come back behind them and consume some of them. Then the governor, like the centurion at the foot of the cross, confesses Jesus. The Holy Spirit announces that Mary is to die on a Sunday just as there occurred on Sunday the annunciation, the birth, and the resurrection of Jesus, and as He will return on a Sunday to judge the quick and the dead. Jesus appears accompanied by heavenly hosts. He announces to Mary that her body will be transported into terrestrial paradise and her soul will be received into heaven among the Father's treasures. Mary asks her Son, as an extreme act of grace, that the prayers that men will address in her name shall always be granted.

Jesus promises this. "Every soul that shall pray in thy name shall not be confounded but shall find mercy, consolation and help in this life and the next." Then, after having blessed the apostles, Mary places her immaculate soul in the hands of Jesus. The funeral rites follow. The Jew, Gephonias, who wanted to overthrow the bier, has his arms cut off by an angel and is healed as he invokes Mary. The Holy Virgin is laid in a new sepulchre at Gethsemane in which she continues for three days as Jesus did, watched by the apostles and angels. On the third day the angels' psalmody ceases, and by this the apostles know that Mary's body has been carried to the terrestrial paradise to be with Elizabeth, Anna, Abraham, Isaac, Jacob, and all the choirs of saints who come to venerate her.

As is seen, this second account differs from the first, not only by its many dramatic characters but because it does not state that Mary's body has been reunited to her soul and carried with it into heaven. The soul has been raised to celestial glory but the body is taken to an earthly paradise where, without being subject to corruption, it will await the day of final resurrection when it will be reunited to the soul as all the saints will be. We have therefore two distinct views in these first apocryphal writings: the immediate assumption of Mary's body in consequence of her anticipated resurrection, or the simple transporting of her body and her incorruption in the earthly paradise.

The later apocryphals from the seventh to the ninth century are divided between these two interpretations. The second of them, less daring, seems to have had a certain ascendancy for some time, at least in the East. A Nestorian legend[1] has it that after the burial of Mary and an attempt by the Jews to set fire to her sepulchre, chariots bright with lights bear her coffin and the cortège to the terrestrial paradise, accompanied by the apostles, prophets, patriarchs, and the other saints, and there it is deposited in a glorious resting place. Transported to Jerusalem, the apostles order the commemorative festivals of Mary. She will be remembered three times a year: the eve of the Sunday after Christmas, because Mary left this world on Christmas day; a second time on the fifteenth of Iyar, on account of the crops, and a third on the fifteenth of Ab, because of the vintage and drought. After giving the world their instructions the apostles are taken again to their respective seats or tombs. In the meantime Jesus descends into the terrestrial paradise, revives Mary and takes her on a journey into the realms beyond the tomb. Then He causes her to die again and leaves her in terrestrial paradise, kept until the last resurrection of the dead. At Jerusalem the Jews succeed in opening the tomb and find it empty. Some are converted, while there is a fight between the Christians and unbelievers for the possession of Mary's burial garments, which the Christians manage to secure. Many miracles are wrought by these relics.

The preceding accounts place Mary's resurrection or her transport to terrestrial paradise soon after her death or three

[1] Published in London in 1899 by Wallis Budge, with the title *The History of the Blessed Virgin Mary*, summarized by Jugie, *op. cit.*, 124–26.

days distant from it. But one writing, attributed to the monophysite archbishop of Alexandria, Theodosius (536–567), inserts between the two events a duration of two hundred and six days, in which Mary's body lies in the tomb, and, contrary to all the foregoing apocryphal theses, knows the corruption common to all humanity.[1] This detail is important, not only for the dogmatic idea to which it refers but because it tends to transpose the commemoration of the Assumption of Mary to the midsummer festival, as happened everywhere in the later course.

This transposition of date makes it necessary also in the pattern of the legend that the apostles be together a second time to make sure of the future resurrection of Mary's body. In fact, in the account of Theodosius of Alexandria, they place themselves right at her tomb on the evening of the 15th of Mesore and attend her resurrection, which takes place like that of Lazarus. Jesus speaks to her in these words, "Arise, body, which by nature is corrupt. Be ever incorruptible! Receive from me resurrection as the first of all creation!" The Ethiopian lectionary on the occasion of the feast of the Assumption, the 16th Nahase, which corresponds to the Coptic 16th Mesore, relates that a year after Mary's assumption the apostles were all carried to heaven together and saw the body of the Blessed Virgin seated in glory at the right hand of her Son. She blessed them, stretching out her hand. Then Jesus celebrated the sacrifice of His holy body while Stephen attended Him. Then Mary mounts upon her chariot of cherubim and is exalted in their presence.[2]

A Latin apocrypha, distinct from *Pseudo-Melito*, adds the detail of the absence of Thomas. The other apostles have deposited the Virgin in the sepulchre in the valley of Jehoshaphat and have been enveloped by a great light. They do not know that in that fraction of a moment Mary's body has been carried to heaven. But Thomas, who arrives at that moment by the mount of Olives, sees her body as it is being carried upwards. He prays to the Virgin who lets fall her girdle for him.

[1] Published in 1886 by Forbes Robinson (*Coptic Apocryphal Gospels*) and more completely by Marius Chaine (*Le discours de Théodose, patriarche d'Alexandre, sur la dormition*: in Revue de l'Orient Chrétien, 1933, n. 44). Summarized by Jugie, *op. cit.*, pp. 128 ff.

[2] The *Ethiopian Sinassario* was published by Ignazio Guidi (1913); cf. Jugie, *op. cit.*, p. 133.

At the sepulchre he does not speak of the vision he has had but affirms abruptly that the body is not in the sepulchre. Peter reproves him. But the sepulchre is opened and found empty. Thomas receives the apologies of his colleagues.[1]

We omit mention of other apocrypha which add nothing substantially new, but we cannot pass over in silence the fine homily of John of Thessalonika, published by Jugie,[2] which appears as an orthodox transcription of the themes contained in the various apocryphal legends. It is distinctive in its tone of humanity and sincere piety. When word spreads that Mary is about to die, those who learn of it run to her and she speaks to them, "Fathers and brethren, let us help one another. Let us light our lamps and watch, for we know not the hour when the thief will come. I do not fear death, it is the lot of everyone, but I do fear the adversary who assails all. . . . Let us therefore help one another and so act that nothing of evil be found in us." Then the women present say to Mary, "O thou our sister who didst become the Mother of God and the First Lady [a] of the universe, why hast thou fear? Thou art the Mother of the Lord. Thou art our hope and our support. If thou art not safe how shall it be with us wretched ones? If the shepherd fears the wolf whither will the sheep flee?" Then Mary comforts them and all lift up their hearts together in prayer. This insistence on the fear of the last passage in this and other accounts evidently is an answer to the need of emphasizing Mary's complete humanity that is complementary to her idealization.

And now what is the value of these accounts? One can adhere at once to the judgment of Jugie, who speaks in the name of the severest Catholic study. "From the historical

[1] This apocrypha was published by Tischendorf in his *Apocalypses apocryphae*, with the heading: *Transitus A.* He considered it to be probably more ancient than *Pseudo-Melito*, while it presents a more developed stage of the legend. For this reason Jugie classifies it among the apocrypha of the seventh century. *Op. cit.*, p. 156.

[2] M. Jugie. *Homélies mariales byzantines. Texts grecs édités et traduits en latin, II. Discours de St. Jean de Thessalonique sur la dormition de la Sainte Vierge*, Vol. XIX of the *Patrologia Orientalis*, pp. 344–438. Jugie identifies the author not with the noted archbishop who attended the sixth Ecumenical Council of 680–81, but with another of the same name who occupied the see between 610 and 649. The writing shows a particular interest in the primacy of Peter, and that is understandable if one remembers that the see of Thessalonika depended upon the Roman metropolis. Cf. *La mort et l'Assomption de Marie*, cit. pp. 139 ff.

[a] *Signora.*

point of view their value is absolutely nothing. . . . From the doctrinal point of view they . . . inform us on the first solutions that Christian piety gave to the problem posed by Mary's death."[1] When, following the Council of Ephesus, people began to reflect upon the dignity of Mary, it appeared impossible to think that her body had remained subject to corruption. Some thought she must have enjoyed the privilege of an immediate resurrection; others that she was laid away in terrestrial paradise in the shade of the tree of life, in expectation of the final resurrection. Our apocrypha are the expression of these pious beliefs which inspire sacred oratory in the festivals dedicated to Mary and the liturgical hymns composed in her honour. And in due course they enter also into learned meditation along the accustomed line of development: first the popular piety, then the worship and finally the theology that reflects and justifies the worship.[2]

We must briefly follow the course of this doctrine.

The Byzantine theologians from the seventh to the ninth centuries show the same uncertainty that we have seen in the apocryphal legends. Mary's soul has been taken to heaven—all agree. Whether her body followed or whether it waited in incorruptibility, this is the question. Some, such as Hippolytus of Thebes, seem to believe in a passage from earthly life to the heavenly without death.[3] The more notable, such as Andrew

[1] Jugie, *La Mort et l'Assomption*, pp. 167, 169.

[2] We remember in passing certain "proofs", the inconsistency of which criticism has recognized: a passage of the *Book of Miracles* by Gregory of Tours which derives from *Pseudo-Melito*, or perhaps from a Syriac *Transitus* even older, a fragment of which has been recovered. There were three homilies of John of Damascus in which the parts referring to the assumption of the Virgin are an evident and recognized later interpolation. There is an insertion in the third chapter of the book of *Pseudo-Dionysius the Areopagite*, of the fifth century, on the *Divine Names*, in which it is written that many brethren assemble "to look upon the body that is the principle of life and the residence of divinity," expressions that must refer to the eucharistic body of Christ and not to that of the Virgin Mary. There is a *Letter to Titus* attributed to *Pseudo-Dionysius* and actually of the eighth century in which the passage just cited is explained in mariological terms. And finally we have the *Eutimiac History*, an apocryphal composition of the ninth century that undertakes to explain the origins of Mary's relics—clothes and girdle—that are kept in the Byzantine sanctuary of Blakhernes. Marcion and Pulcheria ask Juvenal, the bishop of Jerusalem, to let them have Mary's relics and these explain her *transitus*, the lateness of Thomas and the finding of the burial clothes in the empty sepulchre.

[3] Jugie, *op. cit.*, p. 225.

of Crete (660–740), and John of Damascus (d. 749) are quite convinced that the doctrine of the assumption of Mary is without historic foundation or any basis in Scripture, and they present instead the doctrine limited to the incorruption, as a postulate of the dignity of the Mother of God. "It was necessary" (*edei*), "becoming", that Mary should thus be honoured by the Son.[1] It is of interest to note that the doctrine of the Assumption has, in these its first authoritative representatives, the same character of theological construction based on the principles of suitability and analogy which to-day are seen again in the more developed and modern representations. And it can be said that in the East the situation continues thus until the end of the tenth century.

At this point one must refer to the check that the evolution of the cult and theology of Mary had for about a century as a result of the iconoclastic controversy, concerning which there is a somewhat quaint story. Constantine Copronymos one day held up a purse filled with gold to his courtiers and asked them its value. They answered, "A great value." The emperor then emptied it and asked them, "And now has it still any value?" They answered that it had not. Then Constantine continued, "So it is with the Virgin Mary whom you adore without discrimination. While she bore Christ within her she had a value greater than all other women, but from the time that she gave Him birth she returned to the same level as other women and has nothing that is especially significant [a] about her."[2]

The feast and the doctrine of the Assumption of Mary passed from the East to the West, at a time that cannot be set definitely, under the primitive name of *Dormitio* or under the names *Depositio*, *Pausatio*, *Natale*. It was only at the end of the eighth century that it got the title *Assumptio sanctae Mariae* in the sacramentary sent by Pope Hadrian I to Charlemagne between the years 784 and 791, and only at the council of Mainz in 813 did it become an official festival for all western christendom. The object of the festival was properly the blessed death of Mary, her "*transitio*" and the entry of her soul into the glory of the

[1] *Ibid.*, pp. 235, 249.

[a] *nulla di particolare.*

[2] Told by Cedranus, *Historiarum compendium*, II, 1 ff. (*Scriptores Hist. Byz.*, Bonn, 1839) and referred to by Benrath, *Zur Geschichte der Marienverehrung*, Gotha, 1886, p. 5.

heavens. The actual title of the Assumption does not necessarily mean the resurrection of the body or its elevation to heaven. The most ancient liturgical formulae maintain a wise reserve in regard to this, confining themselves to the statement—as does the Gregorian Sacramentary—that the holy Mother of God "underwent bodily death but could not be held by the chains of death".[1]

The same prudence is found again in the theological tradition. We must come down to the ninth century to find two writings of real importance historically and dogmatically; the *Epistle of Pseudo-Jerome to Paula and Eustochium* and the book of *Pseudo-Augustine* on the *Assumption of the Virgin.*

The letter of Pseudo-Jerome is a milestone in the evolution of mariology. Whether through the importance of its content or by the authority of the name under which it presented itself, it was widely credited and in whole or in part was inserted in the Roman Breviary for the festival of the Assumption and of the Immaculate Conception. Erasmus was the first to show that it was an apocryphal writing and to-day no one ascribes it to Jerome any longer. As a result of Erasmus' discovery the Epistle was taken out of the Breviary when this was reformed under Pius V, 1568. It would be interesting to know who its author was. As early as the ninth century the famous theologian Ratramnus accused Paschasius Radbertus of being the forger, and this opinion has had various supporters in our century. The Epistle is assuredly worthy of the great theologian whose name is connected with the first formulation of the doctrine of transubstantiation. It is to be supposed that the antithetic book of Pseudo-Augustine is from his opponent Ratramnus,[2] and then it could be considered that under the shield of two of the greatest fathers of the Western Church the two best theologians of the Carolingian age discussed the worship[a] of Mary.

The letter of Pseudo-Jerome[3] purports to have been written

[1] "Mortem subiit temporalem, nec tamen mortis nexibus deprimi potuit." The verb *deprimi* has a general sense of humbling, depriving; it will be replaced later by the more explicit sense of *retineri*. Jugie, *op. cit.*, p. 203.

[2] Jugie, *op. cit.*, p. 290. It is curious to observe that Roschini attributes this book to Paschasius Radbertus (*Mariologia*, II, p. 307). Actually the elements of internal criticism must not be regarded as very indicative and those of external criticism are almost nil.

[a] *il culto.*

[3] Found among the works of Jerome in Migne, *Patrologia Latina*, XXX, col. 123 ff.

as a sermon for his two disciples Paula and Eustochium on occasion of the feast of the Assumption of Mary. He feels a duty to put his two disciples on guard against the apocryphal story of the *Transitio Mariae* so that they will not think as certain what is doubtful. We know to-day for certain only that Mary has died, "*gloriosa migravit a corpore*". In fact her sepulchre is to be seen in the valley of Jehoshaphat and Paula herself has seen it with her own eyes—the *Pseudo-Jerome* takes its literary fiction seriously—and everyone says she was buried there but now it is empty. It explains these things because:

> "Many of our people are wondering whether she was assumed with the body or whether she went leaving the body behind. But in what way or at what time or by what persons her most holy body was taken from it or where it was transported or whether it was resuscitated is not known, although some maintain that she was already resuscitated and clothed again with blessed immortality in heaven. Many assert the same thing of the blessed John the Evangelist, her servant, to whom as virgin Christ entrusted the Virgin, since in his sepulchre, it is told, there is nothing but manna which is seen to come up. What truth there is in all this we do not know. It is better, then, to leave all these things to God to whom nothing is impossible, rather than to seek with temerity to define on our authority things we cannot prove."

We have here a prudent statement of agnosticism. *Jerome-Paschasius* does not deny it because God can do anything, but neither does he affirm, and in conclusion he prefers not to affirm the resurrection of the Virgin so as not to run the risk of "defining incautiously what can be left unknown without danger".[1]

It would be a mistake to imagine, from this cautious and wise urging, that *Pseudo-Jerome* is any less ardent for Mary's glory. The entire sermon is in highest praise of the Virgin, of her wonderful purity, of her virtue. She was a spiritual martyr through her suffering at the foot of the cross, and if she died in peace, "*in pace vitam finivit*", she was, on the contrary, more than a martyr! Further, he is well persuaded of her glorious assumption—whether with the body or without—because:

> "if there is joy in heaven over every sinner that repenteth, how

[1] *Epistula ad Paulam et Eustochium*, cit. cap. 1–2, "inconsulte definire quod sine periculo nescitur."

much more will there be over the exaltation and glory of such a Virgin! . . . Blessed therefore is such and so great a passage—*talis et tanta nativitas*—blessed the company of citizens of heaven and the wonderful unity of their love (*charitas*): there, above, where none of the angels or archangels are envious of glory,—I do not say of the blessed Virgin Mary, but rather of any of the saints—but each possesses in the person of the other all that is offered freely to all, where there is no distinction of sex, age or nobility of birth, but only the quality of merits gives distinction, as the stars differ in splendour one from another even though all shine with the one light."[1]

What does the disciple *Ratramnus-Augustine* answer to *Paschasius-Jerome*, for it seems logical to think of a dispute?[2] Evidently he cannot contest the fact that from the historical or Biblical point of view there is no sure indication or tradition but recourse must be had to the argument of piety. It is convenient to think this way:

"Christ the power of God and the wisdom of God, to whom belong all things that are His Father's, who wills all things that are, wills all things that are just and right. In consequence it seems right that Mary enjoys unutterable happiness in body and soul in her Son, with her Son, through the Son, (*videtur digne laetari Maria laetitia inenarrabili*) . . . and that she must not have suffered corruption, she who did not become subject to any corruption in giving birth to such a Son. It seems right that she should always continue incorrupt into whom was infused so great grace, that she who produced the whole and perfect life should continue to live on in complete integrity, that she should be with Him whom she carried in her womb, whom she bore, warmed and nursed, Mary genetrix of God, nurse of God, minister to God, follower (*secutrix*) of God, of whom, as I have already said, I do not dare to speak otherwise, not daring to think otherwise."[3]

These two writings, whether by the authority of the names of Jerome and Augustine or by their intrinsic worth, determined for the entire Middle Ages the currents of Catholic opinion in

[1] *Epist.* cit. cap. 14, 15.

[2] Naturally supposing that this identification is admitted, though actually it has no secure foundation. The writing is found in Migne's *Patrologia* among the works of Augustine, Vol. XL, col. 1141 ff., and is entitled: *Liber de Assumptione Beatae Virginis Mariae.*

[3] *Liber de Assumptione*, cap. 8 (Migne, XL, 1148).

regard to the Assumption of Mary. Until the thirteenth century the prudence inspired by *Pseudo-Jerome* was predominant. Beginning with that century the opinion of *Pseudo-Augustine* began to prevail and took the ascendant decisively after humanist criticism had shown that the *Letter to Paula and Eustochium* was not authentic, while the spuriousness of *Pseudo-Augustine* was not clearly recognized until the critical study of the seventeenth century. The influence of *Pseudo-Jerome* is certainly the cause of the cautious silence of theologians such as Anselm of Canterbury or Bernard of Clairvaux and the two popes Alexander III and Innocent III. Other church leaders refer to *Pseudo-Jerome* explicitly or implicitly; Odilo of Cluny and Guibert de Nogent; so do the martyrologies of Adon, archbishop of Vienne, and of Usuard, Notker, and Alain de L'Isle. In the school of *Pseudo-Augustine,* on the other hand, are found Hugh and Richard of St Victor, Peter Damiani, Saint Anthony of Padua, and Abelard. Among the theologians of later centuries were Henry Suso, Jacopo of Voragine and others who considered the Assumption to be a pious belief and the great scholastics differed little from this cautious position.

The most explicit is Albertus Magnus. He thought the Assumption was among the truths which are not directly revealed in Scripture and are not self-evident, but seem to be derived from Scripture, imposed upon reason and not controverted by any contrary Biblical statement or rational argument. Thomas Aquinas does not deal with the Assumption in his theological works—a significant silence. He expresses himself dubiously on the resurrection of Mary and John but ends by stating, "We believe that after her death she came to life again and was taken to heaven."[1] Bonaventura speaks of it especially in his preaching where it is a homiletic argument more than a theological. These positions show no substantial change until the Reformation.

The Reformation did not make the Virgin Mary a particular subject of research or polemic. It dropped mariology entirely and the cult connected with it as not justified by Holy Scripture. But the *Magdeburg Centuries*, which is the first great modern work of church history, appropriated the humanistic criticism of the ancient traditions, particularly in regard to the Assump-

[1] In the explanation of the articles of the Creed, interpreting the angel greeting.

tion of Mary. The Catholic theologians, replying to the Protestants and Humanists, generally presented the Assumption as a definite doctrine but not of faith. Among these Canisius deserves to be remembered because he was the first, it seems, explicitly to declare the evolution of Catholic dogma as an argument of apologetics.[1] But beginning with the sixteenth century it began to be considered rash [a] to deny or cast doubt upon Mary's Assumption. The positions tend to be reversed. In the Carolingian period *Pseudo-Jerome* considered as rash the attitude of those who arbitrarily asserted what could be left unknown without danger. In the seventeenth century historical criticism began to take courage again with the Parisian canonist Pierre Launcy and the historian Lenain de Tillemont, who held the position of *Pseudo-Jerome*. Among the "moderate" opinions of the eighteenth century are to be recorded that of the noted writer of treatises Charles Billuard, and particularly that of Pope Benedict XIV (Prospero Lambertini) who wrote in his work, *De festis Domini nostri Jesu Christi et beatae Virginis Mariae*.

> "The Assumption of the blessed Virgin is not an article of faith. . . . The texts of Scripture that are customarily adduced in its support can be interpreted otherwise and tradition is not enough to elevate this doctrine to the rank of articles of faith. . . . But if it is not an article of faith but only a pious opinion and worthy of being received (*pia tantum et probabilis opinio*) will it perhaps be permitted to accept it or disdain it, defend it or attack it? Certainly not."

We must come down to the definition of the Immaculate Conception in 1854 to find a new element in our question. The doctrines of the Immaculate Conception and the Assumption of the Virgin are evidently connected. It is not to be wondered at, therefore, that in the Vatican Council of 1870 in which papal infallibility was defined, an attempt was made by a number of bishops to get a solemn pronouncement of Mary's Assumption as a verity of faith. They were preceded by a petition started by Queen Isabella of Spain at the instance of her confessor. But the council made no decision. The papal reply to the Queen of Spain admitted, to be sure, that the

[1] Canisius, *De Verbi Dei corruptelis*; cf. Jugie, *La Mort et l'Assomption*, p. 412.
[a] *temeraria*.

Assumption is a consequence of the Immaculate Conception but "the time has not yet come" to define such a doctrine.

From then on the petitioning movement has extended without interruption, assuming in the twenty-year period, 1920–1940, the scale of plebiscites. At the end of the latter year these gathered more than eight million signatures, especially in Italy, Spain and Latin America. It is significant that the nations of western and northern Europe, France, Belgium and Germany, where the most modern and critical standards of Catholic culture are to be found, followed only at a great distance and seemingly without too much enthusiasm. In the figures given by Jugie[1] Spain appears with 1,689,911 signatures as against 137,390 from France. Unanimity is therefore far from being beyond question. Neither are there lacking opponents not of the Assumption, which is taken as a pious belief or a truth believed in by most, but of its "definability" as dogma. We cite only a few; the eminent student of patristics of Munich, Hans Ernst, Gillmann, Bartmann, Father d'Ales and Rivière.[2] We add that some of the more recent popes have taken a moderating attitude toward the petitioning movement and at times an attitude of inhibition: Leo XIII, Pius X who in 1908 declared that the definition of the Assumption still required "much serious study", and Benedict XV.[3] It is of interest to note that the general secretariat of the Marian congregations is in the building used as the headquarters of the Jesuit Order at Rome, an order which from its origin has been the most ardent promoter of Marian piety.

The aforementioned resistance, some of it by men of the highest rank, is not to be interpreted as lack of inclination towards the doctrine of the Assumption of Mary. But in order that a pious belief, however universally shared, can be defined as dogma of the Church, certain conditions are needed in which the Assumption is lacking. The conditions are essentially three: the Biblical basis, the consensus of the earliest tradition, and theological value.

What the position of the Assumption is in tradition we have seen in the preceding pages: until the fifth century, nothing;

[1] Jugie, *op. cit.*, p. 493.
[2] *Ibid.*, p. 487.
[3] *Ibid.*, p. 491.

then traditions diverse and discordant; no real unanimity at any time in history.

The position in regard to Scripture is, if possible, still more hopeless. It is true that Father Aloisio Vaccari believed he could find explicit references to the Assumption in the Bible but against him is the authority of *Pseudo-Augustine*, of Peter Canisius, of Thomas Aquinas and Suarez, all of whom declare that no evidences of it are to be found there. The more serious theologians such as Roschini content themselves with finding some "implicit" evidences in the Scripture. What are these evidences? Essentially three.

The first is the "*Protevangelium*", that is, the foretelling of Genesis 3 : 15 : "I will put enmity between you and the woman, and between your seed and her seed; he shall bruise your head, and you shall bruise his heel." This first prophecy of the victory of the man over sin—that is of Christ inseparable from Mary, the Catholic theologians add—implies also the promise of Mary's victory over death.[1]

The second evidence is the salutation of the angel (Luke 1 :28) and that of Elizabeth (Luke 1 : 42). If Mary is full of grace and blessed among women she must not have been subject to death.

The third evidence[2] is the passage in the Book of the Revelation, chapter 12, concerning the "woman clothed with the sun". [a]The modern mariologists like to turn to this chapter, seeing in it an allegory of the Virgin Mary. But whatever can be thought of their interpretation, it is a fact that none of the early interpreters before the end of the fourth century see the Virgin Mary in the woman of the Revelation. They all understand her to be the Church and so they continue to make most

[1] Roschini, *Mariologia*, II, 2, p. 286. It is to be noted that Catholic theology does not hold the traditional interpretation by which, according to the Vulgate, the promise of victory over the ancient serpent was transferred to the woman ("*ipsa conteret*") and not to her progeny. It is known, indeed, that in the Hebrew "progeny" is masculine and hence it should be translated "he" shall bruise thy head. Roschini, recognizing the error of interpretation, does not attribute to the words "*ipsa conteret*", referring to Mary, a "scriptural" value, but only a "traditional" value. In other words, this argument does not make a part of the Biblical proofs but of those come down from ecclesiastical tradition, and its dogmatic worth remains practically unchanged. Cf. *Mariologia* I, p. 61. It could not be more clearly admitted that tradition is sometimes the codification of error.

[2] For the sake of brevity I omit certain Old Testament texts interpreted allegorically to which Roschini himself does not attribute much value.

[a] See note, p. 177 *infra*.

of their interpretations in the following centuries. Ticonius is the first to suggest the Marian interpretation. But none of the Bible readings for the feasts of Mary contains the twelfth chapter of the Book of Revelation. The least to be said is that such reference is highly uncertain,[a] to say nothing of the point that the woman's flight into the desert, which is a figure for the tribulations of the persecuted Church, would not be a very suitable representation of the glorious assumption of Mary, the more so in that the woman's sojourn in the desert is explicitly limited in time (verse 14). Roschini himself, furthermore, does not seem very enthusiastic about this interpretation, and he confines himself to concluding, "It seems therefore that this argument enjoys some solidity."[1]

There remain the theological reasons, that is, the arguments of "appropriateness" [b] that we have seen at work from the first beginning of the doctrine of the Assumption. Let us ask what is Roschini's exposition of it.[2] These reasons are in three groups. First of all, in so far as concerns the person of Christ, His glory would not be complete if He had left His Mother's body to corruption, neither can it be thought that His filial devotion would have allowed it. (Already *Pseudo-Augustine* had declared that Jesus had certainly obeyed the commandment, "Honour thy father and thy mother.") Moreover, Christ has given greater privileges to His mother, such as perpetual virginity; then why not this? On the Virgin's side are to be considered her conformity with Christ, her blood relationship and personal relations with Him. One is to reflect on the fact that no relics of her have been discovered, and also on her immunity from original sin that brought her back into the condition of Adam before his sin, and the condemnation of sin which is death. There is also the privilege granted to the other righteous (Matthew 27 : 51–53), or promised to those who will be living at Christ's coming again; this could not but be granted to Mary. Finally on the side of men themselves this belief promotes esteem of the Virgin and faith in her and in our future resurrection.

[a] *e per lo meno assai incerto.*

[1] "Videtur itaque argumentum hoc soliditate quadam gaudere", *Mariologia*, II, 2, p. 335 ff.

[b] *convenienza.*

[2] Roschini, *Mariologia*, II, 2, pp. 335 ff.

Now, all this can be fine and edifying, but is it enough to establish the reality of Mary's resurrection, that after all an historical fact happened or did not happen, in regard to which our devout opinions and our arguments of appropriateness have no importance? And if—without meaning any irreverence—God, whose ways are not our ways, had decided otherwise and had not really done that which the Catholic theologians for twelve hundred years have believed He must have done, that which He could not have failed to do, that which they believed it was suitable, right, inevitable that He should do, upon whom would fall the reproach of this disaccord? Upon the Most High or on His servants, who like Job's friends speak imprudently according to the ideas of blind human knowledge?

Martin Jugie, to whom we are indebted for nearly all that we have been explaining in this chapter, seeks, in the systematic part of his masterly work, to maintain that in the complete silence of tradition about Mary's death, the simplest and most devout opinion is that which comes to light in certain ancient writers, in particular Epiphanius. According to this opinion Mary did not die but passed from life to life, gloriously assumed into heaven like Enoch and Elijah, without knowing death. God does not work useless miracles, he observes; why suppose that He caused Mary to die to bring her to life immediately afterwards?

It appears that Jugie is practically alone in offering this solution. If the oldest tradition does not speak of Mary's death it is surely due to the fact that it is quietly presupposed by all, and Roschini is not wrong in stating, with Cardinal Lépicier, that the belief in Mary's death was practically unanimous in the Church.[1] That Mary has indeed shared the lot of mortality with the universality of men is the only certainty that can be drawn from the silence of the Christian tradition and from its evidences. That she was brought back to life and raised to heaven with her body glorified as the first of created beings, who wants to think this is free to do so, but it must be said that there is not a shadow of proof for it.

To come now to the year 1950. The Bull *Munificentissimus Deus*, containing the definition of the dogma of the Assumption, is an important document in the dogmatic development of Catholicism in that it marks a new and accentuated departure

[1] *Ibid.*, II, 2, p. 227.

from the accustomed traditionalism of Catholic theology.

The Biblical and patristic proof of the dogma of the Assumption that is contained in the Bull is extremely weak; one could even say that nothing is done to conceal this weakness, as though it were considered to be of no importance. The Bull cites as liturgical testimony the Latin sacramentaries of the eighth century, and as patristic sources St John of Damascus and other eastern writers, none of whom is earlier than the end of the seventh century. It recognizes, therefore, that if there are earlier clues to the Assumption none of them is certain enough to be made an argument of dogma. The Biblical evidences are still weaker. These are limited to certain passages of the Old Testament that the mediaeval theologians interpret allegorically, as the Bull admits, "with some freedom" (*quadam usi libertate*). They are Psalm 132 : 8 (Vulgate, 131); Psalm 45 : 10 (Vulgate 44); Song of Songs 3 : 6, 4 : 8, 6 : 8–10; Isaiah 60 : 13, and of course the *Protevangelium* (Genesis 3 : 15), and the Hail Mary (Luke 1 : 28). These citations are made without conviction and with detachment. It is clear that for the Bull they have only an historic interest. The dogma is based neither upon the Bible nor upon tradition.

The real foundation of the dogma, according to the Bull, is on the one hand the consensus of the Church of the present time, and, on the other, its theological "suitability".

The argument of the "consensus" of the Church of to-day is developed with such amplitude and solemnity that it is clear that for the Roman theologians it is the only necessary and sufficient one. What the Church believes and what it teaches must be considered as revealed truth. "The Authority of the Church," declares the Bull, "infallibly fulfils its mandate to conserve the integrity and purity of the revealed truth for all time, and to transmit it without adding to it or taking from it. . . . Therefore from the universal consensus of the Church may be drawn a sure and certain argument for affirming the Assumption. It is a truth revealed by God." The premise of the principle is evident: the Authority has been given to conserve the deposit of the faith, therefore whatever it proclaims must be said to be in accord with the deposit of the faith. And if history proves the contrary then so much the worse for history!

In reality the range of this declaration is deeper and more

serious. Father Filograssi, S.J., who to all appearance is one of the principal authors of the papal bull, commenting in the review *Civiltà Cattolica* (Nov. 4, 1950, pp. 287–88) on the Encyclical *Humani generis* of the summer of 1950, repeatedly states that the Spirit of God "conserves truth intact in progression", and referring expressly to the new dogma that had just been defined, adds, "In the case of the Assumption, theology recognizes another notable example of *dogmatic progression* by which the truth is slowly made clear." It is therefore the "modernist" principle of dogmatic development that is expressly invoked on behalf of the new mariological dogma, which confirms the thesis of our Introduction. This fact could have considerable value if it were an indication that Catholicism is beginning to renounce its reactionary dogmatic and if "progression" were really a progression in truth. But, alas, the three sole examples of dogmatic "progression" of the Catholic Church in a century are the immaculate conception, papal infallibility and the assumption of the Virgin Mary!

The other argument on which the definition of the dogma is founded is that of theological "suitability". The assumption is part of the "perfect harmony of privileges" (*perfectum gratiarum concentum*) that the Church recognizes in the Virgin Mary. It is a result of her divine maternity, of her perpetual virginity, and especially of her immaculate conception. And her "co-redemption" also, even though it has not yet been defined dogmatically, is cited as a good argument for the assumption, since to the extent that Mary is associated with Christ in the work of redeeming the world she can be associated with Him in the resurrection. P. Roschini, commenting on the new dogma over the Italian radio, quoted in support of this the thought of the Apostle Paul (1 Cor. 15: 21–22), adding to it thus: "Since by a man *and a woman* (Adam and Eve) came death, so by a man *and a woman* (Christ and Mary) came life, the resurrection of the dead!" With this presumptuous travesty of the thought of Paul it is proven that Mary belongs with Christ to the "first-fruits of the resurrection", that she was raised with Him three days after her death and has been bodily assumed to heaven![1]

But the aspect of this theological "harmony" that appears to

[1] Roschini, *The Dogma of the Assumption*, Rome, 1950, p. 82.

be especially close to the hearts of the authors of the Bull is the divine motherhood. The papal document states, "It seems almost impossible to imagine her to be separated from Christ, . . . who conceived Him, gave Him birth, nourished Him with her milk, carried Him in her arms and pressed Him to her bosom. From the moment that our Redeemer is the Son of Mary, He, as the most perfect observer of the divine laws, could not fail to honour the gracious Mother as well as the Eternal Father. As He was able then to give such an honour to His Mother, preserving her immune from corruption, one must believe that He has actually done so." These statements are a combination of two sentences of Bellarmine and St Francis de Sales, given here in the historical part of the Bull. The theology of the Bull is the sentimental theology of the Counter-Reformation, the pietism of the Jesuits, and this is understandable when one remembers that the Bull has been worked out by the theologians of the Company of Jesus.

In short, the new dogma has as its sole foundation the infallibility of the Roman Catholic Church. Substantially it rests on itself alone, on its own organic internal harmony. The dogmatic force of the Bull is reduced to this. The papal document does nothing to conceal this situation. It may commend itself to respect for its sincerity, but precisely in that way it frankly reveals its intrinsic weakness.[1]

[1] One does not attempt to cite here the abundant literature that has appeared about the proclamation of the dogma of the Assumption. An excellent collection of documents is offered by the review, *Die Oekumenische Einheit*, directed by Friedrich Haller and Friedrich Sigmund Schultz (Ernst Reinhardt Verlag, Munich-Basel, Vol. 2, No. 2). The number has important articles by Heiler and other writers of different confessions, a review of opinions and statements of private individuals and of churches, and a large bibliography. The ideas expounded in these pages are developed more fully in the review *Protestantism* (Rome, Waldensian Faculty of Theology, Via Pietro Cossa, 42; Vol. 4, No. 1). As Catholic comment on the Bull, besides various articles by Father Filograssi in the review *Civiltà Cattolica* (Rome), there are the radio addresses of P. Roschini, collected in *The Dogma of Assumption*, Belardetti, 1950 (see p. 105 *supra*). Among the Protestant voices of continental Europe, besides Heiler's review already cited and the writers listed in it, there are to be remembered *Le protestantisme et la Vierge Marie* (Paris, Je sers, 1950), a symposium of various authors, and the special number of the review *Verbum Caro* (No. 17, 1951), Delachaux et Niestlé (Neuchâtel), containing an interesting article by Max Thurian, *Le dogme de l'Assomption*.

Translator's note: For a study of this dogma by two Roman Catholic laymen who oppose it, see V. Bennett and R. Winch, *The Assumption of Our Lady and Catholic Theology*, S.P.C.K., 1950.

Chapter 6

THE IMMACULATE

"IN the West in the period extending from the Council of Ephesus to St Bernard, mariology is as it were in a state of adolescence. . . . In the twelfth century begins the true scientific evolution of mariology, through works of St Anselm and St Bernard especially."[1] The reasons for this progress are of general character in the main. Not only mariology but all Catholic theology receives a marked impulse in this period that ends with the great systematizations of theology in the thirteenth century. But if we want to seek a particular reason for the development of the veneration of Mary, beyond the internal reasons for its dogmatic development on which we must dwell in this chapter, we must not neglect the impulse that Marian piety receives from the new consideration of woman in cultivated society after the eleventh century begins, particularly from the idealization of woman in the poetry of the troubadours of Provence. Denis de Rougemont, in his book *L'Amour et l'Occident*, has maintained the thesis of the heretical origin of platonic love, love conceived as the cult of a feminine creature idealized and untouchable, passion that is inflamed by denial and consumes itself in it, enjoying its torment since passion begins to die as soon as it is satisfied. He sees in that tormented sublimation of love an aspect of Manichaean dualism flowering again in the heresy of the Cathari or Albigensi, and in the ideal woman of poetry a late arrival of the old gnostic motif of the heavenly Virgin, a secret designation of the Catharist church of the perfected. The cult of the Virgin Mary would be a counter altar of orthodoxy. As the nobility and the troubadours dedicated themselves to the lady of their thoughts, the good Catholics dedicated themselves to the Virgin Mary.[2]

For the purposes of this book it is not necessary to take a position in respect of the interesting hypothesis of De Rougemont.

[1] Roschini, *Mariologia*, I, p. 390.

[2] Denis de Rougemont, *L'Amour et l'Occident*, Paris, Plon, 1939, pp. 85 ff.

Without recourse to the Catharist heresy and its dualism, the long ages of repression of feelings, that goes with the ascetic ideal of mediaeval Christianity, should suffice to explain the idealization of woman in the culture of Europe from the eleventh century. And if one really wants to think of a Manichaean influence it will do to observe that through Augustine a notable infusion of Manichaeism had penetrated into the very body of Catholic Christianity. The Church had no need to seek in the necessity of combating the dualistic heresy the sentimental motivation of the renewed devotion to Mary. It had amply sufficient reason in its own bosom. It is significant, however, that right in this period the Virgin Mary begins to be designated with the name of Madonna, *mea Domina*, my Lady, which is the typical designation of the ideal woman in the new poetry. And it is significant also that the new dogma that becomes the centre of meditation and discussions is that of the immaculate conception of Mary.

The idealization of Mary, one can say, goes back to Ambrose of Milan. Of course expressions of ardent admiration of her can be found even earlier, for example the parallel of Eve and Mary in Justin and Irenaeus. But at the same time there was present also the complementary need to declare the full humanity of the mother of Christ, drawing attention to certain qualities she lacked. Thus Origen, one of the first promoters of Mary, who lived in the gnostic and mystic atmosphere of Alexandria, attributes to her an elevated rank of sanctity but not perfection. Mary belongs to the number of those of whom Jesus predicted that they would be offended at Him. Like the apostles, she too was confused by the catastrophe of the cross, and it was needful that she should thus sin in some measure so that she too should be redeemed by Christ, and His death be truly for all without exception.[1] The same theme, that Mary was capable of sinning as a human, is found again in John Chrysostom, who, commenting on the incident of Jesus' relations looking for Him, considers as "indiscreet" the desire of the mother and brothers who interrupted His discourse to have Him come with them. Chrysostom thinks that at the wedding at Cana Mary was possibly not immune to some feeling of human vanity, wishing to attract to herself recognition from

[1] Origen, *Homilia 17 in Lucam.*

the guests by the miracle requested of Jesus and the showing of her influence over Him.[1]

In Ambrose, the idealization of the Virgin Mary answers the need of offering a model of all the virtues to the Christian youth who are preparing for apprenticeship in asceticism.

> "She was virgin," [he writes] "not only of body but of spirit. . . . Humble of heart, serious in speech, prudent in thought, of few words, zealous in reading. She set not her hope in uncertain riches but in the prayers of the poor. She was intent in work and modest in speech and accustomed to put herself under the judgment of God rather than of men. She harmed no one but desired the good of all; she respected the aged and had no envy of those who were her own age, she avoided vanity, followed right, loved virtue. . . . She had nothing of pride in her look, nothing immodest in her actions, no indolence, she never failed to walk sedately and her voice has never a trace of insolence. Thus her very bodily appearance was the image of her soul, the image of virtue. . . ."

He continues to praise Mary's moderation in eating and the frequency of her fasts; she ate only that she should not die and slept only as long as was strictly necessary and while her body rested her soul kept watch. "Behold the picture of virginity. Mary was such that her life is a discipline for all."[2]

Here we have the ideal portrait of a fourth century nun and it is beautiful and edifying. It would be too much to ascribe any dogmatic value to this homiletic passage. Ambrose has some expressions that are more precise. "Come," he wrote, turning to Christ, "take me not from Sarah but from Mary, so that the Virgin shall be incorrupt but virgin through grace unsullied by any spot of sin."[3] This is a declaration of the purity and sanctity of Mary.

The doctrine of original sin begins to take rigorous form only with Augustine and the Pelagian controversy, and here the problem presents itself whether Mary is to be considered subject to it and, if so, within what limits. Pelagius, discussing the thesis of the universality of sin, opposed Augustine, saying that

[1] Commentaries on Matthew and Luke, at passages cited.
[2] *De Virginibus*, lib. II, cap. 2.
[3] *Enarratio in Ps. 117.*

one must believe that some righteous persons of the Old Testament lived without sin, or at least certainly the Virgin Mary, "concerning whom it is necessary to devotion to confess that she lived without sin". Augustine replies that none of the righteous of the Old Testament was immune to sin, and proceeds, "I make an exception for the Virgin Mary, about whom, for the honour due to the Lord, I do not want to have any discussion when it concerns sins, since we know that she who has been worthy to conceive and bear Him who was without sin has received a greater grace to conquer sin completely."[1]

It is clear that Augustine does not speak of original sin but of actual sins. The question discussed is whether Mary lived without sin, not whether she was conceived without sin. The very allusion to greater grace that she obtained to "conquer" sin seems to imply that a conflict—that was victorious—took place in her. In other passages Augustine teaches explicitly that Mary received physical life "*de peccati propagine*", from the tainted line of Adam and for this reason she was subjected to the common law of death,[2] while Christ was born without sin "by the maternal flesh of sin".[3] Taking account of these affirmations there can be no doubt about the interpretation of another passage that is often discussed. Replying to the pelagian Julian of Eclanum, who accused him of attributing the Virgin Mary's birth to the devil, Augustine answered, "I do not attribute the condition of Mary's birth to the devil because this condition is dissolved by the grace of the rebirth" (*quia ipsa conditio solvitur*

[1] Augustine, *De Natura et gratia*, cap. 36.

[2] Augustine, *De Genesi ad litteram*, lib. X, cap. 18, 32. ". . . et quid incoinquinatius illo utero Virginis, cuius caro etiamsi de peccati propagine venit, non tamen de peccati propagine concepit?" Mary, then, came from the tainted line of humanity but did not conceive Jesus by this line but by the Holy Spirit.

[3] Augustine, *De peccatorum meritis et remissione*, cap. 24. "Solus ergo ille etiam homo factus, manens Deus, peccatum non habuit unquam, nec sumpsit carnem peccati quamvis de materna carne peccati. Quod enim carnis inde suscepit, id profecto aut suscipiendum mundavit aut suscipiendo mundavit. Ideo Virginem matrem, non lege carnis peccati, id est, non concupiscentiae carnalis moto concipientem, sed pia fide sanctum germen in se fieri promerentem, quam eligeret creavit de qua crearetur elegit." The thought is the same as in the passage cited before. Christ was conceived without sin even though the "flesh" of His mother was not without sin, but rather was altogether in the line of Adam's defiled descent. But that flesh of sin He assumed either to purify it or He purified it by the very fact that He assumed it. Indeed He was conceived not according to the law of sin—that is without concupiscence—but by faith in the divine promise announced by the angel.

gratia renascendi),[1] she is therefore saved from the common subjection to evil by that very virtue of regeneration that is given to the faithful and not by any privilege of birth.[2] For this reason the more cautious Catholic theologians do not consider Augustine to be the actual source of the doctrine of the Immaculate Conception, confining themselves to stating that this can be drawn from his premises and that it is implicitly contained there.[3] This interpretation is certainly questionable as we have seen, while it can be admitted, with Harnack, that in conceding to Mary an exceptional position in regard to actual sin, Augustine favoured in a general way the dogmatic development that was to lead to the definition of the Immaculate Conception fifteen centuries later.[4]

Neither can greater clarity be derived from the fathers of the following centuries. It is worth noting that Nestorius, who combated the title Mother of God at Ephesus, admitted that Mary was exempted from all condemnation inherent in original sin, and that meant from the pangs of birth. But Nestorius had sympathy for Pelagianism and there is evidently a sort of elective affinity between this theory that reduces the seriousness of the original fall and the doctrine of the Immaculate Conception that wants to exempt Mary from it. This parallelism is found again in all the following centuries.[5]

One must come down to the Carolingian age to find explicit expressions of Mary's exemption from the condemnation of the primordial fall. Paschasius Radbertus declares that Mary did not suffer the pangs of childbirth because she was free from guilt and therefore from the punishment of Adam's fall, and he maintains by this that she is to be confessed as "uncorrupted

[1] Augustine, *Contra Julianum*, lib. IV, cap. 122.

[2] Catholic theology, as we shall see in what follows, has had to get round the difficulty by distinguishing the situation of fact from that of right. Cf. Roschini, *Mariologia* I, pp. 146 ff.

[3] Cf. the interpretation of Roschini, "Duobus textibus rite perpensis, nobis videtur S. Augustinum immaculatam Conceptionem sufficienter saltem docuisse." *Sufficienter:* that is indirectly, implicitly, with sufficient probability. (*Mariologia*, I, p. 147.)

[4] A. Harnack, *History of Dogma*, Italian translation, Mendrisio, 1914, Vol. V p. 205, n.

[5] For this reason the ironical exclamation "*Miranda res!*" is not justified, with which Roschini refers to this opinion of Nestorius. (*Mariologia*, II, 1, 38.) For the Catholic theologians, even the most erudite as our friend, Nestorius remains fixed for all the ages with the conventional figure of the hardened blasphemer of Mary.

and uncontaminated and free from all contagion of the first beginning", but he conceived such immunity as the effect of a sanctification in her mother's womb.[1] According to Anselm of Canterbury, on the other hand, Mary was not only conceived but born in sin like all the sons of Adam.[2]

In our question, as in all the development of mariology, the popular and liturgical devotion preceded the dogmatic definitions. In 1140 certain canons of Lyons instituted a festival in honour of the immaculate conception of Mary. We can realize still to-day the impression of novelty that such action must have made as we read the famous letter that Bernard of Clairvaux wrote to them on that occasion.

> "Among the churches of Gaul, as all know, Lyons has had preeminence until now, whether for the dignity of its episcopal seat or for honourable studies or praiseworthy discipline. . . . Therefore I am amazed that some of you have wanted to change this very fine character you have by introducing a new ceremony of which the rites of the Church know nothing, that reason does not approve, and ancient tradition does not recommend. Are we perchance more learned or more devout than the Fathers? Do we in temerity want to define what they in their prudence have left in doubt? For it concerns a matter of such a kind that if it had not been their duty not to investigate it the diligence of the Fathers would not have been able to neglect it. But, thou wilt say, one must honour the Mother of the Lord more. Thou sayest well, but the honour of the queen must be judicious. The royal Virgin has no need of a false honour, being well supplied with authentic titles of glory. Honour the integrity of her flesh, the sanctity of her life, admire her virginal fecundity, reverence her divine Son. Celebrate her who in conceiving knew no concupiscence nor pangs in giving birth. Preach her who is to be revered as the angels, desired by the people, foreknown by

[1] Paschasius Radbertus, *De partu Virginis:* "Nullis, quando nata est, subjacuit delictis, neque contraxit, in utero sanctificata, originale peccatum."

[2] Anselm, *Cur deus homo?* lib. II, cap. 16a: "Nam licet ipsa hominis eiusdem conceptio sit munda et absque carnalis delectationis, Virgo tamen ipsa unde assumptus est, est in iniquitatibus concepta et in peccatis concepit eam mater eius, et cum originali peccato nata est, quoniam et ipsa in Adam peccavit, in quo omnes peccaverunt." The thought is put on the lips of the interlocutor of the dialogue, *Boso*, but Anselm does not contest his statement, which agrees with Augustine's ideas already cited. Jesus was conceived without sin, that is without concupiscence, even if the Virgin by whom He was conceived was herself conceived in sin and was born in original sin, in which even she sinned in Adam.

patriarchs and prophets, elect among all, preferred to all. Magnify the inventress of grace, the mediatrix of salvation, the restorer of the ages. Exalt her who is exalted above the choirs of angels in the celestial kingdoms. The Church sings all this of her for me and teaches me to sing. I maintain and pass on with certainty that which I have received from her, but confess that I should have many scruples about admitting what she has not transmitted to us. I have received of the Church what must be celebrated with great reverence, the day when she was taken up from this sad age and received in heaven the joy of a solemn festival. But I have also learned in the Church and from the Church to celebrate the day of her birth without any doubt, holding with the utmost firmness with the Church that she received in the maternal womb the grace necessary that she be born holy. I read, indeed, of Jeremiah that he was consecrated from his mother's womb, and I think no differently of John the Baptist, who, from the womb of his mother, knew the Lord not yet born. . . . That what resulted should have been given to a few mortals cannot be presumed to have been denied to so great a virgin through whom the whole mortal race of men came to life (*omnis mortalitas emersit ad vitam*). Moreover the mother of the Lord was certainly sanctified before her birth (*sancta prius quam nata*); neither is the Church deceived when it regards the day of her birth as holy and celebrates it with exultation every year. I believe that an abundant blessing of sanctification came down in her which not only sanctified her birth but preserved her life from all sin, something that was granted to no other born of woman. Therefore her birth was holy since that great sanctity made it so when she came from her mother's womb.

"What other honours do we believe should be added to this? They say let the conception be also honoured that preceded that honourable birth. But what logic is there in thinking that the conception was holy by the mere fact that it preceded the birth? The conception preceded the birth so that this should take place, not that it should be holy. And from whence would it have derived the holiness to transmit to the birth that was to follow? Was it perhaps not rather because the conception was not holy that it had to be sanctified so that the birth should be holy? Or perhaps it borrowed the holiness from the birth that was to follow it? Now the holiness accomplished in her already conceived could communicate itself to the birth that followed it but certainly could not go backwards to the conception that had preceded it. Whence then the holiness of the conception? Will it be said that the sanctification preceded the conception, that it was conceived already sanctified and that for that reason the conception was also holy, in the same way that it is said that it was sanctified in the maternal womb and that the birth was therefore sanctified also? But there could not be sanctification before existence, nor was there existence before being conceived. Or perhaps in the conjugal embraces the sanctification mingled with the conception itself so that there was sanctification and conception at the same time? But reason does not admit this. How could there be holiness without sanctifying grace, or how could the Holy Spirit associate with sin? Or will it be said that in some way there was no sin where it is certain that concupiscence (*libido*) was not lacking? Pity him who tells himself that she was conceived by the Holy Spirit and not by a man. But up till now this is unheard of. Indeed, I read that the Holy Spirit came into her, not with her, when the angel said, 'Lo, the Holy Spirit will be upon thee.' . . . I say that she gloriously conceived by the Holy Spirit but was not conceived of it; I say that she has given birth as a virgin but was not born by a virgin. If not, where is the prerogative of the Mother of the Lord who is believed to exult in a way that is quite unique by reason of the nature of her offspring and her bodily integrity if the same privilege was granted to her mother as well? This is not to honour the Virgin but to diminish her honour. If then she could not be sanctified before her conception because she did not exist, neither in her conception itself, by reason of the sin that was there, it remains that we believe that already conceived and existing in her mother's womb she received sanctification (*restat ut post conceptum in utero iam existens sanctificationem accepisse credatur*), which, taking away the sin, made her birth holy but not her conception. Therefore if it is granted to a few sons of men to be born sanctified it is not granted to them to be so conceived, so that sanctified conception should be reserved for one alone, for Him who came to sanctify all and coming without sin was to accomplish the purification of sinners. Only Jesus Christ, then, was conceived by the Holy Spirit, since He alone was sanctified before and after conception. Except for Him all the sons of Adam are in the position that one of them truly and humbly confessed himself, 'I was conceived in iniquity and in sin did my mother conceive me.' Things standing thus, I say it is a question whether a conception is sanctified that is not by the Holy Spirit so as not to say it is by sin, or a conception that is not sanctified will be celebrated by festival.

"The glorious one will gladly do without this honour with which sin seems to be honoured or she is to be clothed with a false sanctity. Moreover, a novelty arbitrarily made up contrary to the rites of the Church will not please her, that novelty that is the mother of temerity, sister of superstition, daughter of levity. If you wanted to do these things you should have first consulted the authority of the Apostolic See and not have followed in this way, with thoughtless precipitation, the simplicity of some incompetents! I knew before that there was this error in the thought of some but I feigned ignorance of it, to spare a devotion that came from simplicity of heart and love of the Virgin. But having discovered this superstition among those with knowledge and in a famous and noble Church, of which I am especially a son, I do not know if I could have ignored it without grave offence to you all. Let it be said without prejudice by a better judge. I remit the whole question to the authority and example of the Roman Church in particular, as the other similar questions, always ready to revise my judgment."[1]

We have quoted this letter almost entirely in which St Bernard puts the question in the terms in which it will remain for all the Middle Ages and the Counter-Reformation until the solemn definition of 1854, concerning which one may wonder whether it would have satisfied the saint as to the judgment of the Church.[a]

Bernard of Clairvaux is justly considered one of the greatest promoters of Marian devotion in the twelfth century. He is also in this the typical representative of his age, to which the motives of idealizing woman are not strange, motives present in the new man in the eleventh century and after. He unites in one love the mystery of Jesus and the veneration of His mother together with the ideal of chivalry of the Templars in the service

[1] Bernard of Clairvaux, *Epistula 174 (172) ad Canones Lugdunenses*. We quote the Paris edition of Mabillon, 1839, Vol. I, col. 389–393.

[a] Peter de Celle, a correspondent of Archbishop Thomas Becket and John of Salisbury, in reply to Prior Nicholas of St. Albans. Nicholas was taking the part of the canons of Lyons against Bernard. Peter wrote that he would have liked the Apostolic See to have approved of their idea of the conception.

"Utinam . . . conceptionem Virginis librasset et approbasset et a mari usque ad mare hanc propagasset."

He believed, however, that the doctrinal implications were better as the matter stood.

"Quid est igitur, Virgo singularis omne peccatum vicit, non omne debellendo, sed nullum prorsus sentiendo? Quam victricem appellas, debellatricem appellare cur formidas? An times eam debellare in bello, quam non potes dicere vincere nisi in praelio, aut sine praelio? Segnior est si qua est victoria sine praelio, fortior quae in praelio. Ad ampliorem itaque gloriam, assero Dominam nostram peccatum omne vicisse et debellasse." P. L. CCII, 616, 617, 619, 620.

of the Church and the Holy Virgin. His objections to the theological and liturgical novelty of the Immaculate Conception do not derive from any lukewarmness towards the Virgin Mary, but are bound up with two basic concerns of the Christian faith, the Augustinian conception of sin and the insistence that the honour rendered to Mary should not diminish the Lord's position of absolute uniqueness; and, it may be added, in some measure, the intolerance of the man of wide culture and religious genius for superstitious devotional practices that grow on the traditional ground of Christian piety, changing it in its deeper and more profound convictions.

We shall find again these convictions against the immaculate conception of Mary, but in a more developed form according to the rigorous practice of the schoolmen, in the five short chapters that Thomas Aquinas devotes to our question in the *Summa Theologica*.[1] Thomas has it that the Virgin was sanctified in her mother's womb: not that it is a truth revealed in the Bible, "Concerning the sanctification of Mary, that is that she was sanctified *in utero*, nothing has been handed down to us in the canonical Scriptures which do not mention her birth at all." But accepting the version of *Pseudo-Augustine*—who he thinks is the real Augustine—he gives his opinion on the assumption of the Virgin that it is possible to show rationally (*rationabiliter argumentari*), that she was sanctified in the uterus, and he quotes the angelic greeting, *Ave gratia plena*,[a] and the example of Jeremiah (1 : 5) and of John the Baptist (Luke 1 : 15). It is not revealed truth, then, but a theological proposition: there is a difference that needs to be observed. But Thomas does not think he needs to carry the demonstration farther, or to pass from the sanctification in the maternal womb to the immaculate conception, and he argues:

> "The sanctification of the Virgin cannot be meant to have happened before her animation,—that is, before her soul was united to her body,—for two reasons: first, because the sanctification of which we speak is none other than purification from original sin. . . . But guilt cannot be cleansed except by grace

[1] Part III, quaest. 27, art. 1–6. Cited from Migne, *Patrol. Lat. series secunda*, Vol. IV, col. 245–257.

[a] Also because she bore "the only begotten of the Father, full of grace and truth".

whose subject is the rational creature only. Therefore, before the infusion of the rational soul the Virgin was not sanctified. Secondly, because only the rational creature is susceptible to guilt, the offspring conceived is not capable of guilt before the infusion of the rational soul. And if the blessed Virgin had been sanctified in any way before her animation she would never have incurred any stain of original sin and therefore would have had no need of redemption and salvation which are through Christ, of whom it is said in Matthew 1: 21, 'He will save his people from their sins.' It is not fitting, then, that Christ should not be the Saviour of all men, as is said in 1 Timothy 4. It stands, then, that the sanctification of the blessed Virgin took place after her animation."[1]

And he makes it precise: "Mary contracted original sin but was cleansed of it before birth." She could not be sanctified before her animation, unless one wanted to suppose that her ancestors had received a particular sanctification to this end, since personal sanctification acquired through grace is not transmitted to offspring.

What then, according to Thomas, is the situation of the Virgin Mary in consequence of her prenatal sanctification? It consists simply in this: the incitement [a] of concupiscence, which is in all the sons of Adam the vitiating root of all actual sins, was not suppressed in her in its essence (*sublatus secundum essentiam*), but was bound (*ligatus*), not by virtue of her free will, which did not yet exist in the maternal womb, but by the abundance of grace and by a special disposition of divine providence that took from her all sense of disordered movement. When then, by the operation of the Holy Spirit, she conceived Jesus, the holiness of the child she carried reflected itself upon her (*redundavit*) and the incitement was completely taken away. But she was not freed from death nor from other penal sanctions of original sin, to which she had to submit like all other human creatures.[2] Such doctrine, it is evident, is very circumspect.

The same caution is found in practically all the doctors of the thirteenth century, not only among the Dominicans but also

[1] *Summa Theol.*, *loc. cit.*, art. 2.
[a] *il fomite.*
[2] *Summa Theol.*, *loc. cit.*, art. 3.

in the founder of Franciscan theology, St Bonaventura. Discussing whether the Blessed Virgin could be sanctified "before her animation", that is before her soul was united to the body, Bonaventura answers in the negative, since sanctification is an affair of the soul and is communicated, if ever, from the soul to the flesh and therefore cannot take place before the soul is united to the body. Passing from there to the problem, at what point was the Virgin's soul sanctified, before or after she contracted original sin, he replies by indicating the reasons in favour of the two solutions. It would not be impossible to think that grace had been infused into her in the very instant in which the soul was infused into her flesh. This would certainly conform with the honour of Christ and of the Virgin. It could not be said that such a privilege granted to Mary is repugnant to the Christian faith since it would be a result of the grace that has its origin in Christ and in her would have anticipated that fall which, in the others, it remedies when this has taken place.

Notwithstanding these good reasons—which will be sustained in the following years by the Franciscan school, favourable to the Immaculate Conception—Bonaventura prefers to hold to the other opinion, as "more common, more rational and more certain". It is more common in that almost all believe that the Virgin contracted original sin and due to this she suffered the penalty, sorrow and death. It is more rational because as Augustine says, her own birth preceded her rebirth, as being precedes well being. It is more certain,

> "because it conforms more to faith, piety and to the authority of the saints, who, when they speak of her, exempt only Christ from the universal declaration, that all sinned in Adam. In fact no one is found among those whom we have heard with our ears who has said that the Virgin Mary was immune from original sin. This opinion agrees predominantly with faith and piety in that if the mother is to be held in great reverence and if we are to have a great devotion for her, it follows from this that we owe a much greater devotion to the Son from whom all honour and glory derive. And because it pertains to the excellent dignity of Christ, the fact that he is Redeemer and Lord, and he opens the door to all and died for all, the Blessed Virgin must not be excluded from this universality so that it should not happen that

while she fills the excellency of mother she should diminish the glory of the Son and thus the Son be challenged in his mother; since she prefers that the Son be exalted and honoured rather than she herself, as honour is due to the Creator more than to the creature. Holding to this position for the honour of Christ, which does not prejudice Mary's honour in any way, in that the Son is incomparably superior to the mother, we must therefore believe, in conformity with the general belief, that the Virgin's sanctification took place after she had contracted original sin."[1]

Bonaventura maintains, however, that Mary was sanctified before giving birth.

Such, then, is the opinion of the greatest minds of the twelfth and thirteenth centuries: St Bernard, St Thomas Aquinas, St Bonaventura. Mary was indeed sanctified in the maternal womb, one can believe, even though they have no proofs of it from the Bible or the fathers, but she was not conceived without sin.

Modern students, including Protestants, and Adolf Harnack among them,[2] tend to minimize the importance of this reserve and emphasize the weakness of the position they express. From the time when Augustine, giving up a chivalrous reluctance to speak of sin in connection with Mary—as one declines to discuss the Queen or a first love—had opened the door to the opinion that Mary could have a privileged position in respect of original sin, from that time onward the premises were established for the dogmatic development that was to lead to the definition of the Immaculate Conception. That it has come to this definition is not surprising. Rather, it is to be considered strange that it has taken so many centuries to bring so logical a development to its conclusion. But we must be careful if we seek to understand in their profound motivation the scruples by which a St Bernard and a Thomas Aquinas reject the Immaculate Conception while they do accept her sanctification in the maternal womb. We ask what significance these two positions have, positions apparently so close. What is their significance religiously as symbols of a spiritual attitude and orientation? for we must agree that their difference is this above all else. Sanctification

[1] In III Sent. D. 3, p. I, a. 1, qu. 3. Cf. Roschini, *Mariologia*, II, 2, p. 56.

[2] Cf. Harnack, *History of Dogma*, Vol. VI, p. 390. See also Benrath, *Zur Geschichte der Marienverehrung*, p. 159.

in the maternal womb brings Mary into conformity with other analogous cases and respects in her person the universal laws of sin and redemption. The Immaculate Conception breaks this conformity and introduces a completely new element into the regard for her.

The relation of these two doctrines is analogous to the parallel relation that we have observed with the birth of Jesus. His birth by the Virgin Mary was constantly defended by the Church against the more accessible conception of a birth, however ordained and sanctified by God, through the accustomed way of human generation. The point was that the virgin birth signifies the absolute exception, the complete uniqueness that sets Christ apart, elevating Him above others born of woman who were sanctified or predestined from the maternal womb. It was certainly the intuition of an analogous relationship that impeded the theologians of the scholastic age from attributing the immaculate conception to Mary. They observed a disquieting closeness between an immaculate conception of Mary and the miraculous conception of Jesus. We are aware of this uneasiness in St Bernard's letter. The idea that the only logical way to exempt Mary from the universal human heritage would be to postulate a virgin birth for her as well comes into consciousness and is repelled as sacrilege. In the period following, logical argumentation succeeds in quieting these scruples of faith and devotion but the fact that they could arise is quite instructive of the profound convictions represented in the bitterest dispute that rent Catholicism at the end of the Middle Ages. The opponents of the Immaculate Conception rejected that new dogma for the same reasons for which the Church of the end of the first century had accorded the virgin birth to Jesus when it discarded the Ebionite idea of a birth sanctified in the maternal womb, and instead accorded to Mary the sanctification from the maternal womb because this did not constitute an absolute novelty but rather is the exception within the rule, the privilege that confirms and does not annul the universal law.

The Biblical analogies to which they refer are not really very convincing. The "word of the Lord" to Jeremiah, "Before I formed you in the womb I knew you, and before you were born I consecrated you; I appointed you a prophet to the nations"

(Jer. 1 : 4, 5), refers to the prophet and to his consecration to his mission. There was the idea of a purification from sin, either as entirely absent, or being free from it by the reasoning of "suitability": God had to sanctify in some measure him who was to be His instrument of election. It cannot be a matter of purification from original sin since the idea of original sin is beyond the horizon of the Old Testament, at least as a doctrine rigorously formulated. The annunciation of the birth of John the Baptist has an analogous significance, "And he will be filled with the Holy Spirit even from his mother's womb" (Luke 1 : 15). The Holy Spirit is the spirit of prophecy by which his forerunner will be animated. But for the history of our dogma it is not so important to know what those passages meant objectively as to know how they were understood.

The apocryphal gospels also, which are among the principal sources of the idealization of Mary and of her immaculate conception, keep in the line of Biblical analogies. Anna, the mother of Mary, is sterile like Hannah, mother of Samuel, and like her is rendered fecund by a direct intervention of Providence. The birth of Mary is made to accord with that of the great predestined of the Old Testament, Samuel, or Isaac son of Sarah, the wife of Abraham, who was conceived in her old age by a special divine grace. The theology of the first centuries had seen in those fathers and prophets a typical figure of Jesus, and the apocryphal literature prefigured the birth of Mary in the manner of their birth. And Mary, consecrated to God from the maternal womb, had been brought up upon the steps of the altar in the Temple of Jerusalem and was consecrated to the Lord with a vow of perpetual virginity.[1] All these motives are summed up in the mediaeval celebration of Mary, sanctified from the mother's womb. The traces of this assimilation remain, at least in the more circumspect such as Thomas Aquinas. The sanctification of Mary is only gradual and she continues subject to the penalty of sin, i.e., sorrow and death. She remains, in short, completely human. The earliest fathers, as we have seen, did not hesitate to recognize some form of weakness in her, at least the doubt and scandal in regard to the cross.

The immaculate conception of Mary broke all the analogies and passed all the limitations implicit in that assimilation.

[1] *Protevangelium of James*, cap. 5–7.

Mary, conceived without sin, never had in reality known our human condition. Created an exceptional being in the most rigorous sense of the term, she became the perfect analogy, on the human plane, of her Son, the Redeemer. This idea with its prestige, intuitively easy, lent itself admirably to the liturgical requirements of the cult of Mary which at just that time knew an unprecedented increase. It was to be immensely welcome to the common people, always avid of the miraculous and ready to accept every exaltation of the Virgin the more enthusiastically the more hyperbolical it was. The new dogma, as all know, was defended fervently by the Franciscans who came from the people and lived with the people, while the rival order of the Dominicans, heirs of the Thomist tradition, kept up an opposition continually renewed. In the heated disputes aroused by this doctrine, the Franciscans accused the Dominicans of being enemies of Mary's honour and the Dominicans accused the promoters of the Immaculate of impiety and heresy: of impiety because of their excessive assimilation of Mary to the divine Christ, and of heresy because the Immaculate Conception opens the first and irreparable breach in the Augustinian conception of sin and salvation.

In this severe doctrine the whole Middle Ages lived and trembled and to it it owed its rigorous sexual asceticism and also its tragic conception of life. But in the centuries when humanistic culture [a] began to reassert itself, that conception began to be burdensome for the conscience. There arose a new and more human conception of the relations between the sexes and also a less sombre conception of sin and release from it. If the lay literature is witness of the first, the Franciscans' mirth made itself the organ of the second. Some centuries later the Reformation was to separate sex from sin, in the conception of original sin, abandoning the crypto-Manichaeism, which from Augustine afflicted the nuptials of Christianity, confirming again at the same time the tragic vision of life which was its profound and human value. Catholicism has followed an inverse way. It has mitigated naturalistically the conception of original sin, renewing a Pelagian disguise in various forms, associated with the neo-pagan celebration of the joys of life. But it has maintained on the other hand the sexual Manichaeism,

[a] *civilità.*

at least as a theory and monastic ideal of perfection. The dogma of the Immaculate Conception contained the two principles in the germ. It was the negation at a decisive point of the doctrine of the universality of sin, and at the same time it was the apotheosis of virginal purity elevated to a stature quasi divine. For this reason it was to triumph fatally. It was too Catholic for Thomas Aquinas' Augustinian scruples to prevail over it, or for the consciousness of the inevitable distance between Christ and His mother, that was common to all the great scholars of the classic age of scholasticism, to win against it either.

It is certainly not by chance that the idea of the Immaculate Conception was promoted in the theological field appropriated by that Scotist theology which is the dissolution of the great system of mediaeval faith.

It appears that the personal contribution of Duns Scotus to our question has been exaggerated. Roschini rightly stresses the importance that some earlier doctors had in starting the new doctrine towards its triumph: Henry of Ghent, William Ware the teacher of Duns Scotus, and the Paris theologian Raymund Lull, who was a contemporary of the Scot. The course followed by the dogmatic evolution is instructive. It moves from the universally admitted concept of sanctification in the maternal womb, leads it back in time as far as possible until it makes it coincide with conception itself. By this retrocession it is declared that Mary was subject to original sin at only one instant and then that temporal instant resolves itself into a purely logical instant. If it is true that logically conception must precede sanctification, this precedence is annulled in the reality of time, for the conception and the sanctification coincide. Mary has never been subject to original sin: she ought to have been subject to it, that is all. At this point the concept of the sanctification in the maternal womb is integrally translated into the quite different idea of conception without stain. The exceptional character of the privilege is attenuated, or at least disguised, by the recourse to the grace of God. Christ, perfect redeemer and mediator, argues Scotus, has a method of redemption perfectly sufficient for each one and it is certain that the most perfect must have been reserved for His mother. Now, it is certain that the prevention of evil is more perfect than the repairing of evil. It was then fitting, whether for the Mediator or for the dignity of His mother, that Mary should rather be preventively exempted from original sin than purified from it after having contracted it. "Mary then had the greatest need of Christ the Redeemer. In fact she would have contracted original sin by virtue of her birth if she had not been prevented by the grace of the Mediator. And as the others had need of Christ so that sin already contracted should be remitted them by his merit, she had so much greater need of the Mediator that he should precede sin so that it should not be contracted by her."[1] In conclusion: "She is there the blessed Virgin, mother of God, who was never actually an enemy (of God) by reason of actual sin or original sin, yet would have been an enemy if she had not been preserved."[2]

Duns Scotus wrote these words in 1300, commenting at Oxford on the *Liber Sententiarum* of Peter Lombard. Eight or nine years later, however, shortly before his death, and taking up the same argument, he qualified his statement by introducing a "perhaps" in respect of original sin.[3] Thus, in the final analysis, Duns Scotus' position remained uncertain and the definite expression of his thinking to the end of his life is still that contained in the treatise of Oxford already cited. "Upon this question I say that God was able to effect it that Mary was never in original sin. He was able also to effect it that she remained in sin for a moment or for a certain time and was cleansed of it in the last instant of that time. Which of the three solutions really took place whose possibility I have shown, God knows. If they are not repugnant to the authority of the Church or the authority of Scripture, it seems probable that one is to attribute the most excellent to Mary."[4]

For this reason the modern mariologists, like Roschini, do not consider Duns Scotus to be the author of the theological demonstration of the Immaculate Conception but only of its possibility. But others, before and especially after him, express

[1] In *Commentary on Book IV, Peter Lombard's Sentences*, 1. 3, dit. 3, qu. 1 (about 1300).

[2] *Ibid.*, d. 18, qu. unica. "Est ibi beata Virgo, Mater Dei, quae numquam fuit inimica actualiter ratione peccati actualis, nec ratione originalis; fuisset tamen, nisi fuisset praeservata."

[3] "Numquam fuit inimica actualiter, ratione peccati actualis et forte nec pro peccato originali, quia fuit praeservata, ut supra dictum est." Cf. Roschini, *Mariologia*, II, 2, p. 69.

[4] *Loc. cit.*, dit. 3, qu. 1.

with greater certainty what the great nominalist doctor considered only as a probable opinion. And the way of the elaboration of the dogma is always that which we have observed and shall find in other mariological definitions: first the possibility of the doctrine is affirmed—and in this regard the demonstration is that of Scotus; then the "congruence" or "suitability"—it was right, it conformed with Mary's dignity, the piety of Christ, the righteousness of God that this should happen so; finally it passes to the affirmation of the factual truth of the doctrine proposed. God could preserve Mary from original sin. Now it was "suitable" that He should do so. Therefore He did so. *Potuit, decuit, fecit.* Thus dogmas are built up in Catholicism. Thus, by the admission of the Catholic mariologists, the entire mariology is constructed.[1]

It does not come within the scope of this book to follow the great controversy between Franciscans and Dominicans in the fourteenth and fifteenth centuries in which it can be said that "heaven and earth" took part, because the opposed theological conceptions received supernatural sanctions, unfortunately divergent. There were visions of St Brigid that were favourable to the Franciscans and of St Catherine of Siena that were loyal to the Dominicans. In the historical field the principal theatre of the struggle was the University of Paris, which was troubled in 1387 by the attacks of John of Montesono against the Scotist doctrine of the Immaculate, who was condemned by three hundred theologians. At the same time in the university the most noted proponents of the conciliar theory, Pierre d'Ailly and Jean Gerson, favoured it, "moderns" who were inclined to be critical of Thomism. The reforming council of Basel in 1438 sanctioned the Immaculate Conception as a doctrine that was "devout and consonant with the worship of the Church, the Catholic faith and right reason and sacred Scripture". Unfortunately the council had just been condemned by pope Eugenius IV for its ardent anticurialism, and the definition could not be considered valid. It had, however, a notable influence with the nations that received its decrees. In 1477 the Franciscan pope Sixtus IV sanctioned the feast of the Immaculate, endowing it with special indulgences, but his decree did

[1] Cf. Roschini, *Mariologia*, II, 2, pp. 59, 63, 64, 69, 87. These citations refer only to the Immaculate Conception.

not succeed in making the opposition desist, which, on the contrary, asserted itself most actively in the person of the Dominican general Vincenzo Bandelli. In 1482 the pope forbade, under pain of excommunication, that in any discussion of such doctrine not yet defined by the Church, the adversaries should accuse each other of heresy or impiety. The Sorbonne in 1496 required its tutors to swear to teach nothing contrary to the Immaculate Conception and one hundred and twelve doctors took this sort of antimodernist oath in reverse, for it was precisely the "modern" opinion that they were obliged to observe. At the Council of Trent, Franciscans and Jesuits made an attempt to obtain the definition of the Immaculate but the papal legates broke up the movement for fear of a schism. The council restricted itself to declaring that it did not mean to include the Virgin Mary [a] in its definition of original sin and confirmed the constitutions of Sixtus IV (*Sessio V, De Peccato Orig.*, No. 5).

In the sixteenth and seventeenth centuries, by the influence of the Reformation and, in France, of the Jansenists, the discussions had a renewed intensity and came to the point where Paul V had to forbid all public discussion of that controversial question, and Gregory XV extended the same prohibition to private discussions. In the meanwhile, however, the cult of the Immaculate continued to grow, and Alexander VII, in the year 1661, detailed the object of the feast declaring it to be a pious and ancient judgment that "Mary's soul in the first instant of its creation and infusion into the body, by special grace and privilege of God and in consideration of the merits of Christ . . . was preserved immune from all stain of original sin". Clement XI extended the feast of the Immaculate Conception to the whole Church in 1708. Benedict XIV, while still Cardinal Lambertini, sought a way of mediation between the contrasting opinions, distinguishing between the active and passive conception of Mary and reserving for the latter her immunity from original sin. The distinction is important because it is along that line that agreement among the theologians was finally reached. The Catholic theologians distinguish an "active" conception, that is the act of the parents, and a passive conception, which is the beginning of the life of the foetus, and

[a] The adjective "*immaculatam*" was used.

in this are differentiated an initial moment, the principle of physical life, and a final moment in which the rational soul is infused into the embryo which is said to occur in the third month when it is sufficiently developed. This is the moment of "animation". Now, as we have observed, one of the questions in the discussion was whether Mary had been sanctified before, or after, or in the actual instant of animation. Lambertini pronounced in favour of this solution, which as we have seen was that sanctioned in anticipation by Alexander VII.[1]

It was left for the romantic pope Pius IX to proclaim the dogma of the Immaculate Conception. From his youth he had special reasons for gratitude to the Virgin Mary for by her he had been healed of an infirmity that made him unadapted to the priesthood, and in the revolutionary crisis of 1848 he had attributed his bodily recovery to her. From his refuge at Gaeta he sent out an encyclical, February 2, 1849, asking the bishops about the opportuneness of defining the Immaculate dogmatically. Two-thirds of those questioned showed themselves favourable. Among the other third there were not lacking grave cautions against declaring as a dogmatic and revealed truth what had been only a pious belief of the Church. But the personal inclination of the pope, combined with the pressure of the Jesuits and the weight of the majority of the replies, overcame the last resistance. On December 8, 1854, in St. Peter's, Pius IX, solemnly enthroned, tiara on his head, replied solemnly to the prayers of the dean and college of cardinals that he would define the doctrine of the Immaculate:

> "The doctrine according to which the most blessed Virgin Mary in the first instant of her conception, by the singular grace and privilege of almighty God and in consideration of the merits of Christ, Saviour of the human race, was preserved immune from all stain of original sin, is revealed by God and therefore is to be believed firmly and constantly by all the faithful."[2]

[1] See the lively exposition by Steitz, in *Real Encyc.*, 2nd ed. 1881, art. *Maria.*

[2] Bull *Ineffabilis Deus*: "Ad honorem Sanctae et Individuae Trinitatis, ad decus et ornamentum Virginis Deiparae, ad exaltationem fidei catholicae et christianae religionis, auctoritate Domini Nostri Iesu Christi, beatorum Apostolorum Petri et Pauli, ac Nostra, declaramus, pronunciamus et definimus, doctrinam, quae tenet beatissimam Virginem Mariam in primo instanti suae conceptionis fuisse singulari omnipotentis Dei gratia et privilegio, intuitu meritorum Christi Iesu Salvatoris humani generis, ab omni originalis culpae labe praeservatam immunem,

The solemn declaration is not precise about the particular moment that Mary's preservation from original sin must be thought to have taken place, but from the context of the Bull it must mean that "the first instant of her conception" designated the moment of the "animation" of the Virgin and the mariologists understand the dogma in that sense. It is a matter then of the median solution that we have seen delineated that excludes the idea that Mary can have been sanctified before she had a soul. The conception without stain is intended in a passive sense as preservation from sin and in an active sense as sanctification in the maternal womb.[1] These precise details are necessary to understand the Catholic dogma exactly and we ask our readers to excuse us for these particulars. But the Church has long since forgotten the principle that it is sometimes rash to want to know what can be left unknown without danger.

The modern interpretation of the Immaculate Conception, as we noted, takes up the idea of a sanctification in the maternal womb dear to the schoolmen of the thirteenth century. Therefore some mariologists think St Thomas Aquinas, if he could come back to life, would agree with the definition of Pius IX. But that means, if we are not mistaken, that they have missed the severe Augustinian sense of Thomism, to which belongs essentially the affirmation that Mary really was woman of Adam's descent, even if in a very brief period in her prenatal life, and that she was burdened by the common heritage of malediction from which she could be freed through redemption by her divine Son. The "most perfect" method of redemption thought out for her by the Scotist theology is actually a crossing over to thinking of a quite different order, that is the postulation in Mary of the innocence of Eve before the fall, which is the negation of the Augustinian dogma at a point that is decisive.

In the papal definition the doctrine of the Immaculate is called "revealed truth": a serious and risky affirmation in view of the total silence of the Sacred Scriptures and earliest tradition. It cannot be said that the mariologists' explanations of

esse a Deo revelatam, atque idcirco ab omnibus fidelibus firmiter constanterque credendam."

[1] For the definition of terms, see Roschini, *Mariologia*, II, 2, pp. 19 ff.

this argument are very clear or persuasive. Roschini argues that a truth can be contained in the Sacred Scriptures explicitly or implicitly and the Holy Father has not stated that it is explicit. Besides, a truth contained implicitly in Sacred Scripture can be there objectively (ontologically), or it can be there logically, subjectively, insofar as this trut his believed and professed by the Church. Now

> "it is not always required that these two orders (the objective, ontological and the subjective, logical) should always keep together, and if this is true of what is explicitly revealed so much the more can it be the case of what is implicitly revealed. Indeed it can happen that what is professed and believed explicitly should not appear or even be actually present from the beginning, whether because it is doubted that some truth is included in the deposit of revelation, or whether for some reason or other there is no consciousness of it. The question whether or not this faith was held at the beginning concerning the Immaculate Conception is an historical question and is to be resolved by historical arguments."[1]

If we understand correctly, we must consider as implicitly contained in the Scripture everything which at a given moment of dogmatic evolution will become the faith of the Church even if it is not explicitly contained as an object of conscious faith of the primitive Church, because by the fact that it has become the object of the faith of the Church in time following it must be presumed that it is contained "ontologically", that is objectively, with an objectivity that no one knew until now! One must say then that the criterion of revelation is not what is actually contained in Scripture but what the Church decrees must be sanctioned there in order to conform with the faith. It is clear that it will be possible to define any innovation, with this vicious circle, as divine truth.[2]

The defining of the dogma of the Immaculate Conception is

[1] Roschini, *Mariologia*, II, 2, p. 22.

[2] There are actually truths in the Scripture that are going to be rediscovered or valued late, for example justification by faith, the value of which the Reformation made evident. But this deals with truth that is actually present and ascertainable by the usual methods of historical and theological research. One does not really see how with this method of research it is possible to cause a truth to rise out of the Scripture which is never remotely alluded to!

an event fraught with the greatest consequences. It was the first definition dogmatically pronounced by the pope as such. The dogma of papal infallibility was not yet defined but it was to be a few years later in the Vatican Council of 1870. It is logical to believe that the definition of the Immaculate was in some way a general test [a] of the new papal prerogative and a sounding of Catholic opinion throughout the world to see how it would react to the exercise of such privilege. The applause with which the Catholic world accepted it, except for a strict minority of high personalities who dissented, was such as to permit at once the launching of the decree that completed the evolution of papal authority in the Church. It counts for nothing to object to this interpretation that the pope consulted the episcopal body before declaring the dogma,[1] because he did not declare it in the name of the episcopate but in his own name. It can be presumed that in any dogmatic definition to come the pope will never act without the fullest consultation with the Church, as is seen to-day with regard to the Assumption of the Virgin. This however does not alter the fact that from 1854 as *de facto* date and from 1870 as the date *de jure*, the pope is the normal organ of dogmatic definition for the Church.

The dogma of the Immaculate Conception was important for the mariological doctrine. It has given such an impulse to the development of mariology that one can only compare it in dogmatic importance with the definition of *Theotokos* of the Council of Ephesus, 431. In fact the modern mariologists consider these two definitions to be the theological foundation of the whole Marian doctrine, and if they take back to the divine maternity Mary's mission as mother of mercy, as mediatrix, and "co-redemptress", they see in the immaculate conception the principle of all her personal perfections. Let us ask the concise Marian catechism of Roschini for its explanation.[2]

Mary's perfections consist first of all in the immunity from "incitement" of concupiscence and in immunity from any actual sin whatever. This doctrine was defined at the Council of Trent in canon 23 of the sixth session and drew a sarcastic

[a] *prova.*

[1] Cited in Roschini, *Mariologia*, II, 2, p. 23.

[2] Roschini, *Chi è Maria?* pp. 52–63. Cf. the proof in *Mariologia*, II, 2.

reply from Calvin.[1] She possessed the plenitude of grace by which she received from birth a degree of grace superior to that received by any other saint, rather, than all the saints together at the end of their earthly life, with all the angels included. "The initial grace of Mary—compared with that of all the Saints is as a sun in respect to its ray, as an ocean to a drop."[2] And this grace grew continually, by means of the practice of good works and certain sacraments such as Baptism and the Eucharist. Thus Mary had all the virtues "that become her condition", that is the theological virtues, faith, hope and charity, and the moral virtues prudence, justice, fortitude and temperance, in the sense that the virtues that can be acquired naturally by the agency of the reason and will were infused into her by grace in the first instant of her life.[3] Furthermore, she had all the gifts of the Holy Spirit: wisdom, intelligence, counsel, fortitude, knowledge, piety, fear of God. She had all the fruits of the Spirit: love, joy, peace, patience, meekness, goodness, long suffering, mildness, faith, modesty, continence, chastity. She had the eight beatitudes: poverty of spirit, mildness, hunger and thirst for righteousness, mercy, purity of heart, a peaceful spirit, was persecuted for righteousness' sake. She had all the holy graces, the word of wisdom and the word of knowledge, the gift of faith and the gift of healing, of miracles and prophecy, discernment of spirits, the gift of tongues and of interpretation. She had them "virtually" and she had in actuality those that were appropriate to her condition and mission. She had the knowledge that is acquired to an excellent

1 Johannis Calvini, *Acta Synodi Tridentinae cum Antidoto*, Geneva, 1547. He refers to our question in an incisive note commenting on this canon. After stating that none among the justified can escape all venial sin in the course of life, the council adds the reservation, "unless by a special privilege of God as the Church believes of the Blessed Virgin" (*quemamodum de Beata Virgine tenet Ecclesia*). Calvin observes that the Church includes Augustine who, if in one place he preferred to be silent about the Virgin Mary out of regard for her (*amolliende invidiae causa*) . . . , in other places he almost openly (*prope disertis verbis*) places her in the number of sinners as do Chrysostom and Ambrose who suspected that she was tempted by ambition (*qui ambitione tentatam fuisse suspicantur*). Calvin adds that he recalls these things only to let the readers understand that there is no fiction so silly that it may not be considered an article of faith (*nullum esse tam nugatorium figmentum, quod inter fidei dogmata ab istis asinis non censeatur*). (Calvini, *Tractatus theologici omnes*, Geneva, 1597, p. 358.)

2 Roschini, *Chi è Maria?* p. 55.

3 Roschini, *Mariologia*, II, 2, p. 162.

degree and she had an excellent "infused knowledge", the knowledge proper to the angels. She had "probably" if not permanently the "blessed" knowledge, that is the direct vision of God, which is proper to God Himself.

Such privileges of the soul are accompanied by those of the body. Mary was noble, being of royal descent. She was of a perfect constitution because "she always enjoyed a perennial equilibrium of all the bodily elements". She was therefore immune from all illness. She was most beautiful "with a charming beauty, especially because in her was reflected all the heavenly splendour of her soul".[1] Whoever wishes to have the proven demonstration of this, let him read the pages that Roschini dedicates to the beauty of Mary in his great Latin *Mariologia*.[2] To tell the truth, there would be no need of that for the proof that our painters of the Renaissance have given us is enough. But here he will find the theme treated in orderly fashion, *scholastico more*: first the definition of beauty, objective and subjective, and its three elements according to St Thomas, *integritas*, *debita proportio*, *splendor*; then he will find the thesis, *Virgo singulari corporis pulchritudine excelluit.* "The Virgin excels by the singular beauty of body." Then the proof: (1) by the authority of Scripture, Liturgy, Fathers and Writers: (2) by reason, in syllogistic form: "To beauty there belong the three notes we have recorded, integrity of body, proportion of its members and clearness and beauty of colour. Now these three were in the Virgin Mary in supremely excellent way. Therefore . . ." Therefore the Virgin was beautiful.

Finally, the perpetual virginity and the assumption of the Blessed Virgin are joined to the Immaculate Conception as to their foundation. The circle of Mary's perfections is closed. The dogma, defined a century ago, is the pedestal upon which all the earlier mariological creations now rest.

[1] Roschini, *Chi è Maria?* p. 59.

[2] *Mariologia*, II, 2, pp. 202 ff.

Chapter 7

THE COMPASSIONATE MOTHER

ALFONSO of Liguori, in the preface of the first volume of his "*Glories of Mary*", considers it necessary "to put into clearer light some propositions that can be met there that can appear advanced and perhaps obscure". The first of these is the statement that "God wants all graces to come to us by the hand of Mary".[1] The author tells us in his introduction that this is his own theme, "leaving to other authors the description of Mary's other merits, I have chosen to speak of her great mercy and her powerful intercession".[2] With these words he defined what can be called the peculiar theme of the mariology of the Counter-Reformation. While, as we have seen, the fourth century devoted its attention first of all to Mary's virginity, the fifth to seventh centuries to her divine maternity, the Carolingian epoch to her assumption, and the twelfth to fourteenth centuries to her Immaculate Conception, the period that extends from the Council of Trent to the French Revolution is preoccupied above all else with defining the universal mediation and the compassionate motherhood of Mary in reaction against the Reformation, Jansenism, and eighteenth-century rationalism. The fact that Alfonso of Liguori feels the need to defend the idea of the necessary mediation of Mary as "advanced and perhaps obscure" is enough to show, that notwithstanding all the mariological progressions of the preceding centuries, this was still in the eighteenth century a relatively new idea and open to discussion at least in the form that the Neapolitan saint gave it in his works.

In a broad sense this aspect of mariology is certainly one of the oldest since it goes back to the famous parallel between Eve and Mary, instituted by Justin Martyr and Irenaeus, even if

[1] S. Alfonso Maria De' Liguori, *Le Glorie di Maria*, Instit. Miss. Pia Società di S. Paolo, Rome, 1947, Vol. I, p. 8.

[2] *Ibid.*, p. 14.

"the terms must not be forced" as R. P. Rondet, S.J., wisely observes.[1]

Irenaeus wrote:[2]

> "The fact that the Lord came manifestly into his own possession and sustained it by that creation that he upholds himself, and completed a recapitulation of the disobedience that occurred in connection with a tree through the obedience manifested upon a tree, annulling the consequences of the deceit unfortunately undergone by the Virgin Eve—who was already married to a man—was happily announced by means of a truth declared by an angel to the Virgin Mary, who was also married to a man. Then as the first was misled by the word of an angel so that she alienated herself from God by transgressing his word, so the second received by an angelic message the happy word that she would carry God in her womb, and was obedient to his word. And if the first disobeyed God the other was persuaded to be obedient to Him so that the Virgin Mary could become the advocate of the Virgin Eve. And thus as the human race fell into the chains of death through a virgin, it was also saved from them by a virgin, the disobedience of a virgin having been counterbalanced by the obedience of a virgin. For by the same way the sin of the first created man was amended by the correction of the first-born and the wile of the serpent was conquered by the innocence of the dove and the bonds were loosened by which we were tied to death."

In another passage Irenaeus states:

> "as by her disobedience the virgin Eve was the cause of death for herself and for the human race, so the obedient virgin became a cause of salvation (*causa facta est salutis*) for herself and the human race."[3]

This is one of those many parallels that the doctors of the early Church liked to detect between the Old and New Testaments. As the apostle Paul had put into a parallel the obedience

[1] R. P. Rondet, *Mater Misericordiae.* Report contained in the volume of the Acts of the *Fifth Marian National Congress*, held in Grenoble-La Salette in 1946 in the Centenary of the appearance of Our Lady of Salette, published with the title, *Marie Corédemptrice*, Lyons, ed. du Sud-Est, 1948, pp. 149 ff. We shall have occasion to refer to other worthy studies contained in this volume.

[2] Irenaeus, *Adversus Haereses*, V. 19, 1.

[3] *Ibid.*, III, p. 22.

of Christ and the disobedience of Adam (Romans 5: 12 ff.), so Irenaeus balanced the obedience of Mary against the disobedience of Eve. But as Eve did not have an independent part in the first account of the fall, so Mary had none in Irenaeus' parallel. Her part is that type of testimony to the incarnation that is in the gospel writings and the anti-docetic point of it is evident. Mary, receiving with faith the angel's message that she was "to carry" Jesus, shows that He really was come into the dominion that was His by right to recapitulate in Himself the sin of Adam and annul its results.[1] Her participation in the great event is occasional and passive. It is entirely concluded in the fact that she "carried" Christ. The term "advocata" raises a problem. It is known that the *Adversus Haereses* has come to us in a Latin translation only. What will have been the term, then, used by Irenaeus? *Synegoros*, lawyer, intercessor in its proper sense? *Parakletos*, helper or comforter or consoler as the Gospel of John has designated the Holy Spirit? However it may be, Irenaeus' thought is circumscribed by the historic pair Eve and Mary. Mary rehabilitates Eve or pleads her cause or consoles her. In an apocryphal gospel we have seen that Eve runs to the grotto of Bethlehem to be present at her redemption. There is no indication that Irenaeus allegorizes the parallel further, sees in Eve the symbol of natural humanity or in Mary the universal mother of sinners, or the figure of the Church. His famous parallel creates the impression of an ingenious literary construction more than a considered and intentional theological doctrine.

This is the more noteworthy in that the idea of a solidarity in intercession and the idea of a special value in the intercession of martyrs began to take form at the end of the second century. The same Irenaeus during the persecution of the Church at Lyons had taken a letter to Rome in which the confessors, strong by the authority of their faithful Christian testimony, interceded in favour of the spiritual and unpopular Montanists against whom the bishop of Rome was too severe. During the great crisis of the Decian persecution in 250, the confessors in prison often undertook the responsibility of restoring the poor "lapsed", those who had recanted through weakness, creating

[1] The exclusively anti-docetic intention of Irenaeus' parallel is recognized by Dillenschneider in *Marie Corédemptrice*, p. 75.

difficulties for the regular discipline and the hierarchy of the Church. By virtue of the spiritual unity between the Church militant and the Church triumphant, the idea that the martyrs could help the living with their prayers entered the heritage of common beliefs scarcely noticed. The blessed martyrs in the liturgy of the mass are associated with the living in the prayers made in common with the universal Church (*comprecatio*). But in that solidarity of intercession the martyrs definitely precede the Virgin Mary in time. Later the Virgin is also associated with them and in the first place, the place of honour, as the *Theotokos* the Mother of God. And it is a short way from prayers in communion with the Virgin and the saints to an invocation addressed to the Virgin and the saints. Actually it was not as short as one might suppose. The mariologists give great importance to an old invocation of the Virgin, *Sub tuum praesidium*, the Greek text of which was recovered in a papyrus and seems to go back to the third century. The fact that it contains the term *Theotokos* would lead one to give it a later date; but this is not a decisive argument because we have seen that the title *Theotokos* had possibly been already used by Origen and we may have here a confirmation of such as a possible date. The papyrus is mutilated and can be reconstructed.

"We take refuge under the protection of thy compassion, O Mother of God. Do not neglect our prayers in our troubles, but free us from danger, thou who alone art pure (or revered), thou who alone art blessed."[1]

This prayer entered the Byzantine and Ambrosian liturgies very soon but became general in the West only in the Carolingian period. "*Sub tuum praesidium confugimus, sancta Dei genetrix.*"[2]

With the fourth century we begin to find the title *Mediatrix* used by certain oriental writers, such as Ephraim the Syrian, Epiphanius, Andrew of Crete, John of Damascus. In the West we must come down to the Carolingian epoch to find it in Paul the Deacon, or even to the Cluniac Movement of the eleventh century, Peter Damiani. The reason for this delay in the West must be looked for in the fact that in the Byzantine age the pre-

[1] It was published by C. H. Roberts in *Catalogue of the Greek and Latin Papyri*, John Rylands Library, Manchester, Vol. III, 1938, n. 470. See the discussion by Cecchelli, *Mater Christi*, I, pp. 305 ff. Roberts, on the basis of the term *Theotokos*, does not think it can go back beyond the fourth century.

[2] R. P. Rondet, in *Marie Corédemptrice*, p. 153.

dominant thought about Mary was as *Theotokos*, the Queen of heaven, the *Basilissa* enthroned, the *Panhagia*—all holy—who with Christ, *Pantokrator*, presides, majestically dominating, in the mosaic apses, awesome with glory almost divine. Only with the rise of the new phase of western culture, with the aid of the new conception of femininity that goes with it, does the figure of Mary become humanized and comes to be the symbol of the merciful maternity with Anselm of Canterbury and especially with St Bernard, who must be considered the real creator of modern Marian devotion.

He gives a full and lyric modulation to the parallel of Eve and Mary, as he exclaims at the beginning of a sermon for the Sunday following the feast of the Assumption of Mary:

"A man and a woman have done us grave injury, but thanks be to God, by means of a man and a woman all is restored. . . . The most wise and merciful builder would not destroy that which was damaged but he rebuilt it in every way that was most useful. From the old Adam he has made the new and has transfused Eve into Mary. Christ could certainly suffice and now he is fully sufficient, but for us it was not good that man should be alone. It was more seemly (*magis congruum*) that one of the other sex should be present at our restoration since neither of the two was absent at our corruption. It is certain that the man Jesus Christ is the faithful and most powerful mediator between God and men, but men reverence in him the divine majesty. In him humanity appears absorbed in the divine, not that its substance is changed but because the affections are deified. His compassion is not the only quality that is honoured: his justice is honoured also, for even though he learned compassion by the things he suffered so that he should become merciful, he keeps his power of judgment none the less. In truth our God is a consuming fire. How should the sinner not have fear of perishing in the presence of God as wax melts in the fire?

"And see how the woman who is blessed among women will not be idle. She will find a place for herself in this reconciliation! We have need of a mediator for this mediator and none will be more helpful than Mary. Eve was a cruel mediatrix, through whom the serpent of old infused his pestiferous poison into man as well. But Mary is faithful who gives the saving antidote for men and women to drink. The one was for us a minister of seduction, the other of propitiation; the one suggested falsehood, the other brought redemption. Why should frail humanity ever fear to draw near to Mary? There is nothing severe in her, nothing terrible: she is all agreeableness and offers milk and wool to all. Look carefully at all the gospel narratives and if there is found in Mary anything scolding, or hard, any slightest sign of anger, then put on mistrust and fear to go near her. But if, as is true, you find her full of pity and grace, full of gentleness and compassion, all of which are her attributes, then give thanks to Him who in his most benign compassion procured such a mediatrix for you, in whom there can be nothing to mistrust. For she is made all things to all and is rendered debtor of a most abundant charity to the wise and the ignorant. To all she has opened the bosom of her compassion so that from her fullness all receive, the prisoner freedom (*redemptionem*), the sick healing, the afflicted consolation, the sinner pardon, the righteous grace, the angel joy, the whole Trinity glory, and the person of the Son the support of human flesh, so that none is deprived of her warmth."[1]

Here then is stressed the theme of the dual mediation of Christ and Mary. The theme is unfolded further in the sermon for the nativity of Mary called "The Aqueduct" because in it Mary is compared to a canal through which the divine waters flow to men.

"You are afraid to approach God and in fear of the mere sound of his voice you go and hide in the thickets. He has given you Jesus as mediator. What can such a son not obtain from such a Father? He will be granted his request through reverence for him; for the Father truly loves the Son. Do you perhaps fear to approach him too? He is your brother and your flesh and has been proven in all things without sin so that he should be merciful. Mary has given you this brother. But perhaps you fear the divine majesty in him, for even though he was made man he has remained God. Do you want an advocate close by him? Appeal to Mary. There is pure humanity in Mary, not only pure from all contamination but pure by the singularity of nature. And I say it for certain, she too will be heard for reverence of her. The Son will grant the Mother's request and the Father the Son's. My little children, this is the ladder for sinners, this is my greatest trust, this is all my reason for hope. What indeed? Perhaps the Son can refuse or receive a refusal? Perhaps he cannot hear or

[1] Exordium of the sermon *in Dominica infra Octavam Assumptionis B. V. Mariae*, S. Bernardi *Opera Omnia*, ed. Mabillon, Paris, 1839, Vol. 2, col. 2155–2156.

be heard? Neither the one nor the other. 'Thou hast found grace with God, said the angel.' Great joy! She will always find grace and we have need of grace only. The discreet Virgin did not ask for wisdom as Solomon did, not riches, not honours or power, but grace. The grace by which alone we are saved."[1]

After this we find no cause for wonder in the invocation of Mary that concludes the second sermon *De Adventu Domini*.

"By thee we have access to the Son, O Thou who hast found grace, mother of life, mother of salvation. By thee we receive him who has been given to us through thyself. Let thine integrity at his side make apology to him for the guilt of our corruption, and let the humility pleasing to God secure the pardon of our vanity. Let thine abundant charity cover the multitude of our sins, and thy glorious fruitfulness make us fruitful of merits. Our Lady, our mediatrix, our advocate, reconcile us with thy Son, commend us to thy Son, represent us with thy Son. O blessed one, by the grace thou dost find, by the pre-excellence thou dost merit, by the mercy that thou bearest, cause that he who through thyself condescended to share our infirmity and misery, shall through thine intercession make us partakers of his glory and bliss, Jesus Christ, thy Son, our Lord, who above all things is blessed by God through the ages. Amen!"[2]

We should be rendering a poor service to St Bernard if we wanted to give to these devout paradoxes a greater importance than they really have in his complete thought. It is evident that the reason for the mediation of Mary is turned mainly towards the timid and the weak in faith in whom humility creates paralysing thoughts in their relation with the divine. The monastic cure of souls must always be preoccupied with the religious complexes of inferiority, of fluctuations of spiritual certainty[a] which monastic life feeds abundantly. For those who fear before God's majesty, for those to whom even Jesus Christ appears too tremendous, Bernard recommends recourse to the protection of Mary. Mary is all human, only human: "*pura humanitas in Maria*". Will there not be a light and kindly irony in the thought of the great mystic as he makes humour

[1] *In nativitate B. V. Mariae sermo De Aqueductu*, Vol. 2, col. 2170.
[2] *Sermo II de Adventu Domini*, Col. 1648.
[a] *pusillanimitas.*

over the double sense of the adverb "purely" human? Will there not be something like condescension as he speaks of the "milk" that Mary offers to the children in the faith? St Bernard speaking to adults does not offer spiritual Marian milk but the hard food of the Christ-centred mysticism, of which his eighty-six sermons on the Song of Songs offer an incomparable text. This mysticism of Christ is not food for the faint-hearted.

> "Conformity with Christ marries the soul with the Word, to which it is alike by nature and shows itself alike by choice, loving it as it is loved. If then one loves perfectly, one marries. What is there more joyful than this conformity? What is there more to be desired than the love by which, not content with a human teaching, you approach the word trustfully by yourself, O soul, ask questions of the Word familiarly, and consult him in every matter as much as the mind can and the desire dare? This is truly a spiritual contract, a holy union. I make an understatement—contract. It is an embrace. An embrace in which the wanting and not wanting of the same thing makes one single spirit out of two. There is no need to fear that the difference of the two persons cause the union of the two wills to limp in any way, for love knows not fear (*reverentiam*). Love in fact takes its name by loving, not by honouring. Then let that man honour him who fears holiness (*qui horret*), who feels astonishment, fear, surprise, for all these things are almost entirely absent in him who loves. Love in its abundance translates into itself and subjects all the other sentiments. It loves that which it loves and knows no other. . . ."[1]

This is the real St Bernard, far above the elementary ideas about the necessary mediatrix of the Mediator!

Perhaps the great mystic did not become aware of the transfer of his thought of religious mediation to a sphere in which the result was banal and quite without profound meaning. The idea of Christ the Mediator, as appears in the more reflective New Testament writings of Paul and John, is connected with the serious problem: how is it possible for the divine as such to come into contact with the human? Where do we find a point of entry between the infinite and the finite, the transcendent and the creature, eternity and time? The problem had profound repercussions both philosophical and theological

[1] Sermon 83 in *Cantica*, Vol. 2, col. 3178.

that are already clearly coupled together in the Philonic doctrine of the Word. The solution of that problem is the Man-God. Irenaeus, the first great Christian theologian, stabilized the problem clearly in his definitive terms. In order that Christ can be the mediator of eternal and divine life for men He must be "truly man and truly God". But did not this synthesis of faith perhaps come to dissolve anew in the devout observations of St Bernard which transferred Christ, so to speak, entirely to the divine plane and added Mary's mediatorial capacity in her "pure humanity"? Will she who is "purely human" be able to be the mediatrix of the divine to humanity?

Actually the very concept of mediation had undergone a fatal transformation, being taken from the metaphysical-religious plane where Greek Christianity had developed it, and placed on the ethical-juristic—one could almost say political—plane peculiar to Latin Christianity. The relation with the divine is here represented according to the considerations of honour belonging to feudal society. God is the supreme majesty to whom none may come except through the hierarchy. By way of the Son, who has the keys of His heart, and by His incarnation stands a little nearer to sinners, one can be sure of finding access to the throne of grace. And if Christ is still too close to the majesty of the throne, there is Mary who has the natural power over Him that the mother has over her son, Mary, who by her pure humanity is close to us. And if the mother is not enough? There are the saints. St Alfonso of Liguori, carrying to the end the system of the hierarchical intercession of the heavenly court, expressly states that all intercessions of the saints must pass through Mary.[1] The series is complete, then: the saints intercede with Mary, who asks the Son, to whom the Father cannot refuse anything.

It went even farther. An anonymous book of devotion that had a great vogue in the late Middle Ages, the *Speculum humanae salvationis*, declared that Christ has divided His kingdom with His mother, reserving justice to Himself and entrusting mercy to her. *Regnum suum in duas partes divisit: unam partem retinuit, alteram Mariae commisit.*[2] Mary does not abstain, however, from

[1] *Le Glorie di Maria*, I, p. 145.

[2] Quoted by R. P. Rondet, *Marie Corédemptrice*, p. 159, who considers this idea too artless.

intervening in the other part of His realm, that of justice. She "restrains" the Son.

> "St Bonaventura remembered," [wrote St Alfonso] "that the prophet Isaiah lamented in his day and wrote, 'Lord thou art justly angry with us sinners and there is none who can appease thee for us.' Yes, because Mary had not been born into the world then and before her, said the saint, there was none who dared to restrain God. But now if God is angry with a sinner Mary undertakes to protect him, she restrains the Son that he should not punish but save him. St Bonaventura goes on to say that none can be found more active than Mary to put restraining hands on the sword of divine justice so that it does not descend to punish the sinner."[1]

To this point was that estimate of the Master reduced who in the Gospel of Matthew, 11: 29 is described as "gentle and lowly in heart". As though He could be represented in the pose of the executioner with axe raised, and lo, the sweet Mary lays her gentle hand on the blade so that it should not come down on the head of the guilty one!

Here we have one of the most important of the elements for the understanding of the rise and spread of the mediaeval cult of Mary as Mediatrix, the transformation of the figure of Christ that took place in theology and devotion. In the great christological disputes of the fourth to seventh centuries, the definition of the full and consubstantial divinity of Christ had somewhat obscured the human figure of the Jesus of the Synoptics. The Christ who to-day still fixes His great ecstatic eyes upon us from the Byzantine apses, the *Pantokrator* enthroned, could make one shiver with awe at the holy, but certainly could not draw the trusting devotion of the faithful. The systematic theology of the West, centred in the idea of original sin and the necessity of a difficult ransom, had made Christ the symbol and warrant of all the Latin Church's system of ethics and discipline. That system was rigidly juridical. Nothing is given, everything is bought and paid for, and although salvation is still a work of grace, yet insofar as grace recompenses the appropriate merits which grace itself helps to grow up in men's will, it is a system of retributive justice rigorously calculated upon merit. And

[1] Liguori, *Le Glorie di Maria*, I, p. 100.

this juridical structure of doctrine, characteristic of the Roman spirit, had been fixed again by the code of honour of feudal society. Anselm of Canterbury in *Cur Deus Homo?* gave the theological transcription of the drama of sin and salvation, interpreted in feudal terms of honour: the infinite offence that must be paid for by an infinite sacrifice. He who offers the sacrifice of infinite value is necessarily the highest, greatest, farthest removed from the little modest suffering human. He it is who attracts the confidence of men. The new devotion of the twelfth century had indeed tried to recover a more human vision of Christ, but not all had the capacity of St Bernard's religious genius or the ingenuous piety of St Francis of Assisi. For the mass of the faithful, for those who were children in spiritual things—and they were legion—who could not manage solid food but only the milk of childhood, the way of escape from such concentration of sacred and divine law was the Virgin Mary. In the great theological elaboration of sin and salvation one might say she was untouched; she remained outside the hard Catholic scheme of salvation, so juristic and ascetic. She could be the symbol of a pure compassion beyond all idea of merit or justice. She was able to be that symbol of a pure grace that Christ had ceased to be. She could, in a particular way, by her natural femininity, be exalted through the idealization of woman in the new age. She was able to be this by the parental bond that seemed to assign to her, although lower by nature, a gentle and persuasive power over the terrible eternal judge, her Son.

Once again the transfer to Mary of Christ's attribute of merciful goodness came to nullify the great Christian paradox of salvation. The merciful Christ is the merciful God, God who from on high bends down over the sin and sorrow of humanity to the very point of uniting Himself to it, taking the burden and bearing it in vicarious sacrifice. But Mary was not divine. She was by definition "purely human". Mary's compassion was simply humanity's pity for itself. To be sure, this could be moving and consoling, but it had nothing of paradox or revelation. It is known that humanity is compassionate towards itself: it is known that the eternal feminine is the symbol of this human compassion. The great saving synthesis of God who is the merciful Father, of Christ who is God-Saviour, was dissolved again. All divinity remained on one side and was synonymous with tremendous majesty and severe justice, while mercy remained on the other and was a mercy entirely human. The system of salvation became reduced to a series of hierarchical relationships designed to reduce and neutralize that vindictive justice, and the system worked so well that it came to the point that Mary's rôle was not to give birth to the Saviour.[a] It delegated to her pure humanity the symbolizing of a grace unrelated to merit so that when there was a being so perfect in grace and condescension, was it necessary that God should take human flesh and suffer the cross? Would it not have been enough to ask the heart of a new Eve to protect the poor sinners at the throne of justice?

Of course in what precedes we have accented the colours and emphasized the lines of what was really quite complex. But in substance it would be impossible to deny that such was the motivation of Marian devotion. When Luther some centuries later, in his joy at having found again a Christ who was compassionate, painted in gloomy colours the judicial Christ that had been the incubus of his boyhood, it was easy to accuse him of having knowingly distorted the reality. But the great advance that Marian devotion made from the twelfth century onward is the best confirmation of the substantial truth of his appraisal. Luther recovered the Gospel of the pure mercy of God in Christ, the Gospel of grace without merit and beyond merit. With this, without polemics or attacks, he dissipated the doctrine of Mary's mediating mercy in the new evangelical faith and made it impossible, impossible because superfluous.

The criticism of the mediaeval Marian system was not made by the reformers first of all; it was the work of Erasmus of Rotterdam, humanist and Catholic.[1] Luther, educated in the piety of St Bernard, wrote in his commentary on the *Magnificat* some pages on the humility and faith of Mary that are among the most delicate to be found. Calvin in his commentary on the Gospels entitled "*L'Harmonie évangélique*"—to quote Roschini, *magnifice de B. Virgine loquitur*—speaks most appreciatively of the Virgin Mary.[2] But the Reformation, without dislike for the

[a] Supplied. *Trans.*
[1] Roschini, *Mariologia*, I, p. 391.
[2] *Ibid.*, I, p. 307.

gentle mother of Christ, continued to proclaim with unshaken constancy its apostolic principle: "There is one God, and there is one mediator between God and men, the man Christ Jesus, who gave himself as a ransom for all" (1 Timothy 2:5).

The most violent dispute over Mary's work as mediatrix that took place during the Counter-Reformation was due not to the Protestants but to the Jansenists. It was provoked by the book of a Catholic jurist of Cologne, Adam Widenfeldt, published in 1673 with the title, *Monita salutaria B. Virginis Mariae ad cultores suos indiscretos*. In its French translation, *Avertissements salutaires*, it had a wide circulation in France and had as one result a reform of the Gallican liturgy. The author put on the lips of Mary such words as these:

> "Do not put me parallel with God or Christ. . . . I am your preserver. . . . The praises that come to me for my own sake are vain. . . . Take heed that your *dulia* does not sink into *latria*, breaking the commandment, 'Worship God only.' . . . Those who call me mediatrix and advocate, let them not say it in the same sense in which my Son is properly mediator and advocate. He is the Mediator of the new Covenant. He has satisfied God with his own merits. . . . Let no one attribute this to me. Was I perhaps crucified for you? Then do not call me saviour and co-redemptress. . . . Do not honour me as if God were not enough for you. If you love God you have no need of anything. . . . Blessed is he who, like the apostles, wants to know nothing but Christ and him crucified!"[1]

In the wake of the *Monita salutaria* came a reaction against Marian devotion in which are to be noted some names eminent for knowledge and piety, such as Launoy, Baillet, the church historian Tillemont, and in Italy Ludovico Antonio Muratori. But in the eighteenth century Marian piety made a vigorous recovery especially through the works of Grignon de Monfort in France and St Alfonso Maria de' Liguori in Italy, 1696–1787.

The latter's "*Glories of the Most Holy Mary*", published in 1750, can with good reason be considered the classic text of modern mariology because we find in it a full collection of

[1] Quoted by Roschini *Mariologia*, I, p. 394, 5.

material,[1] mixed and devoid of the most elementary critical sense, a collection of all that the author knows has been said about Mary by theologians great and small, by monks and preachers with a special predilection for edifying stories, all collected without discrimination and with devout complacency. It is a classic of mariology, furthermore, by very tonality of Marian devotion, by its typical mixture of piety and superstition, of devotion and puerility that has accompanied the cult of Mary from its origin, tendencies which seem to be more accentuated the closer we come to our own time.

Alfonso of Liguori hyperbolically exalts Mary's power of intercession:

> "Although Mary in heaven can no longer command the Son, yet her prayers will always be a mother's prayers, and so most potent to obtain as much as she asks. St Bonaventura says that Mary has this privilege with the Son of being most able to secure what she wants. And why? Precisely because . . . they are the prayers of a mother. It is for that reason, St Peter Damiani says, that the Virgin can obtain what she wants, in heaven as on earth, able to lift up even the most despairing to the hope of salvation. Jesus wishes to honour this his dear mother, who has so greatly honoured him in her life, by granting her at once what she asks and desires. St Germain confirms this beautifully as he speaks to the Mother of God. 'You are Mother of God, omnipotent to save sinners, and you have no need of other commendation with God since you are the mother of the true life.' St Bernardino feels no repugnance about saying that all obey Mary's command, even God, really meaning that God grants her prayers as though they were commands. Whence it is that St Anselm speaking with Mary says to her, 'Holy Virgin, the Lord has raised you to such rank that with his favour you can obtain all the graces possible for those who are devoted to you, for your protection, Mary, is all powerful, as says Cosmas of Jerusalem.' 'Yes, Mary is all powerful,' continues Riccardo of San Lorenzo, 'while the queen by every law must enjoy the same privileges as the king. Thus

[1] In point of encyclopædic quantity Liguori is exceeded by Ippolito Marracci (1604–1675) who spent all his life collecting quotations and examples in Mary's honour, and had the misfortune also to be excommunicated for it. Certain of his friends, without his knowledge, published a book of his in defence of the Immaculate Conception during the time when the pope had forbidden discussion of this.
See the bibliography in Roschini, *Mariologia*, I, pp. 290, 291, and for the incident noted, *Osservatore Romano*, Dec. 15, 1949: "*On the borders of a dogma.*"

there is joined together the same power of the son and of the mother of the Almighty.' 'In such a way,' says Saint Anthony, 'God has put the whole Church not only under Mary's protection but also under her dominion.' "[1]

This omnipotence of hers Mary puts at the service of sinners with unlimited maternal solicitude. No sin is so great that she is discouraged by it. As a mother does not shrink from caring for the wastrel son, "so our Mother does not abandon us when we turn to her, whatever the reek of our sins of which we are to be cleansed" (p. 110). She is called Queen of Compassion, because, as St Bernard has it, "she opens God's bottomless pit of mercy to whom she wills, when and as she wills; yes, there is no sinner however great, who is lost if Mary protects him" (p. 24). She "has a heart so benign and merciful that she cannot suffer it to send away unhappy anyone who prays to her" (p. 25). In the revelations of St Brigid she declares, "There is no sinner living, however cursed, who is deprived of my compassion. No one is so finally dismissed by God that if he has called me to his aid he will not return to God and enjoy his mercy." "I am called by all the mother of mercy, and truly God's mercy towards men has made me so merciful towards them. That is why that one will be wretched and always wretched in the other life who in this life is able to come to me who am so pitying with all and desire so to help the sinner, yet with all his wretchedness does not come and is damned" (p. 26).

Alfonso of Liguori adds example to example, more and more edifying, wonderful and incredible, to show the reality and efficacy of Mary's intercession in the most desperate situations. All the legends of the Marian repertory, old and new, pass through his pages: there was the monk Theophilus who by the influence of the devil had written, "renounced Jesus and Mary His Mother", and had then by his penitence obtained the grace of God through Mary: and there was the magpie that having learned to say *Ave Maria* spoke the invocation when taken by a hawk and escaped because the hawk fell dead at the instant (p. 72).

Mary's intercession is naturally efficacious after death.

[1] Liguori, *Le Glorie di Maria*, I, pp. 151, 152.

"Eusebius of Nuremberg tells that in the town of Aragona there was a young girl called Alexandra who was killed through reasons of jealousy and her head cut off and thrown into a well. St Dominic passed a few days after and, inspired by the Lord, he turned to the well and said, 'Alexandra, come out', and lo, the head of the dead girl came out and set itself on the rim of the well and asked Dominic to hear its confession. The holy man did so and then gave her the communion in the sight of a huge crowd that gathered for the wonderful event. Then Dominic told her to tell how she had received that grace. She replied that when her head was cut off she was in mortal sin but the most holy Mary had saved her life through the devotion of the Rosary that she recited. For two days the head stood on the edge of the well in sight of everyone and afterwards the soul went to purgatory. But a fortnight after that Alexandra's soul appeared to Dominic, beautiful and resplendent as a star, and told him that one of the greatest helps that the souls in purgatory have in their punishments is the Rosary that is recited for them, and these souls quickly go to paradise and pray for those who repeated that potent prayer. When this was said St Dominic beheld that fortunate soul leaping jubilantly in the realm of the blest" (p. 206).

Therefore an unlimited trust is to be put in Mary. To find Mary is to find grace (p. 60). She is the hope of the evildoers, of the despairing, the one refuge of sinners, the sure harbour of the shipwrecked, even the protectress of the damned (pp. 62, 103). She is the assurance of pardon, the pledge given by God of His promise to forgive them. She is the Noah's ark in which the sinners are saved (p. 65), the rod of the Good Shepherd (Psalm 23) which leads them in the distresses of death (p. 77), the "propitiatory" of purest gold from which the Lord speaks to men and grants pardon, graces and gifts (p. 86). She is the city of refuge, the city of God, the tabernacle, the hospital of infirm souls (p. 96), the olive that spreads the comforting oil of grace, the vine that gives fruit of sweet odours, the ark of the covenant by which the Israelites obtained victory over their enemies which the devils feared (pp. 119, 120). She is the morning star that announces grace (p. 98), the star of the sea in the tempests of life (p. 99), the moon that stands between the earth and sun and reflects the sun's light (pp. 95, 174), even the sun itself that warms the whole world with its rays (p. 185).

Mary is the kindly conspirer of heaven "who is continually active in matters of mercy, securing grace for all, the righteous and the sinners" (p. 182), the treasurer of all graces "whence it is that our salvation is in her hands" (p. 225). She is "that throne of graces to which the Apostle urges us to draw near with confidence (Hebrews 4: 16) that we may receive mercy" (p. 226): the strong tower in which the sinner can resist the assaults of hell (p. 234).

Mary's intercession is necessary for our salvation: "because God wills that all graces that He dispenses shall pass through Mary" (p. 128), so that one can say of her what Christ said of Himself "that no one could find him unless first the eternal Father had drawn him with his divine grace. And thus, according to Liguori, Jesus speaks of his Mother: "no one comes to me unless my mother has first drawn him with her prayers" (p. 140); and "if Mary is for us who shall be against us?" (p. 78). A sigh of the Blessed Virgin is more powerful than the prayers of all the saints together (p. 158). If Mary does not pray for us none of the saints dare pray, but if she prays for us all paradise prays with her (p. 146). The merits of Christ's blood do not even apply to sinners unless Mary commends them to God (p. 106). Therefore devotion to Mary is the pledge of our predestination, the proof that we are written in the book of life, the certainty of salvation (p. 214), our hope of final perseverance (p. 67). She is then the ladder to heaven, even a better ladder than that of Christ:

> "It is related in the Franciscan chronicle of Brother Leo that he once saw a red ladder at the top of which stood Jesus, and a white one where Mary stood at the top. He saw that some went to go up the red ladder, mounted a few steps and then fell down. Again they began to mount and again they fell. Then they were urged to go up by the white ladder and up that he saw them ascend happily while the Blessed Virgin reached out her hand and so brought them safely to paradise!" (p. 210).

Puerile and grotesque. But all the Marian piety in St Alfonso of Liguori has such characteristics, for which, seen from the point of view of the Gospel and sane piety, it can only be judged a grave aberration. The fact is that this author can be considered the greatest mariologist of the eighteenth century, the renovator of Marian piety, the champion of the faith that decisively routed Jansenism.[1] It is a sad sign.

Must we confine ourselves to this negative judgment? Would there not be in Liguori's mariology some positive element notwithstanding the tares, and could it not be that this would illuminate more than the negative elements do the real reasons for the enormous development of mariology in Catholicism?

Liguori has been accused repeatedly of exercising a demoralizing influence, preaching an easy pardon for the greatest sins by the unlimited mercy of the holy Virgin. One "Ave Maria" is enough even if said "without devotion and half asleep", as in the story of the two students of Flanders (p. 199), to secure protection from the snares of the devil. The same prayer, recited each day by a woman who lives in sin with an adulterous man, is enough, for the Virgin refuses to take a position against her who, in spite of sin, honours her (p. 227), and she opposes the protests of the betrayed wife with a cold refusal! Prayer operates at times in a purely mechanical way, as when it was repeated by the magpie seized by the hawk!

Yet let us look carefully. What is the object of these things? To encourage sinners to persist in their state of sin hoping for a final absolution? That would be too much to affirm. Rather it is to impress the imagination with such an exaltation of the Virgin Mary's mercy as to lead astonished souls to prostrate themselves humble and contrite at the feet of their redemptress. The adulterous woman when she knows the Virgin protects her through these daily Ave Marias, at the thought that "for that wretched act of devotion she showed her so great mercy, went at once and threw herself down before that holy figure and there in the presence of all asked pardon for her scandalous sin and made vows of perpetual continence" (p. 227). This is the necessary end of all Liguori's edifying stories. The manifestation of the Virgin's mercy, unexpected, undeserved, striking, produces conversion and penitence that lead to a holy life and, customarily, soon afterwards to a devout death. The greatness

[1] Roschini, *Mariologia*, I, pp. 297 ff., gives his judgment on the mariology of Liguori: "encyclopædic and progressive, complete, fundamental, full of unction, eminently practical." Cf. Dillenschneider in *Marie Corédemptrice*, p. 89. "With these Glories of Mary he had the distinction of dealing a decisive blow to Jansenism and crowning the effort of his predecessors with even more theological fullness and practical success."

of the grace received is measured above all in relation to the poverty and merit in the sinner: a simple Ave Maria, even if said in a distracted and sleepy way! If in certain instances—such as that of the magpie—this contrast teaches the power "*ex opere operato*" in the Ave Maria, it must be said that in the majority of them it only emphasizes the slightness of merit and the greatness of grace. This is properly the theme that returns with greater insistence in Liguori's book. So much is this the case that this insistence has at times a sound one could call quasi-Lutheran and one thinks of the hazardous paradox of Luther, "*. . . pecca fortiter sed fortius fide.*"

This approach is not as arbitrary as might appear. Even Luther with his famous dictum certainly does not propose a dissolute morality, neither does he urge men to do what suits them on the ground that however large the account it will eventually be settled by the Redeemer, but his expression was simply his way of acknowledging by hyperbole the immensity of the grace of Christ who died for us. The pious stories and learned citations of Liguori do not propose an object any different. And this affinity does not surprise if one considers that whether it is Luther or Liguori they go back to the same fount of piety, St Bernard. Liguori's passages that have a half "Lutheran" sound are precisely those which directly or indirectly derive from some passage of St Bernard's. The Bernardian theme of love for no other reason but itself, of love that loves because it loves: the theme of limitless grace that knows no sin so great that it cannot triumph: a grace that is essentially beyond merit or justice or fear, this is the real meaning of "justification by faith" whether Lutheran or in the Marian piety of Liguori.

The great difference, however, is that in Luther this theme is found concentrated and symbolized in the person of Christ, and the faith that saves is the unconditional faith in His work fully completed and sufficient on Calvary; whereas in Liguori it is summed up and symbolized in the figure of the compassionate Mother, the Virgin Mary, and faith is "confidence" in her who is so good that she does not refuse anyone.

With these observations we are approaching the heart of the problem that we have posed in this book. Is it not extremely significant that the only sphere of theology and of Catholic devotion in which it is possible to speak of a truly free grace, a grace that is not paid for by some "suitable" merit but is given to unworthy sinners, is the sphere of Marian piety? How has this happened? The answer is not hard. It is because the Catholic theological and soteriological system, with its rigid juridical pattern, permits no other way of expression. Christ in Catholic dogma can no longer be the symbol of a total grace because He remains the supreme judge, seated on the rainbow, who terrified Luther as a child, and remains the cold executor of final judgment, painted by Michelangelo in the Sistine chapel with arm upraised to curse unless the pitying mother stops Him. If He is not that, He is, inversely, the crucified one, too mysterious and at the same time too broken by the weight of inexorable divine justice to be truly the comforter, the friend of every day, the merciful one.

The Reformation was valuable as a reaction against this hard juridical theology and it has meant the recovery of the evangelical aspect of Jesus. But let us not forget it, this recovery was possible only at the cost of a revolution that turned Europe upside down and broke its religious unity. It is to be believed that the recovery of a compassionate Christ was bound to be difficult. One wonders whether it was possible only at that price.

Precisely because Catholicism refused to adhere to this rediscovery of the Christ of compassion, precisely because at the Council of Trent it lacked the wisdom to do other than make rigid its juridical system of salvation against the Reformation, there remains for it no other course for the expression of a faith that is simpler and more immediate than to try to get round the immense barrier of mediaeval theology, a barrier conceptual, ritualistic, disciplinary and sacramental, and to do so by throwing itself in the way of Marian piety. For this reason it is fatal that this should continue to develop and should be inspired by all the love and devotion that belongs to this fresh and "evangelical" intuition of the divine mercy: that it should draw its vigour from this by deforming it!

To ignore this simple fact would be useless. Mary is not Jesus and Marian piety is not the Gospel. In Marian piety the great evangelical paradox of a righteous God who can be more than justice resolves itself into its antithetic elements: on one side a divinity all severity and all justice: and on the other a compassion that is all human and without justice. It is a compassion that finds an immortal symbol in the woman and mother but also finds in her its disquieting limitations, for it is outside the ethical, like the maternal instinct that without discrimination is always on the side of the son however depraved, and covers the guilt with indulgent complicity.[1] If there is, as there is, something demoralizing in Liguori's piety, it is not because he preaches in his own way the "*sola gratia*" of the new devotion, but because the grace is not a pity that is divine or human-divine, but only human, only feminine. It is in the last analysis, as we have said before, humanity's pity for itself!

There is something of an historical nemesis in this divergent development. In the years when St Alfonso de Liguori was maturing his Marian devotion, Lutheran pietism was flowering in Germany and, in Anglo-Saxon countries, Methodism, which was affiliated to it. Affinities are not lacking between these movements and the piety of Liguori, affinities psychological and historical, the same sentimental piety, the same lifting up of illumination on the plane of the affections, the same preoccupation with conversion, with the gift of the heart, with the devout life. In the identity of Europe's cultural climate the two movements proceed step for step, declaring themselves against the spiritual positions—in other respects stronger and more venerable—of Lutheran or Calvinist orthodoxy on one side and of Thomism and Jansenism on the other. But evangelical pietism proceeds farther in the revived appreciation of the

[1] This quality of Marian devotion is shown clearly by Charles Brutsch in his book, *La Vierge Marie*, Delachaux et Niestlé, Neuchâtel, 1943. "We are weak and want to be clothed with strength, but we do not like to recognize ourselves as guilty before God and ask forgiveness. Mary with the tender heart does not make our sin against God so pronounced. . . . When, in return, we meet Jesus Christ and lift our gaze to the cross, we cannot do so without feeling the sin that separates us from God. . . . But the cross tells us also that all our sins are pardoned for us" (p. 56).

Right and well said. But it is possible that Brutsch did not sufficiently observe the legalistic and juridical nature of the Catholic thought of sin and redemption. The very contemplation of the cross does not suggest to the Catholic that glorious antithesis of radical sin annulled by an unconditional pardon which inspires evangelical devotion, but remains involved in the calculations of merit *de congruo* and *condigno* in which justice is hardened and grace devitalized. It is true besides, that even the Marian devotion sooner or later falls again into the bonds of *de congruo* merit by acquisition and hence the liberation shows itself in the last analysis to be illusory.

living human Jesus of the Gospels, observing His saving sacrifice with a new emotion and making Him also the perfect model of Christian life, and it started humble artisans and intellectuals, men and women, along the way of imitating Him. Catholic pietism, on its side, promoted Marian devotion hyperbolically, removing itself farther and farther from the authentic conceptions of the Gospel.

Thus the faith that refuses to renew itself, accepting the control of historic truth and Christian consciousness, of necessity must develop by the unauthentic way of religious fabulation, that is, of mythical and legendary invention. In this necessity lies the fatal dialectic of the mariological development in Catholicism that cannot be arrested.

Chapter 8

THE CO-REDEMPTRESS

Motus in fine velocior: movement is swifter at the end. The century that passes between the definition of the Immaculate Conception and our day is without equal in the intense, audacious and organic development of mariology. For this development Roschini assigns certain causes.[1] Most important of these was the action of the Apostolic See, which in the preceding centuries had been more or less neutral in this development and sometimes had wisely sought to moderate it. Now, however, it assumed an increasingly propulsive rôle: Pius IX, Leo XIII, Pius X, Benedict XV, Pius XI, and Pius XII, all in various guises are popes devoted to Mary. Another cause was the publication of numerous patristic and liturgical documents, the revival of Thomism, the discussions with the non-Catholics, the celebration of Marian congresses, the declaring of special days in Mary's honour, the founding of Marian associations, the creation of chairs of mariology. With the last in particular mariology became a section by itself in the organism of Catholic theology, and it develops "scientifically" both in elaborate historical research and in the systematizing of belief. All the themes of the preceding centuries are treated fully with attention and prudence but with a logical consequentiality and a familiarity with conclusions that were unknown in the preceding periods. The Marian system has now its twin pillars in the dogmatic definitions of Mary's divine motherhood and her immaculate conception. On these the entire structure is built up with a feast of abstract logic that leaves the reader breathless and sometimes doubtful of his own or others' complete sanity.

The proper theme of the mariology of the twentieth century is co-redemption; that is, Mary's active collaboration with Christ in the redemption of the world. The importance of this fatal argument cannot be exaggerated. It is not a matter of a

[1] *Mariologia*, I, pp. 396 ff.

marginal aspect such as her assumption, the definition of which may or may not cause a substantial modification of the mariological structure. It concerns a central doctrine, or, better, a culminating doctrine in which the whole preceding development of mariology comes to its conclusive and synthetic formula.

The question of co-redemption is still actively debated among Catholic theologians. Some, for example Goosens[1] and Lennerz,[2] deny it, or at least limit it somewhat. The majority, however, by the natural tendency of mariology toward extravagant [a] solutions, admit it and defend it.[3] To realize the importance that is attached to this doctrine it is sufficient to consider the fullness, tenacity, and detailed exposition that Roschini gives to it in his *Mariologia*,[4] where the subject of the Virgin's mediation, which if I am not mistaken was central in past ages, is settled in a few pages, or rather is absorbed into the subject of co-redemption.

What are the terms of this new problem? There is general agreement among Catholic theologians that Mary has some part in salvation, that "she is not idle", to repeat an expression of St Bernard that we quoted earlier. But in what does her part consist? Of course all consider that as mother of the Redeemer she was the passive instrument by which salvation came into the world. Moreover, all agree in celebrating her merciful power as dispenser of saving grace according to the interpretation—erroneous and excessive—of the angel's greeting, "*Ave Maria gratia plena*". But is her part limited to this? Is the Holy Virgin only the collaborator of Christ in the distribution of graces that He acquired by Himself with His sacrifice on Calvary, or can we believe that Mary has collaborated with

[1] W. Goosens, *De cooperatione immediata Matris Redemptoris ad redemptionem objectivam*, Paris, Desolées, 1939.

[2] H. Lennerz, S.J., *Considerationes de doctrina B. Virginis mediatricis*, in *Gregorianum*, 19 (1938) pp. 419–44. *De redemptione et cooperatione in opere redemptionis*, in *Gregorianum*, 22 (1941), pp. 301–24.

[a] *massimaliste.*

[3] The following treatments are contained in the volume already referred to, *Marie Corédemptrice*: C. Dillenschneider, Redemptorist, *Marie est-elle l'associée de son Fils dans l'humaine rédemption?* (pp. 68–104). R. P. Nicholas, O.P., *La doctrine de la corédemption dans le cadre de la théologie générale de la rédemption* (pp. 105–130). Canon Jouassard, *Marie corédemptrice, conséquences pratiques* (pp. 131–148).

[4] *Mariologia*, II, 1, pp. 251-426.

Him in some way in the acquiring, or more precisely in the language of the school, in "meriting" these graces? Co-redemption true and proper consists in the latter. It is particularly the establishing of a positive solution of this problem that occupies Catholic theologians in these present years.

To do this it is necessary to give a detailed interpretation of all the Biblical or patristic passages that can refer directly or indirectly to a participation of Mary in the economy of salvation.

Of course there is first of all the famous passage, Genesis 3: 15; "I will put enmity between you (the ancient serpent) and the woman, and between your seed and her seed; he (the progeny) shall bruise your head, and you shall bruise his heel." The Catholic theologians now know that the prophecy, "shall bruise your head" (*ipsa conteret*), refers to the woman's progeny and not to the woman, but seeing Christ in the progeny and Mary in the Woman they associate the mother and the Son in the victory over the ancient serpent. "In the words of the *Protevangelium*, the woman is united with the Redeemer not only by the bond of maternity but also by the bond of participation in the struggle and triumph." This interpretation of Roschini's[1] is contradicted by Goosens, who sees in the passage nothing but the announcement of the Redeemer's maternity. It gets support, however, from Pius IX's Bull *Ineffabilis Deus*, which applies the passage to the Virgin, declaring, "she was united with Him (Christ) by the closest and indissoluble bond and through Him she exercised an everlasting enmity against the poisonous serpent, and triumphing over him completely bruised his head with her immaculate heel."[2] She triumphed with Christ, therefore she was co-redemptress with Him. To stand by the literal significance of the papal expressions, however, there is no reason to see in them an allusion to objective co-redemption but only to the holiness of Mary and eventually to her mediatorial function.[3]

There is connected with this interpretation a detailed employment of the well-known parallel of Eve and Mary. "Eve, dis-

[1] *Mariologia*, II, 1, p. 284.
[2] *Ibid.*, II, 1, p. 264.
[3] So Goosens interprets it; cf. Roschini, *Mariologia*, II, 1, p. 264.

obedient, became the cause of death for herself and all the human race; Mary, obedient, became the cause of salvation for herself and all the human race."[1] It is argued: Eve had an active part in the fall of man, a part not only passive, a subordinate part certainly, yet not just a material and unconscious part but rather a moral and "formal" participation. We must therefore believe that Mary has an active part in our redemption, subordinate to Christ's work to be sure, yet moral and formal, a part that is conscious and voluntary, immediate and direct insofar as a moral action produces the result foreseen and willed directly and immediately, though only at a distance in time.[2]

How is this co-operation, active, immediate, and direct, to be explained? It expresses itself in two culminating moments: the nativity of Christ and His death.

Let Roschini now go on:

> "St Luke (1 : 26–39) teaches plainly that the Blessed Virgin, by her free consent, co-operated at the redemptive incarnation. In fact the angel explains to her God's plan to restore the human race and asks her in his name to agree to it so that the plan can follow on. The Blessed Virgin stays free, speaking absolutely, she can give or refuse her consent. She sees on the one hand an ocean of sorrow for herself, and on the other all the generations of men, past, present and future who anxiously await salvation. She stands in the midst as mediatrix of reconciliation between God and men. To her is left the free choice between a mission full of ineffable sorrows and the perdition of mankind. But with the utmost generosity she accepts the sorrowful mission that is offered her so that the human race shall be saved, and she pronounces her 'Fiat', as opening the door to the Incarnation of the Word of God through which our redemption takes its start, indeed, is already virtually accomplished."[3] [a]

[1] Irenaeus, *Adversus Haereses*, III, cap. 22.

[2] Roschini, *Mariologia*, II, 1, pp. 302, 303. He favours the more radical interpretation.

[3] *Mariologia*, II, 1, p. 289.

[a] Cf. I. M. Bover, S.J., *Deiparae Virginis Consensus*, Matriti, 1942.

"Itaque nostra tractatio eo collineat, ut ex Scripturae ac Traditionis documentis ostendat B. Virginem Redemptoris incarnationi consentiendo vere ac proprie hominum Corredemptricem ac Mediatricem fuisse."

He has a short chapter on Liturgy that gives glimpses of Marian devotion as a poetic impulse, e.g. p. 166.

All this is said in a way that is clear, concise and intended to be proven. But it is not a sin of "rationalism" to doubt that Mary at the Annunciation had such a complete understanding of all that awaited her, or that God had in that formal way asked permission to work out the redemption of the world through her. By the discussion given by Roschini himself in support of his interpretation, we know that Rivière "seems to doubt somewhat" this perfect understanding on the part of the Virgin of her mission, and of the sufferings of her Son, and of the fact that she had thus from that moment accepted the destiny of suffering with Him. Bartmann "seems to concede only the physical motherhood". Lennerz and Goosens admit a certain co-operation yet not "immediate and proximate", but only "remote, indirect, mediated, insofar that with her free consent she gave us the Redeemer, who alone redeemed us by His death on the cross." These scholars reduce that co-operation, practically, to her physical mother's relationship to the Redeemer. Roschini sustains the thesis of the immediate and proximate co-operation, however, that is to say, Mary's co-operation with intention and full knowledge, that she agreed not only with clear foresight but with intense desire for it as well. "The Redeemer, then, we say, insofar as He was Redeemer, was such by God's will and was Mary's gift."[1] A gift, and we add at once, a meritorious gift, of the purest and highest merit, although only *de congruo*, that will join itself to the absolute merit *de condigno* of the incarnation of Christ!

The second occasion of the Virgin's co-operation in the redemption of the world is her presence at the foot of the cross. Again we follow Roschini.

Mary stood at the foot of the cross (John 19: 25–27). Why? To comfort her Son? To help Him in that dark hour? But she knew she could be of no help to Him. Yet she stood, "impelled by the duty of offering her Son for the salvation of the world to the extent that it depended on her just as she had brought Him

[a *continued*] "Salvatoris Mater pia
mundi huius spes, Maria,
Ave plena gratia. . . .
Verbum verbo concepisti
Regem regum peperisti
Virgo viri nescia."

[1] *Mariologia*, II, 1, p. 291.

to the light for its salvation, to unite her sacrifice to that of her Son." The very manner of her presence confirms it. She stood on her feet, "*stabat*", "like a priest offering his sacrifice to God for all humanity". As St Anthony says, she stood conforming to the will of God so that one can say of her that she, the earthly mother of Jesus, like His heavenly Father, "did not spare his own Son but gave him up for us" (Romans 8: 32). We add that she stood as mother.

> "In the victim that was offered for the salvation of the whole world there was something of the Virgin herself. The blood that was shed for the remission of sins had flowed from her purest heart, she both knowing it and willing it. Mary had real maternal claims in regard to the Victim, claims of infinite worth. Freely giving up these claims, that is giving up the human life of her son as he himself gave up his own life and his own claims, the Blessed Virgin came to participate in some measure in the constitution of the perfect victim of the redeeming sacrifice, offering something of her own and thereby conferring something of acquired merit.
>
> "The unity of the Virgin constitutes the unity of the sacrifice and redemptive merit. The act of abdication of both (that is of Christ and the *Deipara*) is distinct undoubtedly in what is personal, but is united intimately and indissolubly under a double aspect: (a) by reason of the unity of the divine decree that each asked in fullest wisdom, (b) by reason of the unity of end to which each act was ordained, that is the glory of God and the redemption of the world. In such a way the divine motherhood was the means chosen by God and made into an act in which He united Jesus and Mary to form one single and total principle of our salvation. Thus the divine motherhood becomes a supremely certain sign, by which is manifested the association of Christ and the *Deipara* in the work of our salvation. The Blessed Virgin, then, standing by the cross as mother of the Victim, and giving up her maternal claims upon him,—or better, confirming the abdication already completed in the very moment of the incarnation,—for the eternal salvation of the human race, sacrificed her Son, as much as was in her, and in consequence became the Co-redemptress of the human race."

After this explanation it will cause no surprise to read that Jesus, in speaking to John concerning Mary, "Behold thy Mother", was solemnly declaring "the spiritual motherhood of the Blessed Virgin and therefore her immediate co-operation in the objective redemption, co-operation which, as far as her nature is concerned, is identified with the spiritual motherhood in which the one and the other coincide in the first conferring of supernatural life, that is, in the first acquisition of grace. In the same instant, then, in which men's redemption was completed by the work of Christ and Mary, there took effect also their regeneration to the supernatural life of grace that had been lost by the sin of Adam and Eve."

[Conclusion.] "By these things it is apparent, if we are not mistaken, how in the Sacred Scriptures of both Old and New Testaments, correctly interpreted, the Blessed Virgin shows herself to be the immediate co-operator in the work of redemption, that is, as true and proper co-redemptress."[1]

The least to be said of all this is exactly the opposite: that the Sacred Scripture "*rite interpretata*", that is, read without dogmatic solicitations, and in the light of all we know about the first Christian generations and their ideas, contains absolutely none of these very hazardous speculations. Mary's presence at the foot of the cross is even ignored by the synoptic Gospels, which, until the contrary is proven, are to be taken as the sources that are earliest and most certain from the historical point of view. The account in the Gospel of John has the quality of a delicate intimate incident and has not the accents of a solemn proclamation of sacerdotal dignity and co-redemptive rank on the part of Mary that would be in contrast with all we know of the actual spiritual climate in which the crucifixion took place. What the cross was for Jesus' disciples the synoptic accounts show us realistically. It was a collapse, a scandal, the confusion of all their certainties, a reminder of the flight of the bravest, even the frightened absence of Peter. Only some devout women watch from a distance. The cross represented sentiments closer to mourning and confusion than to transcendent revelations of the faith; these began only after the resurrection. To represent Mary in that atmosphere as a sort of Abraham sacrificing on Mount Moriah is to substitute a quite conventional and even somewhat melodramatic vision for the dark and very human reality. The latter was certainly closer to Origen's interpretation when he thought that even

[1] *Mariologia*, II, 1, pp. 298, 299.

Mary had been subjected to the reproach of all, and the sword which, by the prediction of the old man Simeon, was to pierce her soul had been the tragic doubt in that hour about the messianic mission of Jesus. As for the idea that Mary offered her Son in sacrifice and in this association formed a single offering along with Him, it is entirely beyond the horizon of the New Testament and outside church thought until very recent times.

The story of the Annunciation must also be respected as it is, with its poetic and popular naturalness, and we must drop the idea of reading into it all the Catholic theology of the period since the Council of Trent, with its rigid definition of the collaboration of human liberty with divine grace—in antithesis to the "*sola gratia*" of the Reformation—and the human capacity to deserve *de congruo*, and with appropriate acquiescence, the grace that saves. There is no shadow of evidence that Mary is consulted in the angelic annunciation; or that the divine plan depends for a moment upon her "*fiat*—so be it": or that "speaking absolutely"—that is abstractly—she could have refused. In the Gospel story the annunciation is simply an annunciation, the communication of a sovereign decision that is extremely honourable for Mary—"Blessed art thou among women"—but concerning which she can clearly act only in humble submission, as indeed she does, and without her obedience being invested by her with the least quality of merit. Already in her person the redemption of the world is entirely and exclusively the majestic work of Him who saves.

The interpretation of the life and death of Jesus as a redemptive drama is a process of great historical importance that we can follow sufficiently well in its main lines in the New Testament. It must be recognized that Jesus had a knowledge of the tragic fatality of His death and the redemptive value of His sufferings. He must have meditated often upon the great prophecy of Second-Isaiah about the suffering servant of Jehovah. But the gospel narratives emphasize repeatedly that He was the only one to possess that consciousness, and all the indications of it that He made to His disciples evoked only protests and incredulity. The redemptive interpretation of the drama of the cross arises only in the primitive community after the resurrection, as the recovery of the faith that triumphs over reality, transfiguring it and discovering in it an unexpected meaning of revelation. The canvas of that interpretation is Isaiah 53; the sermons of Peter in the first chapters of the Acts of the Apostles are the ancient and extremely precious document of it. Then the apostle Paul appropriates the traditional material and elaborates it with his ethical and juridical conceptions, rabbinical in origin and not without references to the mystery religions.

So the faith in Christ the Redeemer organizes itself in the apostolic age. Mary has no part in this elaboration either as subject or object. She accepted it passively in its early and Petrine form as did the other members of the Jerusalem community. Probably she had no hint at all of Paul's soteriological speculations. And it is certain in any case that the object of those speculations was Jesus Christ, the Messiah who came in a form so unexpected and perished in a way so scandalous. It was Jesus the Servant of God, the *Kyrios*—Lord, the Son, the first man—Eve is quite absent from Paul's speculations—Jesus in His transcendent mystery, in His timeless origin, in His paradoxical mission as crucified saviour, as the humiliated glorifier of God. Mary's very name is entirely ignored, and does not come even once under Paul's pen. If the idea of a possible co-redemption of Mary had presented itself to his mind he would certainly have rejected it with offence; "There is one Mediator between God and men, the man Christ Jesus" (1 Timothy 2 : 5). Such is his epigraphic sentence. It can leave the mariologists undisturbed who say they do not affirm a mediation of Mary on the same plane as Jesus but only in a subordinate way, but it is certain that the apostle does not contemplate any co-redemption of any degree by the mother of Christ.[1]

If we pass from the New Testament to the patristic field there is equal silence. Irenaeus' famous parallel of Eve and Mary alludes only to the motherhood of Mary who gives the Redeemer to the world with her faith in the divine annunciation. The title "advocate" refers to the restoration of Eve and could

[1] "This text does not disturb us and we have not the duty of taking the edge off it for the needs of our Thesis. It could embarrass us only if we were maintaining for Mary a co-redemption either complementary to that of Christ, or independent of it." Thus writes Dillenschneider in *Marie Corédemptrice*, p. 74. Evidently all the theological difficulties are solved with theological distinctions.

be extended at most to the idea of a ministry of intercession which, however, is not explicitly contained in the term. All those who in various ways look for this parallel in the first century connect it with Mary's motherhood. Mary is not associated with the redemptive sufferings of Christ: if anyone is it is the martyrs, but in a quite indirect form as imitators of Christ, as members of His body, as witnesses of Him. In that sense the apostle Paul speaks of his part in the sufferings of Christ, with an ardent figure of speech, "to fill up that which is lacking of the afflictions of Christ" (Colossians 1 : 24, R.V.); but he attributes no co-redemptive significance to this thought. But Mary did not know martyrdom. The idea that her maternal suffering at the foot of the cross constituted for her a sort of moral martyrdom appears timidly in a passage of Ambrose: "The mother was offering herself to the persecutors. . . . If she had died with her son she certainly believed she would have risen with Him."[1]

To find the definite statement that Mary was spiritually a martyr "and more than a martyr", we have to come down to the letter to Paula and Eustochium of the *Pseudo-Jerome*, that

[1] Ambrose, *De Institutione Virginis*, lib. I, cap. 7. It is worth the trouble to quote the whole passage. "Stabat ante crucem mater, et fugientibus viris stabat intrepida. Videte utrum pudorem mutare potuerit mater Jesu, quae animum non mutavit. Spectabat piis oculis filii vulnera, per quem sciebat omnibus futuram redemptionem. Stabat non degeneri mater spectaculo, quae non metuebat peremptorem. Pendebat in cruce filius, mater se persecutoribus offerebat. Si hoc solum esset, ut ante filium prosternaretur, laudandus pietabis effectus, quod superstes filio esse nolebat: sin vero ut cum filio moreretur, cum eodem gestiebat resurgere, non ignara mysterii quod genuisset resurrecturum: simul quae publico usui impendi mortem filii noverat, praestolabatur si forte etiam sua morte publico muneri aliquid adderetur. Sed Christi passio adiutorio non eguit, sicut ipse Dominus longe ante praedixit: Et respexi, et non erat auxiliator; et attendi et nemo suscipiebat; et liberabo eos brachio meo." (Isaiah 63 : 5.)

As we see from the context, Ambrose wants to show that Mary has the moral force necessary to remain a virgin always, and he argues: she who was bold enough to stay at the foot of the cross could not have changed her mind about virginity. Then the theme develops independently of the context. Mary looked at Christ's wounds devoutly because she was thinking of the redemption that would be derived from them by all. Because she did not fear death she offered herself to it. If it was just that she should not survive her son this is praiseworthy, but perhaps Mary, knowing that by Christ's death a universal good would be provided, held herself voluntarily at His disposal to add with her own death something to the value of the Son's death. But "the passion of Christ had no need of any help!" God Himself had declared "I will free him with my arms!" As is evident, the thought of a co-redemption by Mary is clearly seen and as clearly rejected.

we mentioned *à propos* of the Assumption; that is, to the Carolingian age. And even then nothing indicates that this thought implies co-redemption, as it is certain that this is not held by the concept of martyrdom in general. For the entire patristic age we can accept at once the negative judgment of a competent scholar like Father Dillenschneider: those among the fathers who take up the antithesis Eve-Mary

> "are content to show more or less clearly the Virgin's collaboration at the Incarnation as a work of salvation and life. . . . Outside the antithesis of Eve-Mary it happens certain fathers attribute to Mary the effects of our redemption. . . . But let us take care . . . they maintain Mary's mediation only in the distribution to redemptive graces. . . . And these are put in the perspective of the saving incarnation. . . . As is seen, all these effusions lead of the glorification of Mary's saving work in the mystery of the incarnation. It would be vain to expect anything else from patristic literature. The horizon widens in the Middle Ages . . ."[1]

It widens; not too much, in reality. If to the mediaeval devotion to the cross and the wounds of Jesus is added the devotion of Mary's sorrows, this does not attribute a co-redemptive function to these. Only Arnold of Chartres, abbot of Bonneval, contemporary and friend of St Bernard, sets up a correlation between Christ and Mary "to obtain the common result of the world's salvation" and he is not definite as to how. Albertus Magnus is more explicit and declares that Mary has been "assumed by the Lord to help and be consort, *assumpta in consortium et adiutorium*, according to the word in Genesis, 'Let us make for man a helper like him'," and concerning Mary he makes the definite statement that Mary, "with her consent to the cross, offered Him for us all, and through that most sufficient and pleasing sacrifice only once offered, reconciled the entire human race to God."[2] It is evidently a question of a theological paradox. If one is to interpret it to the letter one would need to say that for Albertus Magnus Mary is not only "co-redemptress" but is the real redemptress of the human race in that she herself offers the redeeming sacrifice, actively com-

[1] Dillenschneider, *Marie Corédemptrice*, pp. 76, 78, 79.

[2] *Mariale*, qu. 42 and 51. Cited in Roschini, *Mariologia*, I, pp. 255, 256. Cf. Dillenschneider in *Marie Corédemptrice*, p. 80.

pleting the sacrifice of which Christ is the object; and nobody could attribute such an idea to the teacher of Thomas Aquinas. The latter, for his part, is even more sober, limiting himself to admitting Mary's necessary consent to the incarnation, a single act that redounded to the salvation of many, that is, the whole human race.[1] Denys of Chartres (d. 1471) was the first to present the idea of the meritorious value of Mary's compassion[2] and believed that through it the Blessed Virgin obtained the right to be heard in her intercessions; that is, we are in the field of general mediation, of "subjective redemption".[3] Suarez, the theologian of the Jesuits, began to associate in general the Virgin's merits *de congruo* with Christ's merits *de condigno*.[4] With this the bases of the new doctrine are set. The principle that Mary has merited *de congruo* what Christ has merited *de condigno* will become little by little a sort of "mariological axiom". But in reality it is not clear that the authors who celebrate the merits of Mary's compassion mean to attribute to them a participation in the very objective act of redemption. Their statements must usually be meant in the limited sense that Mary with her merits has obtained the right to distribute the graces derived from the cross of Christ. The mariologists discuss in particular whether Alfonso of Liguori can be considered as a believer in co-redemption in the proper sense, but there is a clear statement of his that excludes this: "Mary is not our co-redemptress because she redeemed us with Jesus Christ, but because she co-operated with His charity at the birth of the faithful."[5]

Mary's co-operation, then, comes to be situated in the sphere of the rebirth, of the subjective appropriation of salvation and not of objective redemption. There is no reason why the passages of the *Glorie di Maria* which affirm a co-operation on her part in salvation should be meant in a different sense.

[1] III Sent. d. 3, qu. 3, a. 2, qr. 2. Cf. Roschini, *Mariologia*, I, p. 248.

[2] He used an etymological principle—passion with.

[3] The text is in Roschini, *Mariologia*, II, 1, p. 320. Discussion in Dillenschneider, *Marie Corédemptrice*, p. 83.

[4] *De Verbo Incarnato*, passim. Cf. Dillenschneider, *Marie Corédemptrice*, p. 83.

[5] This precision is important because it is not found in a work of edification like *Le Glorie di Maria*, but in a book of discussions with Protestants, *L'Opera dommatica contro gli eretici*, Naples, 1871, p. 189. It does not seem to me that the explanations of Roschini (II, 1, p. 335) and Dillenschneider (*Marie Coréd.*, p. 89) in a contrary sense are persuasive.

The same thing, more or less, can be said of the other texts of the seventeenth and eighteenth centuries. They speak of a co-operation by Mary in the distribution of Christ's merits, in which proposition the more ardent speak of a collaboration in redemption in a general sense, but usually limit that with the complementary statement that Christ alone has merited the world's salvation and that Mary has not wrought our redemption or our salvation, that there is a great disproportion between her offering and Christ's. They say that we are therefore to honour her as co-redemptress "in her own way", that the zeal she had in sacrificing herself for the redemption of the world obliges us to this great respect even though our salvation is not affected by her offering, and that the Holy Virgin, uniting her prayers and sufferings to the sufferings of her beloved Son, has deserved that they be applied to her elect with greater efficacy than what the saints have been able to do in this way.[1]

To sum up. The balance still hangs decidedly in the direction of subjective redemption. We should say, rather, that it does not appear that the problem is seen clearly in all its import, or if it is seen there is a just reserve about pressing it to the extreme consequences. We have had to wait for the mariologists of the end of the nineteenth century and of the twentieth century to put the question in its rigorous terms, with a disregard of caution of which their predecessors would perhaps have disapproved, and, sheltered by the comfortable distinction between merit *de congruo* and *de condigno*, dare the affirmation of a co-redemptress in the proper sense of the term, as, for example, Roschini does.

In the evolution of mariological dogma the extremist theses are always sure to become the official theses sooner or later. No prerogative of Mary, however, has been able to command such consent on the part of the supreme teaching of the Church before being debated and matured for a long time. In the case of co-redemption, the pace has been faster, however. We have already quoted Pius IX's statement about the very close union of Mary and her Son in His sufferings. Leo XIII declares that as Mary was present ministerially (*administra fuerat*) at the

[1] These reservations are contained in a book of Balthassar de Riez, *Les justes louanges de la très Sainte Vierge*, Aix, 1669, p. 207. Quoted by Roschini, *op. cit.*, I, p. 347, and which Dillenschneider considers "*net, trenchant*".

sacrament of human redemption, so she is ministerially present (*administra est*) at the grace derived from it. The passage does not define in what sense Mary participated (*non adfuit tantum, sed interfuit*) in the redemptive sufferings of Christ, and all that it affirms clearly is His universal mediation.[1]

Pius X makes his own the mariological axiom but with an important attenuation: "Mary, as is commonly said, merits for us *de congruo* the things that Christ has merited *de condigno*." The difference in the tenses of the verbs is not without significance. Mary merits to-day, at present, in her work as distributor of graces, that salvation that Christ has merited once and for ever, in the past, on the cross. The onus is on the supporters of integral co-redemption to show that the words of the pope may include objective co-redemption. Benedict XV, more categorically, declares that Mary's presence in Calvary "was not without divine counsel", and that suffering with her Son and virtually dying with Him (*paene commortua*) she offered Him "so that one can justly say that with Christ she redeemed the human race" (*ut dici merito queat Ipsam cum Christo humanum genus redemisse*): even though by literal terms these expressions do not necessarily imply objective co-redemption and the words "one can say" are an invitation not to give the phrase too literal a sense.[2] Pius XI states that "the Virgin, most benign mother of God, after having given us our Redeemer Jesus and after having raised Him, offered Him in sacrifice at the cross and by a mysterious union with Christ and by a singular grace from Him was and is devoutly called our restorer".[3] In this declaration it is hard not to see co-redemption in a proper sense of the term. Finally Pius XII, while repeating with his predecessors that Mary offered Jesus in holocaust together with the holocaust of her maternal rights and of her mother love, confines himself to stating that with this sacrifice Mary merited the title of mother of the members of His body and that as she was "associated as mother with the King of Martyrs in the ineffable work of human redemption, she is forever associated with Him with a power virtually unlimited [a] in the distribu-

[1] Encyclical: "*Adiutricem populi*", on the Rosary (1895) and "*Parta humano generi*" (1901) discussed in Roschini, II, 1, p. 265.

[2] Encyclical: "*Inter sodalicia*", 1918. Cf. Roschini, II, 1, p. 279.

[3] Encyclical: "*Explorata res est*" (1923). Cf. Roschini, II, 1, p. 279.

[a] *quasi immenso*.

tion of the graces that derive from Redemption". These last words are clearly favourable to the limited sense of "subjective" co-redemption.[1]

In the light of these texts it must be said that the Holy See, without committing itself fundamentally, at least did nothing to discourage a definition of Mary as co-redemptress in full sense, and that, giving up its traditional function of moderating dogmatic evolution, it is found practically as the advance guard of this doctrine. Such an impression is accentuated if one considers that the title "co-redemptress" unknown to early church usage and now common is already confirmed by a series of approbations of the Holy Office, from 1913 onwards, and of the Congregation of Rites, from 1908.[2] Thus it is easy to foresee that pursuing the mariological evolution in a sense more radical, and accenting the pressure of public opinion, now accustomed to this new Marian privilege, sooner or later co-redemption by Mary will be defined as a dogma in the more rigorous sense that we have seen. The world will then know that it has not been saved by one only Redeemer and Lord Jesus Christ, but by a unique couple "*indissolubili vinculo conjuncta*" of Christ and His mother and wife Mary.

It is not easy to see what religious and speculative interest is attached to the co-redemption of Mary. It seems to be the action of a generic impulse towards her glorification in terms increasingly hyperbolical, by which no title seems excessive or exaggerated and every new honour is hardly proposed before it can be considered accepted and its critics can expect to be denounced as blasphemers of Mary. But truly, in respect of "glory" Mary has already more than enough without need of coining another title that in its exalted character sounds even more of an impiety than those preceding. Well then, why? And for what? What can Mary's collaboration add to the perfect redemption that Christ completed on the cross?

Let us hear the explanations of a French Dominican.

"What does the suffering of Mary add to that of Jesus? It

[1] The first statement is found in the Encyclical "*Mystici Corporis Christi*"; the second in the radio address to the people of Lusitano for the celebration of Fatima (1946).

[2] Cf. Roschini, *Mariologia*, II, 1, p. 392.

integrates the suffering of humanity more completely. The satisfaction completed by these two efforts is not a bit more meritorious—the second on the other hand not being meritorious except by virtue of the first—but it is richer in humanity. Mary's presence and grief give to Christ's passion an additional intensity (*un surcroix d'intensité*) and a human quality especially that otherwise would be profoundly lacking. The fact of suffering in common as rejoicing in common not only increases the quantity of suffering but makes new chords vibrate. Mary's suffering would be lacking to a redemption that would be the offering to God of all the human sorrow. Jesus could suffer everything except the compassion for His own sorrows. It is needful that every man find in the cross the example of what he must suffer to restore his guilty feelings and his passions. The violent separation of the two beings who love each other: what would death be if not this?

"And if we wish to go further in the same direction that the whole of man should be restored, it was needful that man and woman should be present in the completion of the very work of redemption. In that work of the exaltation of human nature which is the Incarnation, the woman has been exalted with the man, having been made mother of God by the same grace that made man the Son of God. And in that work of restoration of man which is Redemption, the woman suffered voluntarily with the man, offering Compassion with the Passion of Christ. It is the mystery of the new Eve. The only bond by which the new Eve could be united with the new Adam was that of motherhood. But the idea of associating the woman with the man in the work of exaltation and redemption of humanity is deeply tied to that of making man himself, according to his whole nature, the real author of his Redemption."[1]

We have no wish to deny that there is something moving in these thoughts. It is hard to discuss coldly the grief of Christ's mother, or of any other mother, and to wish to set limits to the meaning of this can seem to be lacking in humanity and comprehension. And if one had to construct on a sane plane a theory of the mediating redemption offered to God consisting of the greatest human suffering possible, one would have to take account of these thoughts. But this is not the problem. The problem is to know what value these ideas have from the

[1] R. P. Nicholas, O.P., *La doctrine de la corédemption dans le cadre de la théologie générale de la rédemption*, in *Marie Corédemptrice*, pp. 120–1.

Christian point of view, that is from the point of view of the Gospel. Now, there is nothing, either in the Gospel or in the expressions of faith of the early Church, that gives an opening to this idea, that to the perfect humanity of Christ's sufferings anything of His mother's grief can or should be added.

This same consideration of Christ's sufferings in terms of human emotions, this psychological or moral valuation that would see in Christ's sufferings the totality, at least qualitatively, of human anguish, and therefore cannot think that the mother's anguish is absent from them, all this assuredly conforms with Catholic piety of the Counter-Reformation, and to a degree with mediaeval piety too, with its cult of the cross and the wounds of Christ and the more recent veneration of the *Mater dolorosa*. But in the classic conception of redemption Christ's death on the cross saves the world not because it gathers up in itself the perfect totality of human sufferings, but because it is the death of the Man-God, because on the cross God Himself in the person of His Son assumes Himself the condemnation of man and cancels it. In this most sacred mystery the psychological quality of suffering has no weight. Christ does not redeem the world because He suffered much or all that could be suffered, but because He is "*vere homo et vere Deus*"—once again Irenaeus' formula presents itself inevitably.

To this quality of Christ's sufferings nothing can be compared or equalled or added because it is not a question here of more or less, of a totality complete or incomplete, a suffering masculine or feminine, filial or maternal solitary; or common, because there is here a qualitative leap from the human to the divine, and there is no relation of kinship, nor of divine motherhood, nor of merit *de congruo* that can fill up the hiatus between the divine and the human.

The thought that it is appropriate to associate the woman with the man in redemption as they are in sin is in itself worthy of attention. St Bernard had already formulated it in a brilliant paradox, "It was more appropriate that both be present at our restoration because neither had been absent from our corruption."[1] But long before St Bernard, and much more systematically, this theme had been developed by gnosticism, and it was a particular and basic principle of gnosticism that the mani-

[1] *Sermo in Dominica infra Octavam Assumptionis.*

festations of the divine, either in the intelligible world or in this our base world of sense, be made definite in bisexual pairs. Perhaps no analysis of these ideas, from the psychological point of view, excels in finesse that which Ludwig Feuerbach has made in his *Essence of Christianity*. In his radically immanent—that is atheistic—view of religion he says that the cult of the Virgin Mother is really the projection and symbolizing of the feminine feelings of love and compassion and that for this there must be a female figure of the divine in its actual relations with humanity. In the sensibility that he owes to his Lutheran origin and education he observes, however, that the feminine values of gentleness and compassion are already symbolized in the Son.[1] This proximity to Feuerbach should make the mariologists careful!

In reality there is not the slightest sign that the Gospel or apostolic Christianity felt any need to introduce a symbol of femininity such as that into the doctrine of redemption. It is clear that for them Jesus' humanity was in itself rich enough and universal enough to include the best of humanity. Men and women find in Him the sufficient and complete mirror of the Father's infinite love. The second century Church rejected without hesitation the gnostic speculations on the female principle in redemption as a heresy derived from pagan ideas. It seems a fateful thing that mariology is introducing into the Church again, in attenuated form, many elements of the heresies that the Church condemned in other times.

It appears that this must be said also of Nicholas and the humanistic tendency, basically Pelagian, that comes out in his appraisal of the sacrifice of the cross as offered to God out of human sorrow, of the sorrow of all humanity personified in Jesus and Mary. It appears from the quotation we have made that man redeemed himself on the cross, suffering voluntarily and the woman with him, and the idea of the necessary presence of the woman is tied to the principle "make man himself according to his whole nature, the proper author of his Redemption". It is precisely because man redeems himself that the woman has to be there! This is an interpretation of the

[1] Feuerbach, Ludwig, *Das Wesen des Christentums* (Essence of Christianity). Italian edition, *L'Essenza del Cristianesimo*, A. Banfi, Universale economica, Milan 1949, p. 70.

immanent kind that Feuerbach would probably not have despised.

We have no desire to joke about it. No thought is farther from our mind than to judge a man's theology by one phrase or a taste for paradox separate from its context. This humanizing conception is very accessible to the lay public of to-day, especially to men of the left, who are more or less permeated with sociological interpretations of religion. It is profoundly in harmony with, and indeed in the last analysis it is only the extreme expression of, the doctrine of salvation through works produced by infused grace merited *de congruo* that has dominated Catholicism since the Council of Trent. It is too evident that this lends itself to a humanistic interpretation. What has the authentic Christian message become in it? Is it too much to remember that in the doctrine of redemption as set out in the New Testament and as it came to be fixed in the early and mediaeval Church, it is not man who saves himself by offering to God all the sorrow of humanity concentrated in one person, but it is God who saves man, taking upon Himself man's sorrow and guilt? In this conception there is plainly no need of a feminine person close beside the Redeemer, for the accent falls again not upon the full humanity of his sufferings but on the fact that they are the sufferings of the Man-God.

To appraise these ideas fully and also the legitimacy of our criticism, we must extend the conception of co-redemption to another order of thinking. According to an old idea that the mariologists of to-day have taken up, Mary at the foot of the cross represents the Church. Modern mariologists specify that this means the Church in the rôle of co-redemptress. In a certain sense, all the faithful, insofar as they are members of the mystical body of Christ, are workers with Him in the redemption of the world. As the incarnation continues in the mystical body of the Church so redemption continues in its members. That is how Thomas Aquinas interprets Paul's word about completing in his body the sufferings of Christ. "What was lacking to the sufferings of Christ? There was lacking the similar suffering in Paul's body and in others."[1] All then can work together in redemption, adding the relative merits of their sufferings to the absolute merits of Christ's. Redemption is a

[1] Quoted in R. P. Nicholas, *Marie Corédemptrice*, p. 117.

collective and joint fact. "Basically every good work of ours is a reproduction in us and through us of Christ's work and no other value is added to it than a little humanity. It is only a step from this to say that all Christians are co-redeemers and that the Church is Co-Redemptress in the sense that Christians, or rather the Church, co-operates in the world's redemption and continues in itself the redemptive work of Jesus. Let us stop before we take it."[1]

But the step that our author hesitates to complete he really takes; moreover he has taken it, for it is the presupposition of the whole doctrine.

> "Perhaps to avoid the uneasiness—produced by the title of Co-Redemptress reserved for the Virgin Mary—we would want not to suppress it but rather to generalize it. The whole Church is co-redemptress because it co-operates in the Redemption of men, not only as instrument of Christ's grace, but with the offering of His very sacrifice. But the Virgin is this before the Church is, and the end is the very foundation of the Church, because she collaborates for the acquisition of Redemption itself. Among the co-redeemers she is the Co-Redemptress *par excellence*. She is the first of that order and its model. Among all the associates of Christ she is the Associate *par excellence*. She is the model and type of the Church, the Bride *par excellence*, she in whom the human race is more greatly co-assumed with the holy humanity of Christ. Far from reducing Christ in any way, He would be reduced if she were not what she is, the perfection of the association of humanity with His destiny that is the whole meaning of the Incarnation."[2]

Here we meet an order of ideas of an interest not only speculative but religious and practical. In fact the result of the doctrine of the co-redemption of the Virgin, the imperative of action in which it is translated, is properly this: Become co-redeemers, put into operation the internal mission of the Church, of reviving the Church, of reconquering the paganized world; this is your position and your responsibility; join the Catholic parties, become one of the militant members of Catholic Action; in particular take cognizance of the value of your sufferings for the redemption of the world![3]

[1] *Ibid.*, p. 118.
[2] *Ibid.*, p. 128.
[3] All the "Conferences" for the lay public, men, women, youth, seminarists,

Now, with this extensive ecclesiological interpretation before us, we must make it quite clear just what our dissent is, for not everything here deserves to be rejected outright. On the other hand, much that is useful and interesting is vitiated by a radical misunderstanding that requires a precise statement of our position on the other side.

The doctrine of the Church as the body of Christ is one of the grandest themes that are proposed for the thought of Christians to-day, Protestant and Catholic, and the acquisition of a theory of the Church that is really alive would be one of the most fruitful means for Christianity's future as a living and unitive power in the world. It is certain that to it belongs the idea of a communion of life and work with the Head, Christ, and His members, and that in this communion and in the holy community that derives from it, the faith and life of the believers is made actual in achievement. It is true also that the existence of such a community, permeated by the Redeemer's spirit, is of prime importance for the diffusion of the Gospel in the world through the testimony that draws and convinces, by Christian action, in all sectors of human life. But let us be very careful not to compromise the purity of all this by insinuating an excessive meaning into the concept of the Church, a concept that would not be truly Christian.

In the apostolic writings we have the fairest and most authoritative descriptions of the Church that can be desired, as a living community, spiritual, ardent, completely pervaded by the awareness that it is the Body of Christ, but its existence and its mission are never presented under the aspect of "co-redemption". The respect for the perfect redemption is too great, the redemption irrevocably completed on the cross by the only Redeemer. The loftiest expressions of the primitive Church's consciousness, the most vibrant celebrations of communion with Christ, of the life of Christ in His "members", are always set upon the plane of the redemption that has taken place and is completed, never on that of a redemption in the course of being completed, to which it is possible to add even a "value of humanity" with the proper mixture of merits *de congruo*. Not even the martyr who is celebrated in the literature of the

contained in the second part of *Marie Corédemptrice* develop these principles, particularly as a practical application of the co-redemption of Mary.

second century as the most perfect assimilation of the Christian to the Redeemer, and in the Pauline letters themselves is represented as in communion with the sufferings of Christ, has a co-redemptive value. His is only the imitation, a testimony rendered, a passive communion, a being fully and triumphantly reunited to the Saviour, but never a co-operator by his martyrdom in the expiation of the sins of the world.

We must hold fast to this pure and profound New Testament conception, avoiding all indulgent complacencies about the merit of humanity as a collaborator with divinity in its own self-redemption. To sum up, the Church the body of Christ, pledged with Him in a work of missionary conquest of the world: Yes! The Church co-redemptress in the sense of a collaboration of the human with the divine in the world's redemption. No! Father Nicholas was quite right when he pointed out that the co-redemption of Mary and of the Church is the critical point that separates Catholicism and Protestantism![1]

The foregoing observations show also the limits of our agreement and our disagreement in relation to another interesting idea connected with co-redemption, i.e., Mary as representing the Church or as a symbol of the Church.

The theme of Mary as a symbol of the Church is very ancient and receives considerable favour to-day even among Protestants.[2] But first it must be made clear that the Protestants who are interested in these ideas mean Mary as a pure symbol of the Church, a symbol certainly not without reality to the extent that Mary is part of the Church! For Catholic mariology she is the real source of the Church. She it is whom Christ has given to be mother of all believers, because of her participation at the sacrifice of Calvary and in virtue of her universal mediation. She is the true parent of spiritual Christian life, the channel of grace *par excellence*, the "neck" of the Church that is set below the head, Christ, and puts the head in communication with the rest of the body.[3] In short, on the Protestant side we are in the

[1] *Marie Corédemptrice*, p. 127.

[2] See the sermons of Karl Barth already referred to: *Advent*, French translation, 1948.

[3] Roschini, *Mariologia*, II, 2, pp. 349 ff. He discusses at length whether Mary is a "secondary head" or the "heart" or the "neck" of the Church, and decides for this third interpretation by a series of good reasons of "suitability" and of authority.

realm of allegory rich in spiritual meaning: on the Catholic side, of sacramental realism.

It must be noted, however, that the conception of the Church that comes to be symbolized in the Virgin Mary is typically the Catholic conception. It is the Church virgin and immaculate, that generates in her purest womb the divine-human life of the faithful, and is the exclusive distributor of graces without which there is no salvation. It is the Church that intercedes with results for all those who entrust themselves to her protection and also for those who are outside her, and is broad with generous pardon for the erring who return to her devotedly. She is the mother who upon earth administers the Son's kingdom of grace and triumphs in the heavens as queen with Him. In the last developments of dogma she is His associate in the whole work of redemption, contributing not only to distribute the graces He has merited, but to merit them with Him, even though in a secondary and subordinate way. And we do not forget that fortress that discomfits heresies and assures the victory of the Catholic faith in the world.[1]

This is why it is clearly too much to hope that the interpretation of Mary as symbol of the Church can become the meeting ground of a common appreciation of Mary by Catholics and Protestants. It remains clear that by both parties the doctrine and cult of Mary are rightly considered to be the "critical central dogma" of Catholicism. On the Protestant side there can be nothing but a clear-cut refusal.[2]

[1] Cf. Steitz, art. cit. *Maria* in *Realencyclopädie*, 2nd ed. (1881), Vol. 9, p. 326, also Karl Barth, *Dogmatik*, I, 2, pp. 157–160 (1939). It is interesting to note the progress of this interpretation that Steitz presents as an unconscious process of symbolizing of itself, made by the Church in the elaboration of mariology. Barth quotes from the contemporary German works of mariology that show how this assimilation is consciously accepted to-day. This appears also from the quotations that we have made in this text.

[2] For the Catholic theologians see Nicholas, *Marie Corédemptrice*, p. 127: for the Protestant, see Karl Barth, *Dogmatik*, I, 2, p. 157.

Translator's note to p. 101 *supra*.

Cf. Martin Luther's hymn, "*Sie ist mir lieb die werde Magd . . .*" I am indebted to John Ross for drawing my attention to this. It will be found in Karl Goedeke and Julius Tittmann, *Dichter des Sechzehnten Jahrhunderts*, Vol. 16–18, Leipzig, 1882, p. 93. The imagery is from Revelation 12:

"*Sie tregt von gold so rein ein kron*
Da leuchten inn zwelf sterne . . ."

It is strictly a hymn of the Incarnation.

Conclusion

MARY IN DOGMA AND DEVOTION

IN Catholic dogma the Virgin Mary is a copy of Christ, in His life, His person and His work. The principle of analogy with Christ, expressed clearly in contemporary mariology, has faithfully followed the elaboration of Marian doctrine through the centuries. Like the birth of Jesus, that of Mary was announced by angels and was an exceptional event in which the Holy Spirit had part. If Christ was conceived by a Virgin, Mary was conceived without sin. If Christ is like man in all things except sin, so Mary is in everything perfectly human except in sin. If Christ dwells in the fullness of divinity, then in Mary, through her Son, dwells the fullness of saving grace and supernatural life. Christ is the first-born of many brothers, but Mary is the first-born after Him, of the children born of Him, and, furthermore, she is their Mother, and to that extent she is no longer the mother of Jesus but His wife: she who carries in her fecund bosom all the generations of believers, she who after having given to the light the physical body of Christ, bears His mystic body in all the ages. Christ is the second Adam, Mary the second Eve. Christ is the fountain of living water which gushes forth into life eternal. Mary is the fountain of life, the spiritual mother of the new humanity. Christ is the true vine but Mary also receives this title (John of Damascus). She comes adorned with other titles that the New Testament reserved for Christ; like Christ she is the head of our salvation—*kephalaion soterias* (George of Nicomedia, James the Monk), saviour of the world (Anselm, Bonaventura, Albertus Magnus), propitiator—*hilasterion*—for our sins (Office of Lent), liberator from death, conqueror of death (Gregory of Neo-caesarea), reconciler of God with men (John of Damascus, Liturgy), mediatrix between God and men.[1]

And, they would say, by good right since she participates in

[1] Cf. Benrath, *Zur Geschichte der Marienverehrung*, pp. 91 ff., which he borrows from the encyclopædic works of Marracci and Passaglia.

all His work with maternal and spiritual intimacy. She knows beforehand the sacrifice that is to crown her and accepts it, suffering with Him and dying with Him spiritually at the foot of the cross. The *labarum* of the Marian congress of La Salette, dedicated to Mary, co-redemptress, represents her erect, stretched out upon the body of the crucified, slightly lower than Him, her arms extended under His and partly supporting His in the gesture of offering. Jesus dies leaning His head upon that of His mother, who dies spiritually with Him, offering Him to death. Mary's face is serene and piteous; Christ's face is disfigured with pain. It is clear that He is the victim offered up and she is the officiating priest. And the dying body of Jesus is almost completely hidden by the monastic dress of the sorrowful Mother. What symbols!

But if Mary dies with Him she also rises again with Him. His body does not know corruption. Her assumption to heaven is now believed as a revealed dogma and is the unanimous persuasion of Catholic souls.[a] And if Jesus is seated at the right hand of the heavenly Father, Mary is seated and reigns very little below Him. He intercedes with the Father for men; she intercedes with Him. And if Jesus promises that the prayers made in His name will always be granted, one knows equally that those made in Mary's name are granted. In the economy of eternity she occupies a position apart, superior to all the heavenly hierarchy, immediately below the Holy Trinity. If Christ is begotten by the Father from all eternity, the hypostatic order establishes a bond of relationship between the Trinity itself and Mary. In the end Christ will come again to judge the quick and the dead, but Mary does not judge anyone: wholly piteous and merciful, she remains for all eternity consecrated to her mission of co-redemptress.

Notwithstanding these heavenly prerogatives, Mary is not a divine person but continues exclusively and completely human. The Catholic theologians from Epiphanius to Thomas Aquinas and our contemporary mariologists are quite unanimous[b] on this point. Mary is not a second Christ; she is not a second Word, even though some German mariologists and among us Carlo Cecchelli linger willingly on the thought that Mary is

[a] Not all. Cf. bibliography at the end of Chapter 5. (*Trans.*)
[b] *recisi*.

Sophia as Jesus is the Word. But Sophia is mere immanent wisdom, that wisdom which is the summit of the rational creation and therefore is not an exception to the nature of Mary as purely a creature.[1] Mary is not a second manifestation of the Word made flesh but is the purest humanity in which the Word incarnated itself, humanity as it would have been if there had been no fall, Eve before her error. Furthermore, Mary is humanity clothed again with all the fruits of grace, supernatural humanity as it will be in the final glory.

This perfect humanity is the object of Marian worship.[2] It would be in bad taste to call in doubt the distinction established by Thomas Aquinas between the cult of *latria*—adoration—devoted to God, that of *dulia*—veneration—devoted to the saints, and that of *hyperdulia*, we should say "superveneration", reserved for the Virgin Mary alone.[3] It is sufficiently clear that a pious soul that recites the Rosary knows how to turn in the "Our Father" to the Heavenly Father and in the "Hail Mary" to the most human Queen of Heaven. It is easy to suppose that this knowledge introduces a certain difference, at least conceptual, in the various moments of its devotion, although it is not easy to imagine that sort of psychological oscillations between *latria* and *dulia* corresponding to the various moments of the prayer.

But it is more important to observe that the cult of *hyperdulia* turned toward the Virgin, however one wants to define it, belongs to the highest point in Catholic devotion from the point of view of richness of liturgical content, number of festivals, the exalted tone of dedication which all combine together. The worship of Mary is the cult of veneration, gratitude, love, invo-

[1] Cf. Karl Barth, *Dogmatik*, I, 2, p. 158. He cites in particular Scheehen. For Cecchelli, see *Mater Christi*, Vol. I, passim.

[2] The theme of the worship of Mary would deserve a treatment of its own that could not be included with this book, which is devoted to Marian doctrine, without adding greatly to its bulk. We refer in the following observations to the brief but clear Marian catechism of Roschini cited above.

[3] *Summa Theol.*, Part III, qu. 25, art. 5. It is of interest to note that Thomas Aquinas establishes this distinction, disputing against a more radical opinion that leaned for support upon John of Damascus and *Pseudo-Augustine*, and reasoned thus: the honour that is rendered to the king must be rendered to the king's mother; therefore if one gives to the king (Christ) a worship of *latria*, one must concede it likewise to the Virgin Mary. Thomas replies, "Mater Dei est pura creatura. Non ergo debetur ei adoratio latriae."

cation, service, imitation. It addresses itself to the person of Mary, to the Heart of Mary, to the image of Mary, to the Name of the most holy Mary. It comprehends daily practices of devotion, the Ave Maria, Salve Regina, Angelus Domini or Regina Coeli, the Litany, the little office of the Madonna, the Rosary, the crown of Seven Sorrows, a weekly worship to which by ancient custom is dedicated Saturday, a day consecrated to Mary as Sunday is to Christ. Three months particularly are consecrated to Mary: May, September, October, and various annual feasts, such as the Annunciation, the Immaculate Conception, and the Assumption, which are among the most ardently celebrated in the liturgical year. There is the perpetual worship to which are consecrated the Marian associations—Orders, Third Orders, Confraternities or Devout Unions and Associations of youth, the Scapularies of Mary and the Consecration to Mary. And, finally, there are the occasional cults, the *via Matris Dolorosae* and the Marian congresses.

To become familiar with the whole tone of ardent celebration characteristic of Marian devotion it is enough to enumerate the titles contained in the Litany of Loretto:

> "Holy Mary, holy mother of God, holy virgin of virgins, mother of Christ, mother of divine grace, purest mother, most chaste mother, mother inviolate, mother unsullied, mother amiable, mother admirable, mother of good counsel, mother of our Creator,[1] mother of our Saviour, most discreet virgin, venerable virgin, virgin worthy to be extolled, powerful virgin, merciful virgin, faithful virgin, mirror of righteousness, seat of Wisdom,[2] cause of our gladness, spiritual vessel, vessel of honour, singular

[1] This paradox, that borders on the scandalous, must be meant in the sense that Mary is the mother of the Word by which creation was made, and also in the sense that Jesus Christ, in His consecrated figure both human and divine, is the final cause of creation. These affirmations are clearly orthodox. But was it really necessary for expressing these truths to pronounce a formula that spontaneously brings to mind quite different thoughts? The Creator is God the Father! Nestorius' scruples against the title *Theotòkos* would be even more justified in regard to this other title that is both high sounding and delusive. The character "strange at first sight" of this invocation is admitted by A. Guillaume, S.J., in his explanation of the Litany of Loretto, *Le Litanie della S. Vergine*, Ital. trans. Istit. di S. Paolo, Rome, 1942, p. 176.

[2] Mary is the throne of Solomon in which Wisdom is seated. Sophia—Wisdom—is the Biblical parallel of the Word which incarnates itself in Mary. Guillaume, *op. cit.*, p. 383.

vessel of devotion, mystic rose,[1] tower of David,[2] ivory tower, golden house,[3] ark of the Covenant gate of heaven, morning star, health of the sick, refuge of sinners, consoler of the afflicted, help of the Christians, queen of the angels, queen of the patriarchs, queen of the prophets, queen of the apostles, queen of the martyrs, queen of the confessors, queen of all saints, queen conceived without stain, queen of the most holy rosary, queen of peace."

Or again, consider the *Salve Regina*:

"Hail Queen, mother of mercy; sweet life and our hope, hail! To thee we turn, exiled children of Eve; groaning and weeping in this vale of tears we sigh for thee. Come, therefore, our advocate, and turn to us those merciful eyes of thine. And show to us, after this exile, Jesus, the blessed fruit of thy womb, O merciful, O piteous, O sweet Virgin Mary!"

From this cult the most exceptional benefits are expected: for the individual, because the most holy Virgin protects him in life, in death and after death; for the family, the Church and for civil society. And it is not only useful but necessary, so much so that "for the adults who know Mary sufficiently well, such a devotion is morally necessary to attain eternal salvation, so that for one of these who showed himself positively indifferent or refused to venerate Mary and invoke her, it is morally impossible that he be saved".[4]

It does not appear, however, that there is a great need to inculcate this duty. Marian devotion is one of the most obvious aspects of contemporary Catholicism. If the sacred Mass, with its solemn and ancient liturgy, conceptual materials and Biblical figures and with its Christocentric orientation remains officially the centre of Catholic worship, the heart of the people is rather with the Virgin Mary than with the tremendous and abstract mysteries of the altar. For about one hundred years

[1] Symbol of Mary's beauty.

[2] In this verse and the following Mary is the rock of Zion prefigured by Deborah, Jael and other heroines of the Old Testament, the bulwark of the Catholic Church against heresy. Guillaume, *op. cit.*, p. 351.

[3] Mary is the Temple of Jerusalem in which God reveals Himself: also the sacred Ark of the Covenant that contains the true manna (Christ the Bread of Life), and the Author of the Table of the Laws. Guillaume, *op. cit.*, pp. 373 ff., 385 ff.

[4] Roschini, *Chi è Maria? Catechismo mariano*, p. 77.

the appearances of the Virgin have monopolized practically entirely the spontaneous manifestations of the supernatural in Catholicism. Christ no longer appears except rarely to some ecstatics, but Mary triumphs in fascinating apparitions—officially admitted and sanctioned or no—by revelations that are passionately gathered and commented upon even if they are not distinguished by great depth or independence of surrounding conditions,[1] hardened sinners converted, the incurably ill recovered. It is clear that the inventive faculty of popular piety is oriented predominantly in the direction of the Virgin Mary.

In the presence of this complex of developments, taking account of the tone that is assumed, the ardent devotion, the exalted qualifications and nomenclature of the liturgy,[a] one is compelled to say that although the definition of *hyperdulia* cannot be logically contested—after all, definitions are free—it stands pretty well stripped of significance. What is important—and it is impossible to exaggerate the importance—is that the heart of the Catholic masses is oriented not towards an authentic manifestation of the divine but toward the "pure humanity" of the Virgin Mary. It must be said that by all the traditional religious canons this is the essence of idolatry. The worship of Mary is a comprehensive transfer[b] in the psychological sense from the person of Jesus to that of His mother, taking over to her the sentiments of affection, trust and dependence. This is made possible by the fact that in the figure of Mary there came to be assembled little by little all the attributes that are the object of devotion of love and gratitude in the person of Jesus, but without His divinity. What can be the intrinsic religious value of this? And what will be its fruits for the faith and Christian life of Catholicism? The promoters of the worship of Mary believe that, through the veneration of the Mother, faith in the Son can be revived. They must be more in the current of the reactions of the Catholic spirit than we are but to us it is

[1] So our Lady of La Salette, in common French, addresses some children. "Come hither, my children, do not be afraid. I am here to tell you an important piece of news. If my people will not submit to me, I shall be forced to let my Son's arm go. It is so strong and so heavy that I cannot hold it any longer. How long have I suffered for you!" *Marie Corédemptrice*, p. 212.

[a] *qualificazioni liturgiche.*

[b] *un immenso trasferimento affettivo.*

evident that they are following a dangerous illusion. A burning devotion like the Marian has all the characteristics of a cult that is exclusive and jealous. The progressions of the Marian devotion can contribute to a continually increasing hyperbole in the glorification of Mary, but it cannot be logically presumed that they are contributing to a greater consciousness of the authentic Christian faith, or to a deeper appreciation or an understanding adoption of it.

The most characteristic values of Christianity transferring themselves from the person of Christ to Mary undergo a devitalizing of their potency parallel with the difference in grade between the divine Redeemer and the purely human mother. Mary is not God who descends to humanity to redeem it, but she is the immaculate humanity that by faith and obedience deserves to be received into grace, is glorified in the incarnation, is assumed to heaven, intercedes for herself, pleads herself, has compassion on herself. The divine grace, which in the Biblical writings is the unfathomable and unrestricted *fiat* of God's majesty, is at the orders of the "eternal feminine" to whom nothing can be refused. In Mary humanity governs the Kingdom of Heaven and even gives orders to the Omnipotent.

The Christian values that appear with Mary are not merely reduced in power, although dangerously close to some basic human feelings that have nothing specifically Christian about them. Mary personifies the ideal of the ascetics of both sexes in Catholicism. Mary is the sublime projection of their intimate labours, the goal of their ambit, of their repressions which are the more beloved the more they are grievous. The exceptional importance in the worship of Mary, which all the representations connected with human generation assume, the inquietude with which it feels compelled to make precise every particular of her conception, birth, maternity and perpetual virginity are eloquent symptoms of all that. If there is a figure charged with psychological complexes, with the projection of repressed impulses, it is the Virgin Mary. Mary's humanity should be considered much less as a representation of the ideal humanity than as that of the ascetic ideal of Catholicism, that is of a value extraneous to Christianity!

With the theme of the perpetual virginity there is associated the nostalgia, present in every adult, man and woman, for the maternal protection. It is a typical projection on the religious plane of a humanity burdened with the feeling of inexpiable guilt which is in the process of losing its sense of the Gospel's message of pure grace and to which the "arm" of the Lord has become "too heavy".

These two psychological motives, the potency of which needs no demonstration, have a place of great importance in the elaboration of Marian piety. The personal perfections of the Madonna, from the perpetual virginity sung by the apocryphal gospels, defended by scholars like Jerome and by church rulers like Ambrose, down to the dogma of the Immaculate Conception proclaimed by the Marian pope Pius IX, could all be interpreted as variations of the sublime theme of victory over repressed sexual life. And Mary's mission from the conception of the new Eve, "patroness" in Irenaeus, to the merciful mediatrix of St Bernard and Alfonso of Liguori and to the co-redemptress of contemporary mariology, is none other than a development of the theme of benign maternity, always ready to forgive.

The Catholic mariologists know all this. It is impossible that they do not know it. They must therefore know that the Marian piety, far from being a pure pedagogical transcription of authentic Christian values, constitutes their dilution with a reality sentimental and psychological, respectable to be sure, but typically profane, exclusively human and not religious. Can they hope that by this vehicle, so debatable, a true Christian renaissance can be produced? Or perhaps the values of Christianity are so devitalized for them that they are no longer distinguishable from the pure humanity of the mariological values?

This problem is of disconcerting gravity for the future of Christianity.

The mariological development considered in its complexity is retrogressing from the immense spiritual power that was built up in humanity, from the Hebrew prophets to the incarnation of Christ, to free the idea of God and religious devotion from the spurious elements of a psychological and projective nature that flourish in all pagan religions and form their substratum; religions in which the psychoanalyst has a wide field to follow his investigations. The strenuous revindication of the figure of the holy God, who with the sovereign manifestations of His judgment disconcerts all interested calculations and the eudaemonistic fancies of national or tribal cults, among which divinity is always more or less at the service of men, the God who with expressions of His sovereign grace no less unexpected gives His pardon and dissipates the terrorizing projections of the bad conscience—all this had been the triumph of divinity in itself, of divinity at the state of purity freed at last from the disfigurement of parasitic and psychological forms. The great masculine symbol of the fatherhood of God was the minimum of anthropomorphism, inevitable in every living religious conception which is not disposed to dissolve itself into abstractions of formal logic. Christianity in its ascensional phase had achieved the wonder of maintaining that severe conception of the divine, harmonizing it with the idea of the incarnation. God, sovereign, majestic, had been able to come down to man without losing any of His divinity. The incomparable person of Jesus had made this miracle possible, and the dialectic force of Christianity in the first centuries had systematized it and registered it, at the cost of some contrasts, in the dogma of the Trinity.

The whole development of Biblical religion was a grave warning "Glory to God alone", and this solemn warning was taken up by primitive Christianity, especially by Paul and John. But the thought of the incarnation, the fervent communion of the Church, its consciousness of being the mystical body of Christ, was to open the way to a development in an inverse sense, to a positive valuation, at first subordinate then gradually more and more autonomous, of the human aspects of redemption, the celebration of martyrs, the solidarity and intercession of the saints, the glories of the renewed and supernatural life in the faithful, and finally, as the greatest example, the cult of the Virgin Mary.

The historical development of Catholicism seems, with a decisiveness that steadily increases, to have assumed the task of revaluing the human aspects connected with the Christian conception of salvation, piously justifying before the "sole glory of God" a suitable portion of glory for man as well. In this general perspective the worship of Mary shows its interior coherence, the logic of its development and its essentially[a] Catholic nature, but it is Catholicism in its deteriorating aspect that expresses itself more and more consciously in this development.

The way of the progressive humanizing of Christianity, followed at first unconsciously, then, and especially in modern mariology, with clear awareness, is not without resonance in the contemporary religious consciousness. It can be interpreted as a parallel within Catholicism of the general tendency to the laicizing of faith, followed consciously in other fields by the protagonists of positivism. The religion of humanity, in its liberal or Marxist expressions, is, more than it seems, spiritually related to the impulse that excites Catholicism to promote the purely human figure of Mary to the first plane of popular devotion. Certainly it is to this that it owes its popular favour, and perhaps the consciousness of its promoters of being in the current of living history, of answering to a sort of unconscious invocation of our time and hence the illusion of being able by this way to recover a part of lost spiritual authority to the end of promoting a Christian reawakening. All the humanistic emphasis of Catholicism that finds its theoretical basis in the rethinking of Thomism, in the revaluation of ontological metaphysics, of the principle of "analogy of being", and in particular the tendency that seems to be especially active in French Catholicism to interpret the dogma of the incarnation as a glorification of human nature—all this can find an adequate symbol in the Marian devotion.

It can certainly be said that among the lay beliefs that are proposed for men's adherence in this period when all values are criticized, the cult of the Virgin Mother, still suffused with evangelical suavity and feminine gentleness, can lay claim to a notable rank. But it ought to be clear that precisely this tendential humanism and immanence is oriented in a direction quite different from the original impulse of Christianity, which was theocentric and Christocentric, and that if one wants a Christian revival it must not begin with the contamination of the Gospel by the eternal feminine of the cult of Mary, but one needs to have the courage to initiate the great return from Mary to Christ. Let this be said also not only in regard to the Marian cult but with reference to the necessary reversal of the

[a] *squisitamente.*

official guidance according to which all Catholicism has been developing since the Council of Trent.

This renewal of conscience, this great return, ought not to be impossible. Nothing ought to be impossible for a Church powerfully centralized and disciplined as the Catholic. And it could be done without great gestures of reform and without loud renunciations. How many things simply fall into disuse without being officially abrogated! It would be enough to make the machinery change gears and hold it there with decision and perseverance. It would be enough to stop encouraging the worst exaggerations of the popular Marian devotion or, directly, to stop patronizing them. It would be enough to inculcate from top to bottom throughout the hierarchy, the clergy and the religious orders the principle of a sane return to evangelical simplicity and instruct it to lead the consideration of Mary back to the place that is legitimately conceded to it in a Christian Church; a place that no spirit that is sensible to the values of humanity and gentleness would want to deny her. Perhaps a few decades would be sufficient for the atmosphere of Catholic piety to be made sane again generally—and there is no need to emphasize with what advantage for Christian spirituality and for the cause of the reunion of the divided members of the Body of Christ.

Alas, there is no sign that the Church intends to take this road. On the contrary, the evidence is all the other way. Mariology will pursue its triumphant development. The questions now under discussion, as for example Co-redemption, will sooner or later be defined as dogmas in the most exalted sense for Catholic common people and for the greater offence to the non-Catholics. Already the idea has come up of a feast of Mary's regality.[1] After the feast one will see the dogma too.

[1] The proposal was made by Roschini in an article in the *Osservatore Romano*, Dec. 18, 1949. He refers to a sentence in the discourse of Pius XII on the occasion of the proclamation of the Jubilee of 1950, May 25, 1949. "The omnipotent benediction (of the Lord) . . . is poured out in a special way upon the Holy Year to make it, with the maternal help of Mary Queen of the World, a year of increased faith . . .", etc. Roschini adduces the reason of the "analogous likeness that runs between Christ and Mary, between the mysteries of Christ's life and those of Mary's life", and "the singular opportunity in the current time for such a liturgical feast. It can be said that the powers of the world have tried everything to take the people away from the easy and light yoke of the reign of Christ. Now, if it is true that the shortest way, the surest and most charming way to bring souls

And no one can foresee what new solemnities, what new dogmas will arise in the future from the fecund matrix of popular piety and from the docile instrument of the principles of propriety, eminence, singularity and analogy with Christ. The assimilation of Mary to Jesus will be conducted to its extreme consequences on the plane of pure humanity, that is, however mariologists think of it, the pure humanity of Mary will substitute itself more and more in the popular devotion for the divine humanity of Christ. Parallel with this and as a consequence of it there will be the attempt to integrate Mary more completely in the Trinity. It is already stated that Mary is the "complement of the Trinity", even if only the "extrinsic" complement. It is declared that Mary with her divine Maternity "procures for the divine Persons a new and unique glory"; that "thanks to the divine Maternity of Mary the Father acquired a real authority over the Son who is equal to Him by His nature and His perfections." The statement is made that "the divine Maternity of Mary gives a new life to the Son, a temporal life" and that in the end "thanks to the divine Maternity of Mary the Holy Spirit, sterile as regards the divine processions, receives a fecundity in regard to the Son, contributing to give Him a body. . . ." In short, Mary completes the Trinity; Mary brings to the Trinity a perfection it would not have without her. By this Mary, although by nature "infinitely below divinity", "comes to be introduced, in a certain sense, into the very family of God and seated close to the most Holy Trinity".[1] Evidently Mary brings to the divine Trinity the contribution of humanity, of temporality, of corporeality, necessary for the incarnation. One cannot but think of the divine quaternity of the mediaeval alchemists, of the four thrones enclosed by the sacred oval of divine-cosmic totality. When, in Mary, humanity will be definitely associated with the divine essence, the new gnosis of the incarnation will be complete.

And thus, the figure of Christ at last practically obliterated, Mary, the most human and the deified, the transcendent woman, to whom belongs the task of rendering the divine

to Christ is Mary, it follows also from this that the shortest way, the way most secure and charming to affirm the reign of Christ over souls is that of always affirming the reign of Mary. . . . *Ad Jesum per Mariam. Ad regnum Jesu per regnum Mariae.*" We are in the logic of the system.

[1] Neubert, *Marie dans le Dogme*, pp. 33–35.

Trinity more perfect, will establish sovereignty over the devotion of Catholicism.

Such a substitution of symbols would not be without precedents in the history of religions.

When the good Apuleius, whose conversion to the wise and merciful Goddess we have noted earlier, after she had freed him from the form of an ass into which he had been metaphorically changed because of his passions, decided to consecrate his life to Isis Regina, he was told after his first initiation that to be a perfect devotee of the Goddess he would have to submit to a further double initiation in a way more particularly dedicated to Osiris-Serapis. The autobiographical account lets it be clearly understood that the initiate had no particular interest in Osiris and considered that new initiation as a sort of family duty, the expensive character of which he was not ashamed to deplore, so expensive that to provide the necessary sacrifices he had to sell his wardrobe. But the Goddess, or her husband, repaid him with interest in the result, blessing him in his career as advocate and granting him the honour of being added to the priestly confraternity of the *pastophori*.

Actually in the hellenistic era Isis had come to occupy the first place in Egyptian devotion.[1] Osiris, the oldest god in Egypt, who had gathered around his name the most learned and profound speculations, had come in the course of the centuries to specialize in his functions as sovereign in the world beyond the grave. But the shining and powerful goddess who had resuscitated Osiris killed by Seth, had become the most sought, the most precious and clever, the most propitiated mediatrix of salvation. Against her, in the words of Apuleius, Fortune's intrigues were impotent. And in the great syncretistic unification of the Mediterranean cults in the hellenistic and Roman epoch, the transformation of the religion of Osiris into a universal mystery of salvation was made under the name of Isis and to her was entrusted the task of representing in the new phase of culture the values, even though somewhat profaned, of the ancient cult of Osiris.

If we have recalled this episode of the religious history of the

[1] Nicola Turchi, *Storia delle Religioni*, Bocca, 1922, p. 472. I am grateful to Guido Miegge for having pointed out to me the importance of this evolution of the cult of Osiris.

Mediterranean world we have not done so to affirm a parallel with the possible evolution of the veneration of Mary. The comparisons that one would be inclined to make in the realm of comparative religion are too uncertain. But it cannot be denied that there is a certain analogy. At times it seems that in Catholicism the figure of Jesus Christ as the central religious symbol has become somewhat worn out.[a] Perhaps also Jesus has become too exclusively the Lord of the beyond and the Judge of the final judgment. To give back to Christ His incomparable greatness as founder and Lord of a new human race there would be needed a process of revision in dogma, ethic and liturgy of which Catholicism has many times shown itself to be incapable.

The only way that remains open is that of substituting for the symbols that are in course of psychological deterioration others that are newer and fresher. It is perhaps fatal that in Catholicism there are entrusted more and more completely to the cult of the Virgin Mary those Christian values of humaneness, compassion, inner aspiration, of which it still feels itself to be the trustee. Of course Christ will not be forgotten. He will continue at the centre of official honours. Mary will still be conceived as the Mediatrix between Him and men. They will continue to say that one ascends from Mary to Christ. But the real diffusive and persuasive force, the real religious fascination, the real function of effectively focusing the faith and love and devotion of the masses will be exercised entirely by the Virgin Mary. On that day it will be said that within Catholicism Christianity has given up the field to a different religion.

[a] *abbia subito un certo logoramento.*

INDEXES

INDEX OF SCRIPTURE REFERENCES

SELECT INDEX OF NAMES